Economic Method

Understanding Economics as a Science

Marcel Boumans

and

John B. Davis

with contributions from Mark Blaug,
Harro Maas, and Andrej Svorencik

macmillan

First published 2010 by
PALGRAVE MACMILLAN

Palgrave Macmillan in the UK is an imprint of Macmillan Publishers Limited,
registered in England, company number 785998, of Houndmills, Basingstoke,
Hampshire RG21 6XS.

Palgrave Macmillan in the US is a division of St Martin's Press LLC,
175 Fifth Avenue, New York, NY 10010.

Palgrave Macmillan is the global academic imprint of the above companies
and has companies and representatives throughout the world.

Palgrave® and Macmillan® are registered trademarks in the United States,
the United Kingdom, Europe and other countries

ISBN   978–0–230–21812–3   hardback
ISBN   978–0–230–21813–0   paperback

This book is printed on paper suitable for recycling and made from fully
managed and sustained forest sources. Logging, pulping and manufacturing
processes are expected to conform to the environmental regulations of the
country of origin.

A catalogue record for this book is available from the British Library.

A catalog record for this book is available from the Library of Congress.

10   9   8   7   6   5   4   3   2   1
19 18 17 16 15 14 13 12 11 10

Printed and bound in China

To Mark Blaug

Contents

Preface

We see science as an inherently social activity. This applies even more to a textbook such as this, which is the product of a decade of teaching economic methodology at the University of Amsterdam, and so must be seen as a joint product of our past and current colleagues. On the one hand this is reflected in the contributions to the book by Mark Blaug, Harro Maas, and Andrej Svorencik; on the other it reflects the detailed and constructive suggestions and comments by Dirk Damsma, Floris Heukelom, Murat Kotan, Edith Kuiper, Tiago Mata, Julia Mensink Mary Morgan, Geert Reuten, and Peter Rodenburg. Earlier versions or parts of the book were read carefully by our colleagues from other institutions: Sohrab Behdad, Ted Burczak, Sheila Dow, Zohreh Emami, Nancy Folbre, Wade Hands, Kevin Hoover, Uskali Mäki, and Andrew Mearman. We are grateful for their comments and support. We of course are grateful to our students over the years. We also would like to thank Jaime Marshall, Associate Publishing Director in the College Division of Palgrave Macmillan, for his trust and encouragement.

MARCEL BOUMANS AND JOHN B. DAVIS

AMSTERDAM, 2009

Introduction

Economic methodology is the philosophy of science for economics. Philosophy of science investigates the nature of the assumptions, types of reasoning, and forms of explanation used in the sciences, and economic methodology investigates the nature of the assumptions, types of reasoning, and forms of explanation used in economic science. Yet not only do the issues and concerns that dominate today's discussions of economic methodology in many ways mirror those in contemporary philosophy of science, but economic methodology's emergence as a recognized field of economics in the 1980s was strongly influenced by reactions that were occurring at that time in the philosophy of science against logical positivism (see Chapter 1), particularly in connection with the ideas of Karl Popper, Thomas Kuhn, and Imre Lakatos.

This book uses this historical development in philosophy of science to frame its introduction to the field of economic methodology. Though there have been important contributions to economic methodology in the nineteenth and early twentieth centuries, the relatively late emergence of economic methodology as a distinct field of specialization within economics was very much associated with the philosophy of science's response to logical positivism – and then by its further response to Popper, Kuhn, and Lakatos. We believe that it is important to refer back to these historical origins to understand how many of the current concerns and issues in economic methodology came about. We also believe it is important to understand the questions that face economics as a science in light of the questions that are faced by science in general.

The structure of the book

This book is organized along both chronological and conceptual lines. It is organized chronologically in that earlier historical developments in philosophy of science and economic methodology are examined first, and later developments are shown to build on these – often as reactions or alternatives. Many of these developments did indeed occur first within the philosophy of science, but there were also important early developments in economic methodology. Thus while we often consider economic methodology through the lens of philosophy of science, we also try to set out the distinctive concerns of economic methodology.

1

The conceptual approach can be seen in the way we introduce many of the most basic concepts and theories of scientific explanation first and follow their various refinements, departures, and extensions in both philosophy of science and economic methodology. This reflects our view that the conceptual development gains deeper meaning when it is also seen as a historical development. It also shows that changes in thinking about the nature and goals of the philosophy of science and economic methodology from the logical positivism of the 1930s to the present need to be seen as an evolution in thinking.

There is one significant departure from this chronological and conceptual method of organization that is found in the final chapter of the book which looks at the role of value judgments in economics. The issue of value judgments in science is not absent from the twentieth-century philosophy of science, but it is rarely seen as a prominent theme. Nor is the issue prominent in economic methodology as it has developed since the 1980s. However, it is our view that the role of value judgments in economics is a crucial issue for economic methodology, and one which connects to many other central issues in the field. Accordingly, we have placed this discussion at the end of the book as a kind of capstone discussion in lieu of a conclusion. Since economics is very much a policy science (an aspect that is emphasized by its older name, political economy), we believe it to be important that the book should close on a discussion of the links between the science and specific policy recommendations.

Of course, in such a short introduction to economic methodology there has to be a degree of selectivity about the areas that are to be included. The field of economic methodology has continued to change in the years after the cut-off point for the discussions in this volume, and in some respects its 1980s origins are less visible in contemporary economic methodology than they were even a decade ago. Indeed, as economic methodology has developed as a separate field of investigation, it has taken on many more concerns specific to contemporary economic research such as experimental economics. Consequently, in order to provide a sense of some of these recent distinctive concerns, the end of each of chapter has a number of short sections – foci – that extend the discussion and provide additional applications and topics of interest. They may be skipped as desired without interrupting the main narrative of the chapters themselves.

Three comments on the nature of economic methodology

First, economic methodology should be distinguished from economic method, though the two terms are often used interchangeably. Economic methodology investigates the nature of economics as a science. To explain what this means, for the sake of convenience we will define science as the result of scientific research. The term scientific research covers various scientific practices such as classification, description, explanation, measurement, prediction, prescription, and testing. Research, then, is scientific when it meets specific criteria that are associated with these practices.

Economic methodology investigates these criteria by considering questions such as the following:

- Should all scientific activities satisfy the same criteria, or should, say, a scientific explanation be expected to fulfill different criteria from a scientific description?
- Should a distinction be made between criteria for the social sciences and those for the natural sciences?
- Where do these criteria come from: from scientific research that is generally considered to be successful, like physics?
- Is the determination of these criteria a specific task for philosophers of science or should it be determined principally by practitioners?

This book will look at these questions in relation to the investigation of the nature of economics as a science.

A useful starting point for understanding the distinction between methodology and method is to see explanations in science and economics as attempts to answering *why* questions. This means that economic methodology examines the basis and grounds for the explanations economists give to answer *why* questions about the economy. For example, economists use the shifting of demand and supply curves to answer the question of why prices change. Economic methodology attempts to understand the specific role these relationships play in an explanation.

By contrast, economic method attempts to provide answers to *how* questions, and concerns the techniques and tools that are used by economists when making their explanations and descriptions. This can be illustrated using a particular example: maximization analysis – the assumption that agents maximize some function such as utility or profit – is a particular technique or tool that is used in economics to explain or describe choice behavior. Learning about this tool is a matter of learning *how* calculus techniques provide a certain type of explanation of the choices people make. However, if we ask which criterion this use of maximization analysis addresses in producing a scientific explanation or description in economics, one would be asking a question in the field of economic methodology.

Another example can be drawn from the field of econometrics, which involves the use of mathematical and statistical tools to draw conclusions from economic data. Studying econometrics is a matter of learning *how* to employ its techniques and methods. However, an examination of econometrics from the point of view of economic methodology will take the methods of econometrics as given, and will focus instead on the question of which criteria mathematical and statistical analysis addresses in producing good explanations or predictions of economic data.

Second, economic methodology makes use of both descriptive and prescriptive approaches. *Descriptive* economic methodology aims to describe the different types of economic research practices and their results. For example, one type of explanation uses econometric models to explain relationships in economic data on the grounds that relationships in economic data reflect cause-and-effect relationships in economic behavior. In philosophy of science, descriptive methodology is often denoted as positive methodology, where 'positive' (like 'position') comes from the Latin *positus,* the past participle of *ponere* which means 'put' or 'place.' So, positive methodology concerns the question of how science is actually practiced. Note that this characterization does not necessarily mean that descriptive or positive economic methodology is value-free – an issue which we first encounter in connection with the thinking of the philosopher of science Thomas Kuhn (Chapter 4), and discuss more fully in the final chapter in terms of the relationship between values and description.

In contrast, *prescriptive* economic methodology distinguishes between good and bad explanations in economics and considers how good explanations should be formulated. For example, one view of a good explanation (that advanced by Karl Popper – see Chapter 3) is one that has survived severe testing, on the grounds that good explanations stand up to empirical data, while the rule for producing good explanations prescribes that one make every effort to falsify them. Prescriptive methodology in philosophy of science is denoted as normative methodology, and concerns the question of how science ought to be practiced. Despite this, the line between descriptive and prescriptive economic methodology has not always been drawn clearly. At the same time, since the 1980s there has been a change in the relative interest in descriptive and prescriptive approaches in the field of economic methodology, with a greater emphasis in recent years being placed on the descriptive approach. This turning point is emphasized in chronological terms in the book as we move from Chapter 3 to Chapter 4.

Third, there exists a tension in economic methodology, hinted at above, in that the philosophy of science on which economic methodology has drawn since the 1980s has been strongly influenced by reflections on the natural sciences, especially physics, whereas economics – as a social science – has many different characteristics. As a result one of the most important questions in economic methodology is whether an explanation of the status and character of economics as a social science involves issues that are significantly different from those involved in explaining the status and character of the natural and physical sciences. Some philosophers have suggested that there are no fundamental differences with respect to the nature of scientific explanation between the natural and social sciences. Others argue that social sciences in general – and economics in particular – face additional issues that affect how they arrive at acceptable explanations. This question also begins to take on a particular significance as we move from Chapter 3 to Chapter 4, and remains important through the later chapters of the book.

The aims and nature of this book

This book has two main aims:

- It aims to strengthen students' understanding of the status and character of economics as a science so that that they will be able to reason more clearly as both economists and social scientists. In this sense, economic methodology is a means to carrying out better economics and better social science.
- It aims to introduce students to the wider philosophical issues surrounding our understanding of science and, in particular, economics as a science. That is, economic methodology is an end in itself associated with human curiosity about the nature of the world and how we come to understand it.

It is important that students should also appreciate that because economic methodology is the philosophy of science for economics, the approach of this book is essentially philosophical. Unlike many scientific questions, philosophical questions often have no final and unambiguous answer. This can prove frustrating for economics students who are used to courses which aim to reach clear conclusions.

For this reason economic methodology offers a slightly different view of what it means to achieve mastery of the subject matter: in this particular context "getting it right" means achieving an understanding of the different types of assumptions and reasoning that are involved in economic explanations, determining the respective merits of these explanations, and examining how we justify our conclusions in this regard.

Finally, this book provides an introduction to economic methodology that will give students an understanding of the common ground across which economic methodologists have traveled. Of course, methodologists have used different paths to cross this common ground, reflecting their different starting points and the changing nature of economic methodology and philosophy of science since the 1980s. Because of this, and also because of the changing nature of economics itself, present-day economic methodology is a highly diverse and increasingly complex area of investigation. It is important that students remain aware that economic methodology is in a constant state of development. In these pages we have done our best to record what we believe constitutes the common ground that has been traveled so far.

A story about the famous physicist Werner Heisenberg illustrates how we see ourselves as carrying out this task. Heisenberg is chiefly associated with what has come to be known as the Heisenberg uncertainty principle in quantum mechanics, namely that an electron's position and velocity cannot be determined simultaneously. On one occasion Heisenberg was hurrying to a lecture he was due to give at Cambridge University, when was stopped by the police for speeding. Asked if he knew how fast he was going, he replied that all he could say was where he was at that moment. This book hopes in a similar manner to state where economic methodology is at this moment.

How to use this book

The book is based on a seven-week course that has been taught for more than a decade to bachelor's-level students of economics by a large number of different individuals in the History and Methodology of Economics Group at the University of Amsterdam. Most of these students had completed at most only a small number of economics courses, and thus the challenge has been to teach both basic philosophy of science and economic methodology to individuals who are only just beginning to consider the role of explanation in economics.

In the course of our teaching we have used a variety of books, articles, and other resources. We have found that most of the available materials were too specialized, assumed too much background knowledge, or were too difficult for students beginning their studies, not only at the bachelor's level but also often even for postgraduate students with a sound knowledge of the field.

As a result a few years ago we decided to write our own accessible introduction to the subject. The text has been revised on a number of occasions to reflect our teaching experience. This version, written by Boumans and Davis, is written with a single voice, but builds on the contributions of many group members. Our experience with students at the University of Amsterdam is that, once they have started to come to grips with the particular nature of the subject, they are generally able to gain a reasonable understanding of the field and its relation to the philosophy of science, even if some issues remain difficult.

The seven chapters of the book allow one chapter to be covered each week in this short term format, but also allow the book be used in longer courses when supplemented with or when accompanying other materials.

The focus sections at the end of each chapter provide extensions of the material, and may be used as starting points for further discussion. Indeed we have left the links between the focus sections and the chapters themselves loose enough that they may be addressed as desired. The main thread of the book is to be found in the chapters themselves, and we thus recommend that the chapters be followed in their chronological/conceptual order.

The book includes a number of features that are designed to offer further help to readers. A glossary of important terms is to be found at the end of the book (see pp. 195–9), and each of these terms appears in bold when it first appears. Each chapter is also followed by a set of study questions that are intended to help students test their understanding of the chapter. Many of these questions have been used in examinations at the University of Amsterdam. The readings cited at the end of the chapters also include a brief annotation to explain their relevance to the chapters. These readings act as historical signposts to the development of the subject and offer opportunities for further studying the field of economic methodology.

Relevant readings

Bird, Alexander (1998) *Philosophy of Science*, London: Routledge.
> A comprehensive introduction to philosophy of science, but only as applied to natural science.

Blaug, Mark (1992) *The Methodology of Economics, or How Economists Explain*, 2nd edn, Cambridge: Cambridge University Press.
> Originally published in 1980, it is the first book on economic methodology, creating the field, but only from a Popperian–Lakatosian perspective.

Davis, John, D. Wade Hands, and Uskali Mäki, eds. (1998) *The Handbook of Economic Methodology*, Cheltenham: Edward Elgar.
> Although it is called a handbook, this is more like an advanced level encyclopedia. A very useful supplement to this textbook.

Dow, Sheila (2002) *Economic Methodology: An Inquiry*, Oxford: Oxford University Press.
> An introduction to economic methodology by a leading post-Keynesian economist.

Hands, D. Wade (2001) *Reflection without Rules: Economic Methodology and Contemporary Science Theory*, Cambridge: Cambridge University Press.
> An advanced-level survey of recent developments in economic methodology and a survey of contemporary science theory.

Hausman, Daniel, ed. (2008) *The Philosophy of Economics: An Anthology*, 3rd edn, Cambridge: Cambridge University Press.
> A collection of classic texts in philosophy of economics with a comprehensive introduction by Hausman. It includes several texts that are also discussed in this book.

Chapter 1

The Received View of Science

When we run over libraries, persuaded of these principles, what havoc must we make? If we take in our hand any volume of divinity or school metaphysics, for instance, let us ask, *Does it contain any abstract reasoning concerning quantity or number?* No. *Does it contain any experimental reasoning concerning matter of fact and existence?* No. Commit it then to the flames, for it can contain nothing but sophistry and illusion.

(David Hume, *An Inquiry Concerning Human Understanding*)

Sauberkeit und Klarheit werden angestrebt, dunkle Fernen und uner-gründliche Tiefen abgelehnt. In der Wissenschaft gibt es keine "Tiefen," überall ist Oberfläche ...

(Purity and clarity are aimed at, dark distances and unfathomable depths declined. In science there are no "depths," all over is surface...)

(*Wissenschaftliche Weltauffassung: Der Wiener Kreis/A Scientific Worldview: The Vienna Circle*)

We begin our study with a discussion of a famous interwar movement in the philosophy of science that set the stage for many of the developments that were to occur over the course of the following half-century. What came to be known as the **received view**, also the standard view, derives from the **logical positivist** program in philosophy of science, a broad philosophical movement that originated in Berlin and Vienna in the 1920s and was to last into the 1950s in the United States. In the first half of the twentieth century the logical positivists dominated thinking about philosophy of science. Indeed, much of the current direction in philosophy of science is, in important respects, a reaction against the views of the logical positivists, as we shall see later in this book.

The first key document in the development of logical positivism was the 1929 manifesto of the Ernst Mach Society, *A Scientific Worldview: The Vienna Circle* (*Wissenschaftliche Weltauffassung: Der Wiener Kreis*). The members of what came to be known as the Vienna Circle and signatories to the manifesto included the philosophers Rudolf Carnap (1891–1970), Moritz Schlick (1882–1936), and Viktor Kraft (1880–1975), the sociologist Otto Neurath (1882–1945), the mathematician Hans Hahn (1879–1934), and the physicist Philipp Frank (1884–1966). The label "logical positivism" offers a fair description of the Vienna Circle's philosophical program, since the members actively sought to combine aspects of **logicism** (by which is meant that all scientific language, including mathematics, is an extension of logic) and **positivism** (which meant **empiricism** – in particular, the idea that knowledge arises out of sense experience).

Analytic and synthetic *a posteriori* propositions

The main aim of the logical positivist program was to **demarcate** scientific knowledge, to distinguish science from pseudo-science, and to remove any kind of metaphysical or imagined content from scientific knowledge. Their demarcation rule was to accept only **analytic** and **synthetic** *a posteriori* propositions or statements as scientific knowledge. Analytic propositions are tautological – that is to say, they are true by definition. For example, the statement "All bachelors are unmarried males" is true by definition. Moreover, valid mathematical and logical propositions are analytic. For example, "$1 + 1 = 2$" and "$A \rightarrow A$" (where the logic symbol "$\rightarrow$" means "implies"). All other, non-analytic, propositions are called **synthetic**. If these propositions are shown to be true by empirical research, they are called synthetic *a posteriori* propositions. Examples of such statements might be: "My neighbors' dog is aggressive" and "The colour of the coffee I am drinking is light brown." They are true in light of our experience of the real world.

The eighteenth-century German philosopher Immanuel Kant (1724–1804) also introduced a third category of propositions whose truth is not shown by empirical research and which are not true by definition. These were called **synthetic** *a priori* **propositions**. According to Kant, this category included propositions such as Newton's laws and the proposition that the geometry of our space is Euclidean (for example, that the sum of the angles of a triangle is 180°). Kant regarded these propositions as being universally true.

However, Kant's assertion that such propositions were universally true was to be challenged by developments in mathematics and physics at the end of the nineteenth century and the beginning of the twentieth century. First it was shown that non-Euclidean geometries are mathematically possible and, subsequently, contrary to the teachings of Newton, Albert Einstein's general relativity theory assumed a curved physical space, a theory which would be later confirmed by Sir Arthur Eddington's observations during the solar eclipse of May 29, 1919. These scientific breakthroughs were crucial events for the logical positivists, but also for philosophers such as Karl Popper (Chapter 3) and Thomas Kuhn (Chapter 4), and they will therefore be discussed in more detail in these respective chapters.

As a result of these scientific developments, the logical positivists denied the existence of synthetic *a priori* propositions in science, and asserted that all propositions that are not true by definition should be subjected to investigation by empirical research. Their intention in doing so was, as mentioned above, to purify science of all "metaphysical" or philosophical claims about the world that were neither analytic nor synthetic *a posteriori*. Indeed their experience in Germany and Austria in the period between the two world wars reinforced this goal, since that period was one in which a variety of propositions referring to "Nation" and "Nature" and the like were claimed to be true about the world without evidence, and were used to justify all kinds of xenophobic and discriminatory social policies in those countries.

In their program the logical positivists drew on the work of earlier philosophers, in particular David Hume (1711–1776) and Ernst Mach (1838–1916). These two thinkers had stressed the importance of empiricism, which is the view that experience, especially from the senses, is the only source of knowledge. For the logical positivists, empiricism consisted of two related theses: (1) all evidence bearing on synthetic statements derives from sense perception, in contrast to analytic statements, which are true by definition; and (2) **predicates** are meaningful only if it is possible to tell by means of sense perception whether something belongs to their extension, that is, predicates must be empirically verifiable. Predicates include expressions such as 'is red,' or 'went home.' In grammar a predicate is a part of a sentence or a clause stating something about the subject, such as the predicate 'went home' in 'John went home,' or 'is red' in 'This tomato is red.' The extension of a predicate is the set of all those things of which the predicate is true, e.g. the set of all red things. As a result, the proposition "This tomato is red" is meaningful because by looking at it, one can *see* that this proposition is true.

So, the logical positivist's interpretation of empiricism was that synthetic statements must be meaningful. A synthetic statement is meaningful if it can be judged to be true or false by sense perception, or in other words, when it is empirically verifiable: a non-analytic statement is meaningful only if it is empirically verifiable. This criterion for meaningfulness was called the **verifiability principle**. Note that as a result of this principle, various statements in ethics and religion must be considered meaningless in science. For example, the statement "God created the world in six days" has no scientific meaning.

The ultimate goal of the Vienna Circle, which was stated most clearly in their manifesto *A Scientific Worldview*, was to purge science of all propositions that contain terms that are not meaningful. They believed that the only aspects of the world about which we can acquire scientific knowledge are those that are directly accessible by sense perception (that lie on the "surface" of things). They therefore felt that scientific theories should be formulated so that the bearing of empirical evidence is precise and transparent (the "purity and clarity" that they are aiming for). The logical positivists thus regarded scientific knowledge as possible only insofar as sensory experiences are systematically related to one another.

In their investigations of particular scientific propositions, the logical positivists drew a clear distinction between **syntactics** and **semantics**. Syntactics deals with the formal relations between signs or expressions in abstraction from their signification and interpretation. Semantics deals with the signification and interpretation of the signs or expressions. The distinction between syntactic notions such as well-formed statements, proof, or consistency and semantic notions such as truth and meaning was important to the logical positivists. They saw formal logic as liberating empiricism from psychological and metaphysical garb and as permitting one to distinguish analytic statements, which are tautological, from synthetic statements that must pass the test of observation. The logical positivist view of the task of the philosophy of science was to clean up various conceptual messes inherited from past science by pointing out what were – and what were not – meaningful propositions in a properly formulated empirical science.

The aims of the logical positivists can therefore be summarized as follows:

1.   To formulate precisely such central philosophical notions as a criterion of meaningfulness (the verifiability principle) and the distinction between analytic claims (that are true by definition) and synthetic claims (that must be testable);
2.   To develop precise definitions of central scientific notions such as theory, explanation, confirmation, etc.

Theories and evidence

The logical positivists also made a distinction between what they termed the **context of discovery** and the **context of justification**, a point that was later emphasized by Hans Reichenbach (1891–1953). This means that a distinction should be drawn between the way in which a theory is discovered (which could be for a variety of accidental reasons) and the context of its justification, which involves a rational reconstruction of the theory according to the tenets of logical positivism (on the part of the discoverer and/or anyone else developing the theory) for the purpose of its justification.

The logical positivists argued that philosophy of science should really only concern itself with the context of justification. For them, the context of discovery was irrelevant to establishing the scientific value of a theory. This means that whether or not Newton arrived at the Universal Law of Gravitation because an apple fell on his head, or Kekulé found the molecular structure of benzene by dreaming of a snake with its tail in its mouth was of no relevance to the meaningfulness of both discoveries. For the logical positivists, biographical and historical data about the lives of great scientists should have no place in any serious history of the subject.

Another fundamental distinction drawn by the logical positivists was between theories and the evidence, facts, and data, since theories depend upon the latter for their justification (see Focus 4.3 for more about facts and observation and their relation to theories). **Scientific theories** were accordingly seen as systematic collections of concepts, principles, and explanations that organize our empirical knowledge of the world. In the advance of scientific knowledge, theory and evidence are given different weights and they play different roles: the main problem for philosophy of science, and also for economic methodology based on logical positivist thinking, is to explain the relation between them.

Let us go a little further in assessing what is involved in such a process. According to the logical positivist understanding of theory, also referred to as the **syntactic view**, the proper characterization of a scientific theory consists of an **axiomatization** in first-order formal language.

A first-order formal language consists only of symbols representing variables (denoted by x, y, z, ...), function symbols (denoted by $A(\cdot)$, $B(\cdot)$, $C(\cdot)$, ...), predicate symbols (denoted by A, B C, ...), and the symbols $\neg$ ('not'), $\vee$ ('or'), $\wedge$ ('and'), $\rightarrow$ ('if ... then'), $\forall$ ('for all individuals'), and $\exists$ ('for some individual').

An axiomatization reduces a theory to a set of axioms in the manner of Euclid's treatment of geometry (see Focus 1.1 for a more elaborate discussion of axiomatization). The axioms are formulations of logical laws that specify relationships between theoretical terms. These theoretical terms are implicitly defined by the syntactics, that is, the logical structure of the theory. As a result, the language of the theory is strictly divided into two parts: (i) observation statements (or 'protocol sentences') that describe observable objects or processes; and (ii) theoretical statements. The meaning of the theoretical terms is given by their observational consequences. Any theoretical terms for which there are no corresponding observational terms are regarded as meaningless. The theoretical terms are identified with their observational counterparts by means of **correspondence rules**, which are rules that specify admissible experimental procedures for applying theories to phenomena.

When theoretical terms are completely defined in observational terms, they are said to be operationalized. According to the received view, for a proposition to be meaningful it is necessary that all the theoretical terms are operationalized. To clarify this idea of **operationalization**, we take as an example the term "unemployment," which is defined theoretically as the number of people who are jobless, looking for jobs, and available for work.

In this case it is easy to say who is jobless. However, the definition of the terms "looking for jobs" and "available for work" involves human motivation, and thus cannot be observed as if it were a physical fact, such as oranges being orange. This means that in order to measure unemployment, both "looking for jobs" and "available for work" need to be operationalized. This is done by defining "unemployed persons" as:

- All persons without a job during the survey week who have made specific active efforts to find a job during the preceding four weeks, and were available for work (unless they were temporarily ill).
- All persons who were not working but were waiting to be called back to a job from which they had been laid off.

Next, "actively looking for work" is further operationalized by listing the following "specific active efforts" that can be made "to find a job during the preceding four weeks:"

1. Contacting:
    an employer directly or having a job interview;
    a public or private employment agency;
    friends or relatives;
    a school or university employment center;
2. Sending out resumes or filling out applications;
3. Placing or answering advertisements;
4. Checking union or professional registers;
5. Some other means of active job search.

According to this process, only at this stage of operationalization can unemployment be measured, as is done, for example, by the United States Bureau of Labor Statistics from which the above definitions are taken.

Related to this idea of operationalization and emphasizing very much the idea of meaningfulness, Percy W. Bridgman (1882–1961) developed an extreme form of empiricism, which came to be called **operationalism**. Bridgman was strongly influenced by Einstein's new physics, which he saw as leading to a radical new view of theoretical concepts.

In his *Logic of Modern Physics* (1927), Bridgman stated that: "In general, we mean by any concept nothing more than a set of operations; the concept is synonymous with the corresponding set of operations." This means that the true meaning of a term is to be found by observing what a scientist does with it, not by what a theory says it does or what its author thinks it does. The operations to which Bridgman refers are the ways the term is measured. The consequence of this view is that a term will have a different meaning when it is measured in a different way. For example, time measured by a sundial has a different meaning from time measured by a watch. Operationalism has not taken hold in economics, although Paul Samuelson advocated a version of it for a period, as will be discussed in Chapter 2.

The nature of scientific explanation

In general, as stated above, an **explanation** is an answer to a *why* question. The received view of scientific explanation is more specific: a scientific explanation should show some event or some regularity to be an instance of a fundamental **law**. Carl Hempel (1905–1997) developed this view systematically into what is called the **deductive-nomological (DN) model of explanation** (or covering-law model).

In a DN explanation, a statement of what is to be explained (the *explanandum*) is deduced from a set of true statements that includes at least one law (*nomos*). This latter set of statements is called the *explanans*. Schematically, this can be expressed as follows:

> *Explanans*:
> Laws: L_1, ..., L_m
> True statements of initial conditions: c_1, ...c_n
> _____
> *Explanandum*: E

Where the solid line represents a deductive inference. This model becomes an explanation of, for example, why firm x raised its price if one interprets the symbols as follows: L_1 = all monopoly firms raise price when marginal cost increases, $c_1 = x$ is a monopoly firm, c_2 = marginal cost has increased, and E = firm x raised its price.

The problem with Hempel's definition of an explanation is that according to this model not all deductive inferences can be considered to be explanations. Consider the following example:

> Nobody who takes birth control pills as directed gets pregnant.
> George takes birth control pills as directed.
> _____
> George does not get pregnant.

If it is assumed that George is a man, then nobody would regard the argument above as explaining *why* George does not get pregnant. It does not matter whether or not George took birth control pills. In this instance taking pills is not causally relevant for the explanation of George not getting pregnant. An explaining law should accordingly identify causally relevant factors, but Hempel's DN model, which focuses merely on (logical) **deduction** from a law, does not require this.

There is, however, an even more fundamental problem with this model of explanation. It requires that the generalizations in the *explanans* be laws. But how can we be certain that this is the case?

To study this problem, let us have a closer consideration of what laws are. Generally we suppose that a law is true, but for the current discussion this is not relevant, and we can simply refer to "law-like" statements as statements that are just like laws – though we do not know whether they are true. The idea of "law-like," then, is just the idea of a regularity. The problem, however, is that many regularities appear to be accidental. As a first attempt to distinguish law-like statements from accidental regularities, let us try to see whether a syntactic definition of a law-like statement might help. All law-like statements, then, have the logical form of a universal conditional:

$$\forall x \, [A(x) \rightarrow B(x)]$$

(Read as: For all x, if x is A, then x is B. The clause introduced by "if" is known as the "antecedent," and the clause introduced by "then" is known as the "consequent.") This syntactic definition, however, is still insufficient to distinguish law-like statements from accidental regularities. Let us, then, also impose a number of semantic requirements which can be illustrated with the following example.

Compare the following accidental generalization,

"All of the coins in Smith's pocket are dimes,"

with its formulation in the more expanded form according to the syntactic definition above:

"For all x, if x is a coin in Smith's pocket during the time period a, then x is a dime during a,"

where a designates some definite period of time. Compare this with a commonly acknowledged example of a universal law:

"All copper expands on heating,"

which can also be formulated according the syntactic definition given above,

"For all x and for any t, if x is copper and x is heated at time t, then x expands at time t."

One clear difference between these two examples is that the accidental generalization contains designations for a particular individual object and for a definite date or temporal period, while the universal law does not. So a necessary requirement for a universal law is that the domain of the antecedent is not restricted to things falling into a fixed spatial region or a particular period of time. Law-like statements, that is, are required to be unrestricted generalizations.

Another difference between the two examples is that the implication arrow ("→") in the syntactic expression of the universal law above denotes a necessity. All the elements appearing in the antecedent must necessarily also appear in the consequent. This is clearly not the case for the accidental generalization: a coin put in Smith's pocket during the time period *a* would not necessarily turn into a dime. This is to say that a law-like statement has no exception.

Yet these additional semantic requirements are still insufficient to rule out the example of George not getting pregnant as a scientific explanation. To rule this out other semantic requirements about causal relevance are needed. In the literature on laws, however, each time additional semantic requirements were proposed, new arguments were developed which escaped all existing semantic requirements. And so it seems that a law-like statement cannot be sufficiently well defined in a semantic way.

In the logical positivist program, however, laws are essential to scientific explanations. They are also essential to predictions. Because laws are universal with respect to time, they comprehend the future as well as the past, so they are equally able to offer an explanation of what *has* happened and to predict what *will* happen. Explanation and prediction are two sides of the same coin which can be equally demonstrated with the DN model. This is known as the **symmetry thesis**. On the one hand, scientific explanation involves filling in what is missing above the inference line:

?

initial conditions
_____
explanandum

laws

?
_____
explanandum

On the other hand, prediction involves filling in what is missing below the inference line:

laws

initial conditions
_____
?

According to the logical positivists, without laws there are no scientific explanations and no scientific predictions, and science can only provide descriptions of individual phenomena.

The difficulty, perhaps impossibility, of semantically defining a law, however, is seen as presenting a greater problem for philosophers than for scientists. Indeed, it is still the widespread belief of scientists that the ultimate goal of science is to discover laws.

Laws are seen as the icons of our knowledge, and as concise descriptions of Nature's mechanisms which are to be acquired by critical observations of patterns and processes in Nature. If philosophers, then, have difficulties in deciding why a general regularity ought to be considered a law, scientists are simply concerned with determining what general regularities *are* laws.

However, logical positivists became aware only gradually of a more problematic tension between their aim of empiricism and the scientist's aim of discovering laws. In the remainder of this chapter, therefore, we consider this tension in relation to the problems of induction and demarcation.

Further difficulties in the logical positivist program

The problem of induction

David Hume (see p. 11) argued that observations or experimentation only allow the acceptance of singular statements about the properties of particular things at particular times and places. For this reason he asked how we can place any certainty on generalizations from single statements – that is, on the process of induction? And in those cases in which our generalizations imply singular statements about events that have not yet observed, what is their basis?

Let us consider the famous case of the black swans. It was once believed that all swans are white, because for centuries every swan that had been observed in Europe *was* white. Thus, the statement "all swans are white" was generalized from many particular observations at many particular times and places of swans being white. Then, in the seventeenth century black swans were discovered in Australia.

So, because it is always possible that a future observation might not conform to a past generalization, as Hume argued, observation can only justify singular statements. This is what is called the **problem of induction**. It is primarily a problem concerning how singular claims about unobserved things and generalizations about them are to be supported or justified.

This problem of induction challenges the evidential support for laws that was so central to the empiricism of the logical positivists. As we have seen, the logical positivists' methodological rule is to include only analytic propositions or synthetic propositions based on sense data. The problem of induction, however, implies there are no universals, including laws, that can be based on sense data. This in turn implies that laws should be removed from science, which would mean that science is reduced to the provision of descriptions only. This created a dilemma for the logical positivists, to which they offered two different responses:

1. **Instrumentalism**. This is the view that laws are merely useful instruments whose value is measured not by whether they are true or false (or correctly depict reality), but by how effectively they explain and predict phenomena. It means that laws are employed in science on account of their usefulness rather than because they can be verified as true. Thus they should be evaluated in terms of their usefulness. We return to this pragmatic view in connection with the methodological thinking of Milton Friedman (Chapter 2).

2. **Confirmationism**. A different approach is to say that laws do not express certain knowledge about the world, but instead express probabilistic knowledge. Probability concerns the likelihood (or chance) that something is the case or will happen and probabilistic statements have the following logical form:

$$\forall x\,[A(x) \xrightarrow{\;y\%\;} B(x)]$$

(Read as: For all x, if x is A, then there is a probability of $y\%$ that x is B.) Probability statements should be based on empirical research, where the more evidence there is for members of A having property B, the larger y is. For that reason this probability measure is sometimes called the degree of confirmation of a statement. This gives a particular interpretation to the meaning of laws in science that has not only been fundamental to empirical research in the natural sciences, but is practically the only meaning of laws in economics, such as "the law of demand," that the quantity and price of commodities are inversely related.

Demarcation

The logical positivist's aim to demarcate truly scientific knowledge from other kinds of knowledge is an aim that will also be discussed in later chapters. The recurrent problem, however, is to determine whether or not such an aim is feasible.

Consider, for example, Newtonian classical mechanics, which was considered by the logical positivists to be the prototype of scientific knowledge. Take one of Newton's famous laws: $F = m \cdot a$. This law consists of three terms: F force, m mass, and a acceleration.

In order for it to be meaningful, for each theoretical term appearing in this law, correspondence rules should be defined that tell us how these theoretical terms are identified with their observational counterparts. To do this, acceleration is translated into two terms: time and position, which can be operationalized by a clock and a meter measure respectively. Mass can be operationalized as follows: we imagine a procedure for weighing bodies with a balance and standard weights, and we define mass as equal to the weight determined according to this procedure. A fundamental problem arises, however, when we try to measure force. There is no procedure independent from the law itself to measure force. In fact, force is operationalized by this relation itself, which therefore ought rather be looked upon as a correspondence rule instead of a law.

So, there is something odd with the concept of force, which was admitted by Newton himself. Newton proved, with the aid of mathematical calculations, that a planet has an acceleration in the direction of the sun that is inversely proportional to the square of the distance to the sun. Based on these calculations, he introduced the concept of gravitational force as the cause of this acceleration. There was no evidence for this force, and Newton himself found this idea of gravity as action at a distance through empty space absurd. Nonetheless he stuck to it, and the introduction of the concept of gravity by Newton is – ironically – considered one of the greatest triumphs of mathematical natural science.

If we are to accept the verdict of history, the logical positivist has to admit that some terms have no meaning apart from the particular theory that implicitly defines them, that is, they cannot be independently operationalized in observational terms. For this reason the logical positivist attempt at demarcating science from non-science fails. At the same time, the restriction of scientific statements to analytic and synthetic *a posteriori* fails because theories such as Newton's use statements that are neither.

Indeed, this basic problem was to prove even more serious. Even when theoretical terms can be operationalized, there is often more than one procedure or operation for doing so. Which procedure or operation, then, provides the correct meaning of the relevant theoretical term? Inflation, for example, can be measured by either the consumer price index or by the producer price index, though they do not produce the same rate of inflation in the short run. Another problem is that in some cases meanings are not fully captured by correspondence rules; hence such rules can at best be considered only to be partial interpretations of these terms.

The case of Newtonian mechanics proved to be even more peculiar (or should we say typical?). Isaac Newton (1642–1727) wrote his masterpiece *Philosophiæ Naturalis Principia Mathematica* before he reached the age of 25, and he was appointed Professor of Mathematics at Cambridge in 1669 and Master of the Royal Mint in 1696. In 1936, a very large part of Newton's unpublished writings was sold at auction. The famous economist John Maynard Keynes (1883–1946), "disturbed by this impiety," managed gradually to reassemble about half of them, and so was able to study these writings. At the Newton Tercentenary Celebrations in 1946, Keynes presented the remarkable conclusions he had drawn following his study of these papers. He revealed that of the approximately one million words in Newton's handwritten papers more than half related to the subject of alchemy: the magic of transmutation, the philosopher's stone, and the elixir of life. According to Keynes, "Newton was not the first of the age of reason. He was the last of the magicians, the last of the Babylonians and Sumerians … ." It appeared that the concept of force, as action working at a distance through empty space, was nothing other than a magical term! The demarcation line separating science form pseudo-science thus appeared to cut straight through the prototype of modern science!

Looking ahead

Despite the flaws in the logical positivist program, for several decades it remained the dominant view of scientific knowledge. Many accepted the view that to be called scientific a statement must be either true by definition or confirmed by empirical observation. Moreover, logical positivist thinking came to dominate the way economists thought about their own theories. To regard them as scientific they somehow had to be shown to be empirically adequate. The economic methodologist most influential in this regard was Terence Hutchison (see Focus 2.1), whose arguments became well known among economists in the 1930s. The logival positivist program, however, offered little explanation of how theories about economic phenomena related to the possible evidence for them, and by the 1950s this had become a central dispute in economics. In the next chapter we turn to this debate about the role played by empiricism in the development of economic methodology.

Exercises

1 Describe the syntactic and semantic requirements an empirical generalization must fulfill to be called a scientific law.
2 Carl Hempel developed a model of scientific explanation. Give a description of this model. Give also an example of a scientific explanation. Show how this explanation can be turned into a prediction.
3 Within the logical positivist program, two alternative answers were developed to the Humean induction problem. Give a short description of each.
4 According to classical empiricism, the empirical foundation of science is sense data. Modern empiricism no longer upholds this naive view. Give an explanation why this classic view is naive.

5 Describe operationalism. What is the main problem with this form of empiricism?

6 Does the following argument satisfy the logical positivist's requirements for a scientific explanation? Give a short explanation of your conclusion.

> If experts predict a solar eclipse at time T, then a solar eclipse takes place at time T.
> The experts predict a solar eclipse at time T.
> _____
> A solar eclipse takes place at time T.

7 The standard example of the *modus ponens* form of argumentation is:

> All men are mortal.
> Socrates is a man.
> _____
> Socrates is mortal.

Can this classic argument be considered as an explanation of Socrates being mortal?

8 Work out whether the following statements are analytic, synthetic *a priori*, or synthetic *a posteriori*:
   a. There exist no round squares.
   b. There exist no unicorns.
   c. There exist no synthetic *a priori* statements.
   d. In the long run, the economy moves to potential GDP.
   e. If inflation becomes expected by the public, the price-adjustment schedule is shifted upward by the amount of the expected inflation.

Relevant readings

Hausman, Daniel M. (1992) "An Introduction to Philosophy of Science," in *The Inexact and Separate Science of Economics*, Cambridge: Cambridge University Press, pp. 281–329.

A complete but densely written survey of the received view.

Keynes, John Maynard (1951) "Newton, the Man," in *Essays in Biography*, New York: Horizon Press, pp. 310–23.

Though there are many good biographies of Newton, this is the only one that we are aware of that has been written by an economist.

Focus 1.1   Axiomatization

A theory is is said to be axiomatized if a small number of its statements are singled out and all the other statements are deduced from them. This means that axiomatization concerns only the syntactics of a theory; it is a way of re-structuring a theory as a deductive system (a theory's semantics concerns the meaning given to its terms). The statements from which the rest of the theory can be deduced are given a variety of names; they are called assumptions, axioms, laws, postulates, or principles – sometimes indicating their status. For example, using the term "assumption" suggests a much weaker claim to truth than using the term "law."

Within the logical positivist program, the axiomatization of a theory is an important step to be taken in its assessment for the reason that it enormously simplifies its verification. Following the restructuring, one only needs to verify the theory's first principles. If they are proven to be true, the statements that can be deduced from them are also true. For logic and mathematics (analytic systems), this implies that the axioms should be tautologies. One such example of a logical axiom is: "A $\rightarrow$ A $\vee$ B" (read as: "if A, then A or B"). By contrast, in the case of the empirical sciences (synthetic systems), the assumptions have to be verified by empirical evidence. For example, in consumer theory it is assumed that consumer preferences are transitive: "For any three bundles a, b, and c, if a $\geqslant$ b and b $\geqslant$ c, then a $\geqslant$ c" (read $\geqslant$ as "is preferred or indifferent to").

The prototype of an axiomatic system is Euclid's *Elements*, his axiomatization of geometry. Following a list of 23 definitions, Euclid's *Elements* states the following five "postulates":

1. A straight line segment can be drawn joining any two points.
2. Any straight line segment can be extended indefinitely in a straight line.
3. Given any straight line segment, a circle can be drawn having the segment as radius and one endpoint as its center.
4. All right angles are equal to one another.
5. If a straight line falling on two straight lines make the interior angles on the same side less than two right angles, the two straight lines, if extended indefinitely, meet on that side on which the angles are less than the two right angles.

If these postulates are seen as abstract descriptions of experience, we can see that there is a difference between the first four postulates and the fifth. The first four are derived from the experience of drawing with a straight edge and a compass. The fifth postulate is different in that we cannot verify empirically whether or not those two lines meet, since we can only draw line segments, not lines. We can extend the segments further and further (according to the second postulate) to see if they meet, but we cannot continue this extension ad infinitum. Apparently even Euclid acknowledged the questionable nature of this postulate, for he postponed the use of it for as long as possible, only introducing it during the proof of his twenty-ninth proposition.

Non-Euclidean geometry arose from attempts to prove Euclid's fifth postulate, the so-called parallel postulate or axiom. In fact, non-Euclidean geometry is a geometry in which the parallel postulate does not hold. Nikolai Ivanovich Lobachevsky (1792–1856) was one of the first to reject the parallel axiom to see whether the resulting geometry would lead to a contradiction. It did not, and the geometry he elaborated is now known as Hyperbolic or Lobachevsky geometry. Carl Friedrich Gauss (1777–1855) arrived at the same conclusions, and saw its most revolutionary implication, namely that non-Euclidean geometry could be used to describe the properties of physical space as accurately as does Euclidean geometry. Thus the latter geometry does not necessarily represent physical space; its physical truth cannot be guaranteed on *a priori* grounds, as Kant had assumed.

Developments such as the creation of non-Euclidean geometries caused mathematicians to question whether or not their subject had any real foundations. As long as mathematics dealt with – or was believed to deal with – concepts that had physical meaning, then its rigor could be said to have an empirical basis. By the end of the nineteenth century, the developments outlined above had led to an acceptance of the view that all mathematical axioms are arbitrary. In response to this crisis, David Hilbert (1862–1943) sought to reintroduce rigor into mathematics by demanding that mathematical systems, including geometries, be consistent. As long as mathematics was regarded as telling the "truth" about nature, the occurrence of contradictory theorems could not arise. When non-Euclidean geometries were created, however, their apparent variance with reality did raise questions about their consistency. This problem was solved by showing that the proof of the consistency of the non-Euclidean geometries depends on the proof of the consistency of Euclidean geometry. Hilbert did succeed in proving the consistency of Euclidean geometry on the assumption that arithmetic is consistent. But the consistency of the latter had not been established, and, as was shown later in the work of Kurt Gödel (1906–1978), *could not* be established.

In economics, the first example of axiomatization is perhaps Ragnar Frisch's (1895–1973) very first paper in economics, published in 1926, in which three axioms define utility as a quantity. However, the work more often regarded as having introduced axiomatization into economics is John von Neumann and Oskar Morgenstern's *Theory of Games and Economic Behavior* (1944). Following von Neumann and Morgenstern, rational choice theory today rests on a set of axioms that describe – or, rather, define – choice. For example, one of the axioms always referred to in the rational choice literature is the axiom of transitivity: $x_1 > x_2$ and $x_2 > x_3$ imply $x_1 > x_3$, where ">" means "larger than," but often also denotes "preferred to."

There is a tacit but strongly held belief in economics that axiomatization leads to the development of better science. Whether or not this conviction is justified, even the most influential axiomatizer of economics, von Neumann (1903–1957), warned against the use of too much "de-empiricization," his term for axiomatization: "at a great distance from its empirical source, or after much 'abstract' inbreeding, a mathematical subject is in danger of degeneration." According to von Neumann, the unempirical character of Euclid's fifth postulate was the "prime" reason for it to be questioned. He found it "hardly possible to believe in the existence of an absolute, immutable concept of mathematical rigor, dissociated from all human experience."

Relevant readings

Frisch, Ragnar (1926) "On a Problem in Pure Economics," reprinted in in J.S. Chipman, L. Hurwicz, M.K. Richter, and H.F. Sonnenschein (eds), *Preferences, Utility, and Demand*, New York: Harcourt Brace Jovanovich, 1971, pp. 386–423.
   The first important example of axiomatization in economics. It is also the first publication in which the term econometrics appeared.
Heath, T.L. (1956) *The Thirteen Books of Euclid's Elements*, New York: Dover.
   Euclid's *Elements* constituted the paradigm axiomatic system for many centuries.
von Neumann, John (1961) "The Mathematician," in A.H. Taub (ed.), *John von Neumann: Collected Works*, Oxford: Pergamon Press, pp. 1–9.
   Von Neumann's personal view on (the foundations of) mathematics, including Hilbert's axiomatization program.
von Neumann, John and Oskar Morgenstern (1944) *Theory of Games and Economic Behavior*, Princeton, NJ: Princeton University Press.
   The original book on the theory of economic games, which moreover showed how the axiomatic approach was applicable to economics.

Focus 1.2   Models

At the fifth European meeting of the Econometric Society, held in 1935, Jan Tinbergen (1903–1994) presented a paper titled "A Mathematical Theory of Business Cycle Theory." The paper discussed three issues:

1.   The presentation of a simplified business-cycle "mechanism,"
2.   An analysis of its various "influencing coefficients," with a view to discovering those which might be modified by policy,
3.   An analysis of the conditions which would have to be satisfied in order to achieve the aims set by various types of policy.

In the published version, Tinbergen used the term "model" rather than "mechanism" – one of the first instances of an economist using this term to denote
a mathematical product of empirical research. It marked the beginning of a
new practice in economics, which is today loosely termed modeling.

In previous work the term "model" had been used to denote a substantive
analogy as distinct from a formal analogy (Nagel 1961: 110). In substantive analogies, a system of elements possessing certain already familiar
properties that are assumed to be related in known ways is taken as an exemplar
for the construction of a theory for some second system. For example, in
1935 Frisch used the term "model" to indicate that a pendulum is used as a
substantive analogy to the business-cycle mechanism. In formal analogies,
the system that serves as the recipe is some familiar structure of mathematical relations (see Focus 6.1 for further discussion of analogies).

To understand what was intended by the new practice of modeling,
let us first take a closer look at Tinbergen's article. In it the model was
intended to be a simplified representation of an aspect of reality, namely the
business-cycle mechanism, and was constructed to investigate problems in
business-cycle explanations and in business-cycle policy.

The problem faced by the economist was one of finding the right degree
of simplification in order to achieve an appropriate balance between
approximating reality as closely as possible while keeping the model at a
manageable size. In his article Tinbergen recommended the investigation
of a wide range of different models as the specific model discussed in the
article could only provide incomplete answers.

The intellectual tradition that led to Tinbergen's use of the concept of
a mathematical model is rooted in work by the physicist Heinrich Hertz
(1857–1894). Hertz called a model in this sense of representation, an image
(*Bild*). These representations should fulfill specific requirements. First,
and most fundamentally, the consequences of (that is, the inferences from)
a representation of a mechanism must be the representation of the consequences of that mechanism. Hertz also had two additional requirements.

1. First, a representation should not contradict the rules of logic. For
    example, the assumptions of a representation should not contradict
    each other.
2. The representation should be most "appropriate," that is, it should con-
    tain as many as possible of the relevant essential relations and at the
    same time be as simple as possible. Appropriateness can only be tested
    in relation to the purpose of the representation, since one representa-
    tion may be more suitable for one purpose and another for another.

Depending on the relative importance given to these two requirements,
two different modeling traditions have evolved from Hertz's account of
models.

An approach that emphasized the logical requirement evolved into the semantic account of models. Like the syntactic view discussed in Chapter 1, its starting point is a theory reduced to a set of axioms. The problem with the syntactic view, however, is that one can usually specify more than one procedure or operation in order to attribute meaning to a theoretical term. Moreover, in some cases the meanings cannot be captured fully by correspondence rules, hence the rules can only be considered partial interpretations for these terms. A solution to these problems was provided by the semantic approach: models, rather than correspondence rules, should provide the interpretation of the axioms. A model is an interpretation of a theory in which all the axioms of that theory are true. The semantic view thus allows for different representations, because it is usually possible to produce more than one interpretation. One consequence of this approach is that whenever the axioms are incompatible a model cannot exist. This logical requirement of models is the most important criterion for the assessment of theoretical models.

In contrast, an emphasis on the requirement of appropriateness evolved into the tradition of models that was pioneered by Tinbergen. These models were often built for practical (that is, policy) reasons. Consistency, therefore, sometimes had to be sacrificed in favor of empirical relevance, or as Clive Granger (2003 Nobel Prize laureate with Robert Engle, "for methods of analyzing economic time series") once said when discussing the "quality" of models: "a theory may be required to be internally consistent, although consistency says little or nothing about relevance."

Whereas in the semantic view models are defined in terms of their logical and semantic connections with theories, with the latter being the real focus of interest, in current economic methodology, increasing attention is paid to the separate and independent role models play in economic research practice.

The most pronounced view on this independent role is the "models as mediators" account advanced by Mary Morgan and Margaret Morrison (1999), who have shown that models function as instruments of investigation that help us to learn more about theories and the real world, because they are autonomous agents. In other words, they are partially independent of both theories and the real world. We can learn from models because they represent either some aspect of the world or some aspect of a theory, or both. The "quality" of these instruments therefore lies not so much in their veracity, as in how "satisfactorily" they fulfill their research aims and criteria. Morgan offers five statements that cover these aims and criteria:

1. *To measure theoretical laws*: models must satisfy certain theoretical requirements (economic criteria).
2. *To explain (or describe) the observed data*: models must fit the observed data (statistical or historical criteria).
3. *To be useful for policy*: models must allow for the exploration of policy options or make predictions about future values.

4. *To explore or develop theory*: models must expose unsuspected rela-
    tionships or develop the detail of relationships.
5. *To verify or reject theory*: models must be found to be satisfactory or
    not over a range of economic, statistical, and other criteria.

Relevant readings

Granger, Clive W.J. (2003) "Evaluation of Theories and Models," in *Econometrics
    and the Philosophy of Economics: Theory–Data Confrontations in Economics*,
    edited by Bernt P. Stigum. Princeton and Oxford: Princeton University Press,
    pp. 480–6.
    A pragmatist view of the assessment of models by a 2003 Nobel Prize laureate.
Hertz, Heinrich (1956) *The Principles of Mechanics Presented in a New Form*,
    New York: Dover.
    A classic of modern physics, containing an influential account of representations.
Morgan, Mary S. (1988) "Finding a Satisfactory Empirical Model," in Neil de
    Marchi (ed.), *The Popperian Legacy in Economics*, Cambridge: Cambridge
    University Press, pp. 199–211.
    Based on her history of econometrics, Morgan showed that it is more their
        quality than their veracity by which models are assessed.
Morgan, Mary S. and Margaret Morrison (eds) (1999) *Models as Mediators*,
    Cambridge: Cambridge University Press.
    Based on case studies in physics and economics, Morgan and Morrison arrived
        at an account of models alternative to the dominant semantic view.
Nagel, Ernest (1961) *The Structure of Science: Problems in the Logic of Scientific
    Explanation*, London: Routledge and Kegan Paul.
    The standard received view account of explanations, including a semantic view
        account of models.

Focus 1.3   Formalism

Mark Blaug

When it is applied in areas such as the arts, literature, and philosophy the term
"**formalism**" means an emphasis on form rather than content or meaning.

    In the area of mathematics, however, the term has taken on a particular
meaning. In mathematics, formalism refers to a specific school in the philosophy of the subject which emphasized axiomatic proofs through theorems. It is associated in particular with the works of David Hilbert, whose
Foundations of Geometry replaced the traditional axioms of Euclid by an
equivalent but much more rigorously defined set of theorems.

    Hilbert's philosophy of mathematics called for a style of mathematics
in which one plays with symbols devoid of meaning according to certain
formal rules that are agreed upon in advance. This style of mathematics
was in turn associated with the name of Nicolas Bourbaki, a collective
pseudonym for a group of mainly French twentieth-century mathematicians,

who expounded modern advanced mathematics grounded rigorously on set theory. (Bourbaki was known as the name of the group but it was actually a clever joke played on the mathematics establishment, making mathematicians believe that Nicolas Bourbaki was a real person.)

Yes, but the question may well be asked: what does all of this have to do with economics? In 1959, Gérard Debreu (1921–2004; 1983 Nobel Prize laureate, "for having incorporated new analytical methods into economic theory and for his rigorous reformulation of the theory of general equilibrium"), a student of mathematics in France, but then living in the USA, published a slim 102-page volume, *The Theory of Value: An Axiomatic Analysis of Economic Equilibrium*, which gave a clear example of how the Bourbakian program might be applied to economics. The ideals of the program are expressed eloquently in the preface to the book:

> the theory of value is treated here with the standards of rigor of the contemporary formalist school of mathematics. The effort towards rigor substitutes correct reasoning and results for incorrect ones, but it also offers other rewards too. It usually leads to a deeper understanding of the problems to which it is applied, and this has not failed to happen in the present case. It may also lead to a radical change of mathematical tools. In the case under discussion, it has been essentially to change from the calculus to convexity and topological properties, a transformation which has resulted in notable gains in the generality and simplicity of the theory.

And now for the punch line: "Allegiance to rigor dictates the axiomatic form of analysis where the theory, in the strict sense, is logically entirely disconnected from its interpretations" (Debreu 1959: p. x).

For an illustration of what is implied by Debreu, let us consider a popular interpretation of the so-called First Fundamental Theorem of modern welfare economics, first labeled as such by Kenneth Arrow (1972 Nobel Prize laureate with John R. Hicks, "for their pioneering contributions to general economic equilibrium theory and welfare theory") in 1962.

The First Fundamental Theorem sets out a proposition that is repeated in every economics textbook: a perfectly competitive economy maximizes social welfare by a so-called Pareto-optimal allocation of resources that meets with unanimous approval, meaning that it is an allocation that makes it impossible to reassign inputs and outputs in order to make an individual better off (in his or her own judgment) without making at least one person worse off. This proposition can be proved mathematically at various levels of difficulty, but it can also be set out in diagrams and in words, as we have done above. The miraculous nature of the proposition is that it seems to give us a definition of social welfare without the need for any interpersonal comparison of the welfare of individuals.

So what? Well, it appears to some commentators and textbook writers to support the unqualified superiority of free markets over state intervention. All it requires is the interpretation of one of its assumptions – that a *perfectly* competitive economy corresponds to actual economies – as being absolutely correct. Perfect competition is a regime in which all firms are too small to influence the price at which they sell their products so that price is determined by the demand and supply of all buyers and sellers. Does this accord with reality – or is it pure formalism?

In reality, many firms choose to "make" the price and not just "take" the price by, say, introducing a new version of the product and then advertising it, or by locating at a new point of sale and so attracting new customers, or else simply by marketing the same product in a more skilful fashion. In short, perfect competition is by no means a realistic assumption.

None of this matters, however, if we drop the ambitious idea of defining social welfare and instead focus our attention more modestly on evaluating the effects of an economic change – such as a new tax or the removal of a protective tariff. Granting that any such changes will always produce both gainers and losers, then provided the gains are larger than the losses, we may be able to show that the change *improves* the overall level of social welfare. In other words, it may be a potential Pareto improvement (PPI). This language of PPI soon became the orthodox language of textbooks and it is in this form that students nowadays learn welfare economics.

Is this practical – that is, could governments discover who were the gainers and losers (in their own judgment) from any given economic change? Further, could they find out whether the gains were larger than the losses in order to arrive at a net figure for the welfare effect brought about by a particular change? A moment's consideration of the situation will show that no government in the real world would ever be able to identify all of the gainers and all of the losers without questioning every single individual – which is clearly impractical.

So, the First Fundamental Theorem of welfare economics is an analytic proposition that cannot possibly be turned into a practical policy proposal. It is what 1991 Nobel Prize laureate Ronald Coase ("for his discovery and clarification of the significance of transaction costs and property rights for the institutional structure and functioning of the economy") has aptly labeled "blackboard economics," that is, propositions that can be written on a blackboard, but simply cannot be implemented in the real world. If, nevertheless, you find yourself convinced – or at least swayed – by the First Fundamental Theorem, you have in fact succumbed to formalism!

Relevant readings

Debreu, Gérard (1959) *The Theory of Value: An Axiomatic Analysis of Economic Equilibrium*, New Haven: Yale University Press.
A clear example of the Bourbakian approach in economics.

Chapter 2

Methodologies of Positive Economics

By the middle of the twentieth century, economists and econometricians had developed a considerable interest in establishing a proper methodology for empirical research in economics. These ideas were developed and expressed principally in lengthy and often-heated debates that were strongly influenced by the ideas of logical postivism.

Because of the rise of Nazism in Germany and its expansion across much of Europe, the leading proponents of logical positivism had moved to the USA during this period, gaining substantial influence there during the 1940s and 1950s in the field of philosophy – but also in economics. Yet it was not only philosophers who emigrated; many econometricans also traveled across the Atlantic at this time, coming to play major roles in the development of the discipline over the next few decades.

These econometricians shared the scientific ideals of the logical positivists, having a deeply held belief in mathematical rigor and the empirical testing of theories. In this chapter, we will focus on those debates that were stimulated by – and occurred in relation to – the emergence of econometrics as a new form of empirical research, particularly as it was shaped by the writings of three leading econometricians: Jan Tinbergen, Trygve Haavelmo, and Tjalling Koopmans. These were:

(i) the Keynes–Tinbergen debate about the new method of econometrics;
(ii) the measurement-without-theory debate, comparing the method employed by the National Bureau of Economic Research with the econometric approach of the Cowles Commission;
(iii) Friedman's essay about a positive methodology for empirical research as an alternative to the Cowles Commission approach; and
(iv) Samuelson's descriptivism, which was proposed as an alternative to Friedman's methodology.

These debates show that there was not – and indeed still is not – a single agreed-upon methodology for carrying out of empirical research in economics, nor indeed is there one systematic account. Each of the methodologies discussed here was developed within the practice of empirical research. Only much later did economists begin to produce more systematic accounts of economic methodology – of which Mark Blaug's *Methodology of Economics*, first published in 1980, is one of the best known.

The new discipline of econometrics

The 1930s saw the development of a new academic discipline, **econometrics**, which was intended to develop empirical methods that would offer an alternative to the experimental methods of science. The principles of econometrics were defined implicitly by the constitution of the Econometric Society, which was founded in 1931:

> The Econometric Society is an international society for the advancement of economic theory in its relation to statistics and mathematics. The Society shall operate as a completely disinterested, scientific organization without political, social, financial, or nationalistic bias. Its main object shall be to promote studies that aim at a unification of the theoretical-quantitative and the empirical-quantitative approach to economic problems and that are penetrated by constructive and rigorous thinking similar to that which has come to dominate in the natural sciences.

In words of the person who coined the term, Ragnar Frisch, econometrics involved the bringing together of three separate disciplines: economic theory, statistics, and mathematics. In the USA, the Cowles Commission for Research in Economics was set up in 1932, being funded by Alfred Cowles (1891–1984) specifically to undertake econometric research. The Society's journal, *Econometrica*, was published by the Commission. The Cowles Commission's econometric approach, developed in the 1940s and 1950s, became the standard approach that is found in most econometric textbooks.

One of the most popular of these textbooks, Jack Johnston's *Econometric Methods*, identifies the main purpose of econometrics as putting some empirical flesh and blood on theoretical structures. For Johnston, this involves three distinct steps:

1. First, the model must be specified in explicit functional – often linear – form.
2. The second step is to decide on the appropriate data definitions, and to assemble the relevant data series for those variables included in the model.
3. The third step is to form a bridge between theory and data through the use of statistical methods. The bridge consists of various sets of statistics, which help to determine the validity of the theoretical model.

The most important set of statistics consists of numerical estimates of the model's parameters. Further statistics enable assessment to be made of the reliability or precision with which these parameters have been estimated. Further statistics and diagnostic tests will help to assess the performance of the model.

The Keynes–Tinbergen debate

The first two macroeconometric models (see Focus 1.2) were constructed by Jan Tinbergen (together with Ragnar Frisch, the first Nobel Prize laureates in Economic Sciences in 1969, "for having developed and applied dynamic models for the analysis of economic processes").

Tinbergen's first model was of the Dutch economy, published in 1936. In the same year Tinbergen was commissioned by the League of Nations to perform statistical tests on business-cycle theories. The results of this later study were published in a two-volume work, *Statistical Testing of Business-Cycle Theories* (1939). The first contained an explanation of this new method of econometric testing as well as a demonstration of what could be achieved, based on three case studies. The second volume developed a model of the United States, the second macroeconomic model in the history of economics.

Tinbergen's first League of Nations study provoked a great deal of controversy. It was circulated in 1938 prior to its publication, and generated lively discussions about the role that econometrics could play in the testing of economic theory. It was John Maynard Keynes's (1939) critique of Tinbergen's first volume that sparked off the debate about the role of econometrics and what it might be able to achieve.

Keynes's attack, phrased in his usual rhetorical style, was such that the historian of econometrics Mary Morgan (1990: 121) concluded that "he had clearly not read the volume with any great care" and revealed ignorance about the technical aspects of econometrics. (In his reply to Keynes, when discussing the technique by which trends are eliminated, Tinbergen (1940: 151) even remarked: "Mr. Keynes does not seem to be well informed. ... A glance ... at any elementary text-book on these matters could have helped him.")

Notwithstanding Keynes's possible ignorance of econometric techniques, his response highlighted a number of important concerns about this new method. According to Keynes, the technique of multiple correlation analysis which had been adopted by Tinbergen was solely a method for measurement. It contributed nothing in terms of either discovery or criticism. The implication was that if the economic theorist does not provide the modeler with a complete set of causal factors, then the measurement of the other causal factors will be biased.

Am I right in thinking that the method of multiple correlation analysis essentially depends on the economist having furnished, not merely a list of the significant causes, which is correct so far as it goes, but a *complete* list? For example, suppose three factors are taken into account, it is not enough that these should be in fact *veræ causæ*; there must be no other significant factor. If there is a further factor, not taken account of, then the method is not able to discover the relative quantitative importance of the first three. If so, this means that the method is only applicable where the economist is able to provide beforehand a correct and indubitably complete analysis of the significant factors.

(Keynes 1939: 560)

Moreover, Keynes argued that some significant factors in any economy are not capable of measurement, or may be interdependent.

Another of Keynes's concerns was the assumed linearity of the relations between these factors. He also noted that the determination of time-lags and trends was too often based on trial and error, and too little informed by theory. And last but not least was the **problem of invariance**: would the relations found also hold for the future? These questions remained central to the subsequent debate, and need to be considered in any discussion of econometric methods.

Tinbergen's response was technical, rather than methodological. He gave a very detailed description of how he had solved each problem by explaining the techniques he had employed. The implication was that through the adoption of these techniques he had overcome any methodological problems (see the Introduction above for the distinction between method and methodology).

Tinbergen's reply was largely dismissed by Keynes, who ended the exchange with a proposal for an experiment:

It will be remembered that the seventy translators of the Septuagint were shut up in seventy separate rooms with the Hebrew text and brought out with them, when they emerged, seventy identical translations. Would the same miracle be vouchsafed if seventy multiple correlators were shut up with the same statistical material? And anyhow, I suppose, if each had a different economist perched on his *a priori*, that would make a difference to the outcome.

(Keynes 1940: 155–6)

The simple answer to Keynes's question is "No." In the middle of the 1990s Jan Magnus and Mary Morgan attempted to carry out Keynes's suggested experiment.

The basic idea of the experiment is very simple, namely to take a specified data set and let several researchers carry out the same set of applied econometrics tasks, but with their own (different) methods, approaches and beliefs. Our overall aim was to assess, within the environment of our experiment, the differences between the several ways of doing econometrics in a practical application.

(Magnus and Morgan 1999: 4)

The results of the experiment were significant. Even in relation to the simple first task of measurement, the eight participating teams produced different versions of the variables, constructed different models, used different elements from the data sets, and adopted different measurement procedures.

Taking into account all of these concerns, Keynes came to the conclusion that econometrics was not yet a scientific approach:

No one could be more frank, more painstaking, more free from subjective bias or *parti pris* than Professor Tinbergen. There is no one, therefore, so far as human qualities go, whom it would be safer to trust with black magic. That there is anyone I would trust with it at the present stage or that this brand of statistical alchemy is ripe to become a branch of science, I am not yet persuaded. But Newton, Boyle and Locke all played with alchemy. So let him continue.

(Keynes 1940: 156)

In his London inaugural lecture "Econometrics – Alchemy or Science?," David Hendry admitted that "it is difficult to provide a convincing case for the defence against Keynes's accusation almost 40 years ago that econometrics is *statistical alchemy* since many of his criticisms remain apposite" (1980: 402). The ease with which spurious correlations can be produced by a mechanical application of the econometric method suggests alchemy, but, according to Hendry, the scientific status of econometrics can be upheld by showing that such deceptions are testable. He, therefore, comes up with the following simple methodology: "The three golden rules of econometrics are test, test and test" (p. 403). In his view, rigorously tested models, which offer adequate descriptions of the available data, take into account previous findings, and are derived from well-based theories justifying the claim to be scientific.

Laws in economics

As we saw in the previous chapter (see pp. 15–17), in the logical positivist's theory of knowledge (or **epistemology**), laws are crucial in terms of both explanation and prediction. The particular problem in the case of economics and the social sciences, however, is that in these instances laws have to be found outside an experimental setting or laboratory, which creates considerable difficulties in terms of controlling the environment and making separate studies of the causal relationships between variables.

One of the earliest papers to make a significant contribution to the development of econometrics was Trygve Haavelmo's (1944) "The Probability Approach in Econometrics." (In 1989 Haavelmo (1911–1999) was awarded the Nobel Prize in Economics "for his clarification of the probability theory foundations of econometrics and his analyses of simultaneous economic structures.") One of the central themes of the paper was the problem of how to uncover laws outside the setting of the laboratory. The issue was explained in terms of "judging the degree of persistence over time of relations between economic variables," or, speaking more generally, "whether or not we might hope to find elements of invariance in economic life, upon which to establish permanent 'laws'" (p. 13). It results from the fact that real economic phenomena cannot be "artificially isolated from 'other influences'" (p. 14). We always have to deal with passive observations, and these are "influenced by a great many factors not accounted for in theory; in other words, the difficulties of fulfilling the condition 'other things being equal'" (p. 18).

To clarify this problem of uncovering laws outside the laboratory, let us examine the matter through the use of a simple example.

Assume that we would like to find an explanation for the behavior of an economic variable y. Let the behavior of y be determined by a function F of all possible and independent causal factors x_i:

$$y = F(x_1, x_2, \ldots)$$

Then, the way in which the factors x_i might influence y can be represented by the following equation:

$$\Delta y = \Delta F(x_1, x_2, \ldots) = F_1 \Delta x_1 + F_2 \Delta x_2 + \ldots$$

(The Δ indicates a change in magnitude. The F_i indicates how much y will proportionally change due to a change in magnitude of factor x_i.)

Suppose now that we are trying to discover a law that could explain the behavior of y. In principle, there are an infinite number of factors, $x_1, x_2, \ldots$, that could influence the behavior of the variable, but we hope that it will be possible to establish a constant and relatively simple relation between y and a relatively small number of explanatory factors, x.

In a laboratory, we could artificially isolate a selected set of factors from the other influences – in other words we would ensure that **ceteris paribus conditions** are imposed. (*Ceteris paribus* is a Latin phrase translated as "with other things the same.") In this instance, $\Delta x_{n+1} = \Delta x_{n+2} = \ldots = 0$, so that a simpler relationship can be investigated (n is often a very small number, e.g. 1, 2, or 3):

$$\Delta y = F_1 \Delta x_1 + \ldots + F_n \Delta x_n$$

Then, in a controlled experiment the remaining factors, x_i, can be varied systematically to gain knowledge about the F_i in terms of whether F_i is stable for different variations of x_i, and, if so, establish lawful relationships between y and the x_i's.

Having only passive observations available, that is, observing the behavior of the variable only passively without being able to control influences, Haavelmo's distinction between potential and factual influences is fundamental for judging the degree of persistence of a relationship over time. When an F_i is significantly different from zero, then factor x_i is stated to have "potential influence." The combination $F_i \cdot \Delta x_i$ indicates how much the "factual influence" of a factor x_i is upon y. The problem with passive observations is that it can only be observed whether a factor has "factual" (that is, actual) influence. There may be many factors having potential influence but whose influence is never actually observed. So, if we are trying to explain a certain observable variable y by a system of causal factors, there is, in general, no limit to the number of such factors that might have a *potential* influence upon y. Haavelmo's response to this risk of too much complexity (caused by too many explaining fators) was an optimistic observation that "Nature may limit the number of factors that have a non-negligible *factual* influence to a relatively small number" (p. 24).

Thus, the relationship $y = F(x_1, \ldots, x_n)$, which contains only a limited number of factual influences (n), explains the actual observed values of y, provided that the factual influence of all the unspecified factors together are very small as compared with the factual influence of the specified factors $x_1, \ldots, x_n$. However, the problem does not lie in establishing simple relations, but rather in the fact that the relations found empirically, derived from observation over certain time intervals, are "still simpler than we expect them to be from theory, so that we are thereby led to *throw away* elements of a theory that would be sufficient to explain apparent 'breaks in structure' later" (p. 26). The cause of this problem is that it may be impossible to identify the reason for the factual influence of a factor, say x_{n+1}, being negligible, that is $F_{n+1} \cdot \Delta x_{n+1} \approx 0$. We cannot always distinguish whether its potential influence is very small, $F_{n+1} \approx 0$, or whether the factual variation of this factor over the period under consideration is non-existent, $\Delta x_{n+1} = 0$. We would like to "throw away" only the factors whose influence was not observed because their potential influence was negligible to begin with. At the same time, we want to retain factors that are important but whose influence is not observed; but if $\Delta x \approx 0$, then we will not be able to measure that influence, and we will not know that it is important unless we have other (often theoretical) grounds for thinking this.

Haavelmo understood that statistics is not sufficient to deal with this problem of finding the complete list of potential influences; rather, it is "a problem of actually *knowing something* about real phenomena, and of making realistic assumptions about them" (p. 29). To solve this problem, the theorist should first suggest "fruitful hypotheses as to how reality actually is" (p. 31), and subsequently the econometrician should test these hypotheses. He, therefore, introduced Neyman and Pearson's theory of statistical testing (see Focus 3.3) into econometrics, for which this paper became renowned.

The measurement-without-theory debate

Another of the early econometric debates started with a lengthy book review written in 1947 for *The Review of Economic Statistics* by Tjalling C. Koopmans (1910–1985, 1975 Nobel Prize laureate with Leonid Kantorovich, "for their contributions to the theory of optimum allocation of resources"). In 1949, under the general heading "Methodological Issues in Quantitative Economics," a number of publications advancing the debate appeared in the journal: a response from Rutledge Vining, "Koopmans on the Choice of Variables to be Studied and of Methods of Measurement," was followed by a "Reply" from Koopmans, and finally a "Rejoinder" from Vining.

The subject of Koopmans's review was *Measuring Business Cycles*, by Arthur F. Burns and Wesley C. Mitchell, and published by the National Bureau of Economic Research (NBER), of which Mitchell was the director between 1920 and 1945. At this time Koopmans was a senior research figure, and midway through the debate (1948) he became director of the Cowles Commission. So, his original article was more than a book review. Koopmans was mounting a full critique of the NBER empirical approach while simultaneously defending the Cowles Commission's econometric approach.

Koopmans's critique was based on Haavelmo's "Probability Approach." He accused Burns and Mitchell of trying to measure economic cycles in the absence of any economic theory about the workings of such cycles: "The toolkit of the theoretical economist is deliberately spurned" (Koopmans 1947: 163).

Koopmans put forward three arguments to explain the implications and limitations of the NBER's "empiricist position."

1. His first argument is that for the purposes of systematic and large-scale observation of a many-sided phenomenon such as the business cycle,

"theoretical preconceptions about its nature cannot be dispensed with, and the authors do so only to the detriment of the analysis" (p. 163). He compared this empiricist position with Kepler's discovery of the more superficial empirical regularities of planetary motion, which fell short of the deeper "fundamental laws" later discovered by Newton. Newton's achievement was based not only on the regularities observed by Kepler, but also on experiments conducted by Galileo.

However, Koopmans believed that economists are unable to perform experiments on an economic system as a whole, and that it is therefore impossible for many economic problems to separate causes and effects by varying causes one by one, and studying the separate effects of each cause. According to Koopmans, instead of experiments, economists possess "more elaborate and better established theories of economic behaviour than the theories of motion of material bodies known to Kepler" (p. 166), because the evidence for these theories is based on introspection, on interviews, and on inferences from the observed behavior of individuals.

In general, economic variables are determined by the simultaneous validity of a large number of structural equations describing behavior and technology. Any observed empirical regularity between a number of variables may be the result of the working of several simultaneous structural relations. Because so many empirical relations are valid simultaneously, it may be difficult – or even impossible – to uncover the more fundamental structural relationships. In the absence of experimentation, the identification of these structural relations is possible only if the set of variables involved in each equation, and perhaps also the manner in which they are combined, is specified by economic theory.

2. Koopmans's second argument against the NBER's empiricist position was that it offered no evidence for the assumption that the empirical relations found would be invariant across time. As long as the dynamics of economic variables are not based on structural relations of behavior and technology, it was difficult to know how reliable they would be for the purposes of prediction or as a guide for economic policy.

> The movements of economic variables are studied as if they were the eruptions of a mysterious volcano whose boiling caldron can never be penetrated. There is no explicit discussion at all of the problem of prediction, its possibilities and limitations, with or without structural change, although surely the history of the volcano is important primarily as a key to its future activities. (p. 167)

Ironically, thirty years later, Robert Lucas (1995 Economics Nobel Prize laureate, "for having developed and applied the hypothesis of rational expectations, and thereby having transformed macroeconomic analysis and deepened our understanding of economic policy") was to use similar reasoning in his criticism of the Cowles Commission approach. Policy evaluation requires "invariance of the structure of the model under policy variations" (Lucas 1977: 12).

The underlying idea, which has become known as the Lucas Critique, is that, according to the methods adopted by the Cowles Commission, those estimated parameters that had been regarded previously as being "structural" in the econometric analysis of economic policy are actually dependent on the economic policy pursued during the period of study. Hence, the parameters in use may change in line with shifts in the policy regime, meaning that the relations are not stable under policy variations.

3.   Koopmans's third argument against a purely empirical approach is that statistical analysis of the data requires additional assumptions about their probabilistic characteristics that cannot be subject to statistical testing from the same data. These assumptions need to be provided by economic theory and should be tested independently.

In summary, Koopmans's critique of Burns and Mitchell's study is that:

the decision not to use theories of man's economic behavior, even hypothetically, limits the value of economic science and to the maker of policies, of the results obtained or obtainable by the methods developed. This decision greatly restricts the benefit that might be secured from the use of modern methods of statistical inference. The pedestrian character of the statistical devices employed is directly traceable to the author's reluctance to formulate explicit assumptions, however general, concerning the probability distribution of the variables, i.e. assumptions expressing and specifying how random disturbances operate on the economy through the economic relationships between the variables.

(Koopmans 1947: 172)

In a defense of "empiricism as a fundamental part of scientific procedure," Vining replied by offering three points that challenged Koopmans's arguments.

1.   His first point is that he doubted whether "the method of Koopmans's group" would lead to the uncovering of the fundamental invariant relationships:

Is it not something of a mighty jump to imply that the postulated preference function of an individual is in some sense analogous to the

general laws of thermodynamics, the dynamics of friction, etc., etc.?
Is the Walrasian conception not in fact a pretty skinny fellow of
untested capacity upon which to load the burden of a general theory
accounting for the events in space and time which take place within
the spatial boundary of an economic system? (p. 82)

He asserted that the theory about the behavior of economic agents had
not been given in sufficient detail. Vining stated that the Cowles model
was therefore a "pretty skinny fellow" upon which to base so much
high-powered statistical estimation.

2. He questioned the position that empirical research should be evaluated from the point of view of social usefulness. However, Vining did
   not offer any further discussion of this point.
3. The third point was that Cowles' version of statistical economics, if it
   includes only the estimation of postulated relations, had little or no role
   to play in the discovery of economic hypotheses. According to Vining,
   statistical theory should play a similar role in economic research to that
   played by microscopy in biology: "It must aid us in seeing our materials, and methods of arranging our data must be discovered by which
   there will be revealed any orderliness that exists in the welter of motion
   and confusion shown by the disorderly units of the study" (p. 85).

Like the earlier Keynes–Tinbergen debate, this measurement-without-
theory debate has had an echo for several decades.

Finn E. Kydland and Edward C. Prescott (2004 joint Economics Nobel
Prize laureates, "for their contributions to dynamic macroeconomics: the
time consistency of economic policy and the driving forces behind business
cycles") summarized Koopmans's critique of Burns and Mitchell's study
as involving two basic criticisms.

The first is that it provides no systematic discussion of the theoretical reasons for the inclusion of some variables rather than others in their
empirical investigation. They were in broad agreement with Koopmans
in respect of this criticism: "Theory is crucial in selecting which facts to
report" (1990: 3). However, they strongly disagreed with what they saw as
his second criticism: that Burns and Mitchell's study lacks explicit assumptions about the probability distribution of the variables, that is, assumptions
about how random disturbances operate through the economic relationships between the variables, the probability model, which the economist
must then estimate and test. According to Kydland and Prescott, Koopmans
convinced the economic profession that to do otherwise is unscientific:

"We think he did economics a grave disservice, because the reporting of
facts – without assuming the data are generated by some probability model –
is an important scientific activity" (Kydland and Prescott 1990: 3).

The Cowles Commission and Milton Friedman's methodology of positive economics

As has been mentioned in the context of Keynes's critique of Tinbergen's method (see pp. 33–5), econometric modeling always runs the risk of incompleteness: some of the variables that have been omitted for empirical reasons may later turn out to play a significant role in economic relationships.

Haavelmo had also pointed to the possibility that the empirically observed relationships may be simpler than was suggested by theory. This problem could be avoided by building models that were as comprehensive as possible, and based on *a priori* theoretical specifications.

It was the view of the Cowles Commission that to understand a particular aspect of economic behavior, it is necessary to have a complete system of descriptive equations. These equations should contain every relevant observable variables, be of a known form (preferably linear), and have estimatable coefficients. However, little attention was given to either the issue of selecting the variables or what form the equations should take. It was thought that in each case this information could be supplied by economic theory.

The Cowles Commission's solution to the problem of incompleteness was thus to construct increasingly comprehensive models, which were to include as many potential influences as possible. In the 1940s, Lawrence R. Klein (1980 Nobel Prize laureate, "for the creation of econometric models and the application to the analysis of economic fluctuations and economic policies") was commissioned to construct a Cowles Commission-type model of the United States economy in the spirit of Jan Tinbergen's macro-econometric modeling method. The aim was to build increasingly comprehensive models to improve their predictability so that they could be used as reliable instruments for economic policy. The implications of a policy change could then be forecasted.

One of the earliest results of this project were three models that comprised between three and 15 equations. Soon after the publication of these models, they were subjected to a series of tests by Carl Christ.

These studies were among the first to be assessed on the assumption that econometrics models should be tested according to their performance in making successful predictions. An important part of their tests was a comparison of the predictive power of Klein's 15-equation model against that of simple extrapolation models, the so-called "naive models."

In the course of Christ's tests two naive models were used:

- The *first model* states that next year's value of any variable will equal this year's value plus a random normal disturbance ε_t^l with zero mean and constant variance (also called 'white noise').

- The *second model* states that next year's value will equal this year's value plus the change from last year to this year plus "white noise" ε_t^{II}.

These two models can be expressed in mathematical terms as follows:

$$\text{Naive model I:} \quad y_{t+1} = y_t + \varepsilon_t^I$$
$$\text{Naive model II:} \quad y_{t+1} = y_t + (y_t - y_{t-1}) + \varepsilon_t^{II}$$

These naive model tests achieved remarkable results. In each of the two cases the naive model predicted about two-thirds of the variables better than did Klein's 15-equation model. In a defense of the econometric modeling approach, Christ put forward the argument that an econometric model is preferable to a naive model because it "may be able to predict the effects of alternative policy measures or other exogenous changes …, while the naive model can only say that there will be no effect" (p. 80).

To illustrate the issue, it is illuminating to compare econometric models with those models that are widely employed in weather forecasting. It has been suggested that when comparing daily forecasts over a period of an entire year a very good forecasting device, even better than the most sophisticated models used by meteorological institutes, is the rule of thumb that tomorrow's weather will be the same as today's weather. This is an insight shared by the economist Kenneth Arrow. Invited to explain his *Life Philosophy*, he related the following autobiographical anecdote:

> It is my view that most individuals underestimate the uncertainty of the world. This is almost as true of economists and other specialists as it is of the lay public… Experience during World War II as a weather forecaster added the news that the natural world was also unpredictable. An incident… illustrates both uncertainty and the unwillingness to entertain it. Some of my colleagues had the responsibility of preparing long-range weather forecasts, i.e., for the following month. The statisticians among us subjected these forecasts to verification and found they differed in no way from chance. The forecasters themselves were convinced and requested that the forecasts be discontinued. The reply read approximately like this: "The Commanding General is well aware that the forecasts are no good. However, he needs them for planning purposes.

One important critique of the Cowles Commission's approach that reflected Arrow's insight came from Milton Friedman (1912–2006, 1976 Nobel Prize laureate "for his achievements in the fields of consumption analysis, monetary history and theory and for his demonstration of the complexity of stabilization policy").

Friedman (1951) was very critical of the Cowles Commission program but he did express approval of Christ's post-model tests, in particular the naive model tests. "Economics badly needs work of this kind. It is one of our chief defects that we place all too much emphasis on the derivation of hypotheses and all too little on testing their validity" (p. 107). The validity of the equations should not be determined by high correlation coefficients:

> The fact that the equations fit the data from which they are derived is a test primarily of the skill and patience of the analyst; it is not a test of the validity of the equations for any broader body of data. Such a test is provided solely by the consistency of the equations with data not used in the derivation, such as data for periods subsequent to the period analyzed.
>
> (Friedman 1951: 108)

For some time Friedman had been critical of this kind of econometric modeling. In a review of Tinbergen's work for the League of Nations (1940), Friedman asserted that, "Tinbergen's results cannot be judged by ordinary tests of statistical significance," because the variables

> have been selected after an extensive process of trial and error *because* they yield high coefficients of correlation. Tinbergen is seldom satisfied with a correlation coefficient less than .98. But these attractive correlation coefficients create no presumption that the relationships they describe will hold in the future.
>
> (Friedman 1940: 659)

Friedman did not regard naive models as competing theories of short-term change; rather, he saw them as standards of comparison, what might be labeled the "natural" alternative hypotheses – or "null" hypotheses – against which we test the hypothesis that the econometric model makes good predictions, such as in a Neyman–Pearson test (see Focus 3.3). On the basis of Christ's exercise, then, one should reject the latter hypothesis.

However, Friedman rejected Christ's argument that these models are preferable to naive models because of their ability to predict the consequences of alternative policy measures. Friedman claimed that it was possible that naive models can also make such predictions, simply by asserting that a proposed change in policy will have no effect. The assertion that the econometric model can predict the consequences of policy changes, according to Friedman, is a "pure act of faith." And "the fact that the model fails to predict one kind of change is reason to have less rather than more faith in its ability to predict a related kind of change" (1951: 111).

Friedman interpreted the disappointing test results as evidence that any attempt to produce an accurate econometric model of the entire economy was a premature enterprise at that point in the development of the discipline, and could not be achieved until adequate dynamic models of parts of the economy had been developed:

> As I am sure those who have tried to do so will agree, we now know so little about the dynamic mechanisms at work that there is enormous arbitrariness in any system set down. Limitations of resources – mental, computational, and statistical – enforce a model that, although complicated enough for our capacities, is yet enormously simple relative to the present state of understanding of the world we seek to explain. Until we can develop a simpler picture of the world, by an understanding of interrelations within sections of the economy, the construction of a model for the economy as whole is bound to be almost a complete groping in the dark. The probability that such a process will yield a meaningful result seems to me almost negligible.
>
> (Friedman 1951: 112–13)

Friedman's lack of faith in the macro-econometric program sent him off in another research direction – namely, that of partitioning, a so-called Marshallian approach. As Alfred Marshall (1842–1924) put it,

> Man's powers are limited: almost every one of nature's riddles is complex. He breaks it up, studies one bit at a time, and at last combines his partial solutions with a supreme effort of his whole small strength into some sort of an attempt at a solution of the whole riddle.
>
> (quoted in Friedman 1949: 469)

This Marshallian approach of partitioning was echoed in Friedman's comment on macro modeling:

> The direction of work that seems to me to offer most hope for laying a foundation for a workable theory of change is the analysis of parts of the economy in the hope that we can find bits of order here and there and gradually combine these bits into a systematic picture of the whole.
>
> (Friedman 1951: 114)

This approach has been employed increasingly in applied economic research. Over recent decades many applied modelers have shifted their interest in macro modeling away from the economy as a whole to single parts of the economy, such as the consumption function, for which economic theories were relatively well developed.

Marshall's partitioning approach was based on his use of the *ceteris paribus* clause – something that is made clear by the sentence immediately following the quote given above.

> In breaking it up, he uses some adaptation of a primitive but effective prison, or pound, for segregating those disturbing causes, whose wanderings happen to be inconvenient, for the time: the pound is called *Cæteris Paribus*.
>
> (Marshall 1925: 314)

Marshall considered this method to be particularly appropriate in the early stages of economic analysis. The advantage of the use of the *ceteris paribus* pound was that issues could be handled "more exactly."

However, Marshall did note that the more a theory was narrowed in scope "the less closely does it correspond to real life" (p. 314), since it would not recognise the interrelationships between different parts of the economy. In the next stages of development of the theory it was to be hoped that a correspondence to reality could be regained. "With each step of advance more things can be let out of the pound; exact discussions can be made less abstract, realistic discussion can be made less inexact than was possible at an earlier stage" (p. 315).

For Friedman, a model should be evaluated on the basis of its ability to predict rather than its **realisticness** (see Focus 6.3). This methodological standpoint was spelled out in his famous article, "The Methodology of Positive Economics" (1953). Friedman's anti-realisticness position was stated most clearly in his famous dictum:

> Truly important and significant hypotheses will be found to have "assumptions" that are wildly inaccurate descriptive representations of reality, and, in general, the more significant the theory, the more unrealistic the assumptions (in this sense).

In terms of Friedman's argument the use of the term "unrealistic" was unfortunate. It meant that his methodological standpoint has been interpreted as an economic version of the doctrine of "instrumentalism" (see Chapter 1). The use of the term "unrealistic" in this dictum was understood by many philosophers of science (and many economists) as referring to a specific view about the truth status of the assumptions. In this sense "unrealistic" means that the truth value of the assumptions is irrelevant. This misinterpretation of Friedman's standpoint was endorsed through the example of a specific kind of assumption, an "as if" assumption (p. 19):

> Consider the density of leaves around a tree. I suggest the hypothesis that the leaves are positioned as if each leaf deliberately sought to maximize

the amount of sunlight it receives, given the position of its neighbors, as if it knew the physical laws determining the amount of sunlight that would be received in various positions and could move rapidly or instantaneously from any one position to any other desired and unoccupied position.

The assumptions made in this example are "as if p" assumptions where p is an analogous mechanism (see Focus 6.1 for more on the concept of analogy). In other words, p is a simulacrum: something having merely the form or appearance of a certain thing, without possessing its substance or proper qualities; or p is a simulation model, the assumption of the appearance of something without having its reality. In other words, p in this example is an unrealistic representation of the mechanism behind the distribution of leaves on a tree.

Because of this incautious interchange of the terms "realistic" and "realism" (see Focus 6.3), and by focussing on the tree leaves example, Friedman's standpoint could easily be confused with instrumentalism.

However, taking Friedman's paper to be a defense of instrumentalism but reading the whole paper more carefully, the philosopher of science Alan Musgrave (1981) showed that it was possible to distinguish between different kinds of assumptions in Friedman's paper. According to Musgrave, an instrumentalist position stems from the failure to distinguish three other types of assumptions – negligibility, domain and heuristic.

1. A *negligibility* assumption means that a factor that could be expected to affect the phenomenon under investigation actually has no detectable effect.
2. A *domain* assumption means that an expected factor is absent, and so is used to specify the domain of applicability of the theory concerned.
3. A *heuristic* assumption is made if a factor is considered to be negligible, in order to simplify the 'logical' development of the theory.

It is possible to use Musgrave's distinction between different kinds of assumptions to show that Friedman's position is a critique of the need for models to be realistic, but that nevertheless it does not represent a rejection of realism.

Consider another example he employs, namely a Galilean fall experiment. The point of departure here is the same as in Haavelmo's "Probability Approach," namely the problem of being unable to carry out controlled experiments, and so being dependent solely on passive observations. The idea behind a controlled experiment is to create a specific environment – a laboratory – in which the relevant variables are manipulated in order to take measurements of particular parameters with the aim of discovering the relationship, if any, between the variables. However, it is impossible to set up laboratory conditions to investigate macroeconomic relationships.

We can only be passive observers who must unearth law-like relationships by inferring from the data supplied by Nature the underlying "design" of the experiments that Nature performs. This approach will always fall short of a controlled experiment. We can only observe experiments as they occur in the open air, and are not able to manipulate any of the relevant objects.

> Unfortunately, we can seldom test particular predictions in the social sciences by experiments explicitly designed to eliminate what are judged to be the most important disturbing influences. Generally, we must rely on evidence cast up by the "experiments" that happen to occur. The inability to conduct so-called "controlled experiments" does not, in my view, reflect a basic difference between the social and physical sciences both because it is not peculiar to the social sciences – witness astronomy – and because the distinction between a controlled experiment and uncontrolled experience is at best one of degree. No experiment can be completely controlled, and every experience is partly controlled, in the sense that some disturbing influences are relatively constant in the course of it.
>
> (Friedman 1953: 10)

Galileo had designed his experiments in such a way that although they were carried out *in the open air* with *specific* objects, the law he found would apply to *all* bodies in a *vacuum*. The empirical regularity derived by Galileo from his fall experiments is a very simple one:

$$s \propto t^2$$

meaning that distance (s) is proportional to time (t) squared. From this empirical finding he inferred a law of falling bodies that states that the acceleration of a body dropped in a vacuum is a constant and is independent of factors such as the mass, composition, and shape of the body, and the way in which it is dropped.

The question to be considered at this point is: to what extent can the law of falling bodies be applied outside a vacuum? According to Friedman, to answer this question it is important to take into account the kind of object that is to be dropped. In this instance Galileo's law works well if it is applied to compact balls: "The application of this formula to a compact ball dropped from the roof of a building is equivalent to saying that a ball so dropped behaves *as if* it were falling in a vacuum" (p. 16). Air resistance is negligible in the case of compact balls falling relatively short distances, so they behave approximately in the manner described by Galileo's law. In other words, it is safe to apply the *negligibility assumption* in the case of compact balls.

The problem, now, is to decide for which objects the air resistance is negligible. Apparently, this is the case for a compact ball falling from the roof of a building, but what if the object is a feather, or if the object is dropped from an airplane at an altitude of 30,000 feet? One of the standard criteria for laws is that they must contain no essential reference to particular objects or systems (see Chapter 1). In contrast to this standard view, Friedman argues that a specification of the domain of objects and systems for which a generalization applies should be attached to the generalization.

In dealing with this problem of specification, there are two possible options:

1. To use a more comprehensive theory – the Cowles Commission approach – "from which the influence of some of the possible disturbing factors can be calculated and of which the simple theory is a special case" (p. 18). However, the additional accuracy produced by this approach may not justify the extra costs involved, "so the question under what circumstances the simpler theory works 'well enough' remains important" (p. 18).

2. To select the phenomena for which the theory works. That is to say, to indicate the domain for which the "formula" works: for example, the law of falling bodies (outside a vacuum) holds for compact balls but not for feathers, where the air resistance becomes a significant factor. This means that one should specify the domain for which a formula holds, but that this should be done independently of this formula to keep the formula as simple as possible. Thus, one should not incorporate this specification into the formula itself. Having a simple formula that has been successfully used to model and explain certain phenomena, it is a separate – empirical – question what the full range of phenomena is that can be explained by this formula. So the aim is not to build increasingly comprehensive models – as the Cowles Commission program aimed to do – but to keep the model as simple as possible by indicating separately which phenomena belong to its domain. Empirical research should be aimed at investigating the reach of its domain.

> The important problem in connection with the hypothesis is to specify the circumstances under which the formula works or, more precisely, the general magnitude of the error in its predictions under various circumstances. Indeed, ... such a specification is not one thing and the hypothesis another. The specification is itself an essential part of the hypothesis, and it is a part that is peculiarly likely to be revised and extended as experience accumulates.
>
> (Friedman 1953: 18)

Summarizing Friedman's strategy for finding explanations, a hypothesis or theory should consist of three distinct parts:

1. A model containing only those forces that are assumed to be important – in other words, each model implies negligibility assumptions;
2. A set of rules defining the class of phenomena for which the model can be taken to be an adequate representation – these are (independent) domain specifications;
3. Specifications of the correspondence between the variables or entities in the model and observable phenomena.

Accordingly, Friedman is not an anti-realist. He is only opposed to any approach which aims to produce realistic models as "photographic repro-ductions" of the economy, an approach which he unfortunately – and misleadingly – labels as "the realism of assumptions" approach. The ref-erence to a realistic assumption here means as comprehensive as possible a description of reality. The uselessness of striving for such realisticness was illustrated in a hyperbole:

> A completely "realistic" theory of the wheat market would have to include not only the conditions directly underlying the supply and demand for wheat but also the kind of coins or credit instruments used to make exchanges; the personal characteristics of wheat-traders such as the color of each trader's hair and eyes, his antecedents and education, the number of members of his family, their characteristics, antecedents, and educa-tion, etc.; the kind of soil on which the wheat was grown, its physical and chemical characteristics, the weather prevailing during the growing season; the personal characteristics of the farmers growing the wheat and of the consumers who will ultimately use it; and so on indefinitely.
>
> (Friedman 1953: 32)

For Friedman the relevant question to ask about the assumptions of a theory is not whether they are descriptively realistic, "for they never are," but whether they are "sufficiently good approximations for the purpose in hand" (p. 15).

To clarify Friedman's position within the framework developed above, a comprehensive explanation of the motion of a falling body can thus be represented by the following equation:

$$\Delta y = \Delta F(x_1, x_2, \ldots) = F_1 \Delta x_1 + F_2 \Delta x_2 + \ldots$$

Where y is the motion of a body, x_1 is gravity, x_2 air pressure, and $x_3, x_4, \ldots$ are other specifications of the circumstances (such as temperature, mag-netic forces, and so on).

The law of falling bodies states that in a vacuum (where air pressure, $x_2, = 0$; but the notion of "vacuum" in this law in fact also supposes that interference by other disturbing causes is absent: thus x_3, x_4 and so on are also equal to 0) all bodies fall with the same acceleration regardless of mass, shape, or composition: thus F_1 is equal for all bodies.

However, in the open air, the shape and the substance of the falling body determine which of the interfering factors can be considered to have a negligible influence (i.e. $F_i \approx 0$). For example, air resistance is negligible for compact balls falling relatively short distances, so they behave as if they are falling in a vacuum. However, in the case of feathers the air pressure does interfere. Similarly, magnetic forces will act on steel balls but not on wooden balls. Thus, one has to specify the class of phenomena for which a specific model is an adequate representation.

Musgrave (1981) conjectured a sequence in the use of the assumptions: "what began as a negligibility assumption may be changed under the impact of criticism first into a domain assumption, then into a mere heuristic assumption; and that these important changes will go unnoticed if the different types are not clearly distinguished from one another" (p. 386). So, for example, in a simple Keynesian income-determination model one makes the initial statement that governments do not matter because they have only a negligible effect on income. If empirical research appears to show that governments do matter, one can nevertheless decide to ignore government in the model for the purpose of simplification.

In contrast to this view, our reading of Friedman's methodology is that any model based on negligibility assumptions should be maintained, and the domain of phenomena for which the model holds should be explored empirically. Friedman thus advocated a Marshallian partitioning, not on the basis of *ceteris paribus* assumptions as is assumed generally, but according to a combination of negligibility assumptions and domain specifications. For example, he asserts that competitive firms maximize profits by equating marginal revenues to marginal costs (negligibility assumption), because the failure to do so is exceptional or is tantamount to bankruptcy or failure to survive (domain assumption).

Samuelson and the descriptivism debate

The May 1963 issue of the *American Economic Review* (*AER*) contained a session on "Problems of Methodology," stimulated by Friedman's 1953 essay. However, what began as a discussion of Friedman's methodology soon turned, in subsequent issues of the *AER*, into a wider debate on the unusual position of Paul A. Samuelson (1970 Nobel Prize laureate "for the scientific work through which he has developed static and dynamic economic theory and actively contributed to raising the level of analysis in economic science").

Samuelson (1963) first labeled Friedman's position the "F-Twist," thereby avoiding Friedman's name, because he hoped that his view was based on a "misinterpretation" of Friedman's intention. He described this position as follows: "A theory is vindicable if (some of) its consequences are empirically valid to a useful degree of approximation; the (empirical) unrealism of the theory 'itself,' or of its 'assumptions,' is quite irrelevant to its validity and worth" (p. 232).

According to Samuelson, in the area of theory, unrealism (in the sense of factual inaccuracy even to a tolerable degree of approximation) is a demerit, or even a "sin." He then criticized the "F-Twist" by outlining his own methodological view, which has come to be known as **descriptivism** and can be stated as follows: a valid theory is equal to its complete set of empirically valid consequences.

To explain his view, Samuelson first defined a theory (call it B) as a set of axioms, postulates, or hypotheses that stipulate something about observable reality. The complete set of consequences of B is then called C. The minimal set of assumptions that give rise to B is called A. Thus, the following relation applies: $A \leftrightarrow B \leftrightarrow C$.

Before we continue with Samuelson's account, we need to take a closer look at the elementary logic involved in order to achieve a better understanding of his position. The meaning of the logical symbol $\leftrightarrow$ is that the implication is in both directions: $\rightarrow$ and $\leftarrow$. The meaning of a logical symbol can be defined by a truth table, such as the one given below which gives the implication for 'if P, then Q':

	P	Q	$P \rightarrow Q$
1	true	true	true
2	true	false	false
3	false	true	true
4	false	false	true

It should be noted that the logical implication, as defined by this truth table, does not map well onto intuitive notions of implications. For example, the definition of logical implication implies that any statement with a false premise (rows 3 and 4) is nonetheless true! The table shows that the proposition $P \rightarrow Q$ is only false when P is true and Q is false (row 2). So, truth can only lead to truth (row 1). This explains why scientists aim for true assumptions. As soon as we have them, everything that can be deduced from them in a logically correct way is also true, and we do not need further empirical research to establish their truth. However, the table shows also that a false proposition might lead to a truth proposition (row 3). So a false 'theory' might have (logically derived) true consequences. Truth can be deduced from a false 'theory,' so the truth-value of a 'theory' is irrelevant for the truth-value of its consequences (rows 1 and 3 show that both a true 'theory' and a false 'theory' can have true consequences). Note that a false 'theory' can also have false consequences (row 4). The truth-value of the consequences, then, should be determined by empirical research and not by the assessment of the 'theory.' What Samuelson labeled the F-twist is the position in which one considers a 'theory' to be important, even if it is not true, because its consequences are true.

To understand Samuelson's position let us take a closer look at the following truth table that defines the equivalence relation, $\leftrightarrow$:

	P	Q	$P\leftrightarrow Q$
1	true	true	true
2	true	false	false
3	false	true	false
4	false	false	true

This table shows that if the complete set of consequences of a theory is equivalent to this theory itself, $B \leftrightarrow C$, for a true theory it is necessary to have a set of true consequences (row 1), and for a false theory it is necessary to have a set of false consequences (row 4) – the equivalence relation comes apparently much closer to our intuitive notions than the implication relation.

Consider now a wider set of assumptions that includes A as a proper subset, so that it implies A, but is not fully implied by A, and call this set $A+$. Then $A+ \rightarrow A$ and

$$A+ \leftrightarrow B+ \leftrightarrow C+.$$

If C is empirically valid, but $C+$ is not valid for the part that is not in C, then we should jettison that part of $A+$ that is not in A. In other words, because of this equivalence of theory and its complete set of consequences it is always clear where to repair a theory when one finds a false consequence.

A year later, Fritz Machlup (1964) reacted to this position by stating that for Samuelson it calls for us "to reject all theory" (p. 733). According to Machlup, a theory is much more than simply its consequences; if this were not the case it could never explain observed facts. Moreover, using the DN model of explanation (as discussed in the previous chapter), an explanation is not only a deduction from a theory alone, it is always a combination of one or more theoretical relationships and the assumed conditions.

Because in Samuelson's view theories are equivalent to the full set of their consequences whose validity should be tested empirically, theories cannot provide explanations but only descriptions. Note that to derive explanations according to the DN model, we need laws. But the complete set of consequences of any law is simply too large to ever be tested empirically, much less verified. This is the problem of induction (Chapter 1) and means that empirically valid theories can never contain laws. This might be the reason for Samuelson's assertion that

> Scientists never "explain" any behavior, by theory or by any other hook. Every description that is superseded by a "deeper explanation" turns out upon careful examination to have been replaced by still another description, albeit possibly a more useful description that covers and illuminates a wider area.
>
> (Samuelson 1964: 737)

According to Samuelson, Newton's principal achievement was to improve upon the descriptions that had been given by Kepler:

> Kepler's ellipses gave better descriptions of the planets than did the epicycles of the Greeks. Newton showed that the second-order differential equations related the accelerations of bodies to the inverse square of their distances from neighboring bodies could still better *describe* astronomical observations. After Newton had described "how," he did not waste his time on the fruitless quest of "why?" but went on to run the Mint and write about religion.
>
> (Samuelson 1964: 737)

This view of theories does not exclude the possibility of making predictions: "A *description* of an empirical *regularity* provides the basis of *prediction*, which will be as accurate or inaccurate as is the regularity described" (Samuelson 1965: 1167).

Another problem with Samuelson's view is that what is considered to be the consequences of a theory are not only the implications of an isolated theory, but rather of a theory coupled with statements of initial conditions, auxiliary theories, and *ceteris paribus* clauses. The falsity of one of these consequences does not necessarily falsify the theory, but could imply a false statement of, for example, the initial conditions (see the discussion of the Duhem–Quine Thesis in Focus 3.1).

Another difficulty with the notion of descriptivism is that most scientists, including Samuelson himself in some of his other writings, make use of theoretical idealizations and simplifications that contain many false empirical implications – such as in the case of Samuelson's overlapping generations model, where he holds that life consists of only two periods: a productive period followed by a period of retirement. When this apparent conflict between Samuelson's prescriptions and practice was pointed out in the debate in *AER*, Samuelson made the following justification: "Scientists constantly utilize parables, paradigms, strong polar models to help understand more complicated reality. The degree to which these do more good than harm is always an open question, more like an art than a science" (Samuelson 1964: 739).

The philosopher Daniel Hausman used the label "methodological schizophrenia" to describe this contradiction between methodological pronouncements and practice. Although he does diagnose this as a disorder in Samuelson's work, he considers it to be characteristic of much of contemporary economics.

Finally, we note that Samuelson's descriptivist view of theories – his idea that scientific theories simply describe the empirical evidence and do not go beyond the evidence to explain any deeper, underlying, or hidden causes of the phenomena – is the only empiricist view in economics which comes close to Bridgman's operationalism (see Chapter 1). Though Samuelson never referred explicitly to Bridgman, the language he uses suggests that he has operationalist ambitions. For example, the original version of his *Foundations of Economic Analysis* carried the subtitle "The Operational Significance of Economic Theory," and the introduction of the *Foundations* states explicitly that the second fundamental purpose of this work is the derivation of operationally meaningful theorems (the first is a general unification of theory).

Looking ahead

Though there had been a number of views and disagreements with respect to empirical research methodologies in economics from the emergence of econometrics to the period of the debates between Friedman and Samuelson, broadly speaking from this point onward empiricism became a dominant influence on the way economists justified their work, and it has remained central to contemporary economic methodology.

Thus we see a shift in economic methodology from the *a priori* deductivism found in earlier thinking to a general commitment to empiricism: theories must be supported, in some form or other, by empirical evidence. This is one important legacy of the logical positivist movement, emphasizing the empiricist (or positivist) part of the program. Another important legacy of logical positivism, however, arose from the logicist (formalist) part of its program: an emphasis on the syntactic requirements of a theory (see Focus 1.3). The main requirement of this syntactic part of the program was axiomatization (see Focus 1.1). The two aspects of the logical positivist program, formalism and empiricism, led in opposite directions in regard to the assessment of theories (a similar distinction in requirements can be observed in the literature on models, see Focus 1.2). So, the debates in this period displayed considerable ambivalence in relation to the nature of theory and the relationship between theory and evidence.

The logical positivist syntactic view of theory was not widely adopted by those economists who built on the empirical tradition; however, it was greeted with enthusiasm by economists who believed that theories only had proper foundations when they were axiomatized. The most successful and exemplary result of this program is Gérard Debreu's (1959) *Theory of Value: An Axiomatic Analysis of Economic Equilibrium* (see Focus 1.3). So, the logical positivist program actually induced a division of standpoints about the methodological status of theory and also about what basis it ought to have in empirical evidence. One influential response came from Karl Popper, whose view of economic methodology will be discussed in the next chapter.

Exercises

1   In his discussion of Milton Friedman's paper on methodology, Alan Musgrave made a distinction between different kinds of assumptions. Give short descriptions of each of them.

2   Friedman's methodological aims are interpreted in various ways. They can be seen either as a call for instrumentalism, or as a critique of too much realisticness. Give arguments for each of these interpretations.

3   Give a criterion of Samuelson's descriptivism according to which theories can be considered as empirically valid.

4   In one of the examples in his *Methodology of Postivist Economics* paper, Friedman uses "as if" reasoning. Explain what this involves.

5   In what respect is Samuelson's descriptivism different from Bridgman's operationalism?

6   While the assumptions of a model do not need to be true, the model can still be empirically adequate. Describe how it can be shown that the model is empirically adequate.

7   According to Friedman's methodology, an important criterion for assessing a theory is its predictability. The more precise the prediction, the better the theory. To achieve more precise predictions, one has to develop more comprehensive models. This contradicts another Friedmanian criterion for the assessment of theories, namely their simplicity. Describe what Friedman's position is with respect to the tension between these two criteria.

8   For technical or ethical reasons, many economic phenomena cannot be investigated in a laboratory. This makes it difficult to find economic laws. Give a brief decription of the alternative research strategies that were suggested by Haavelmo, Koopmans, and Friedman.

Relevant readings

Christ, Carl F. (1994) "The Cowles Commission's Contributions to Econometrics at Chicago, 1939–1955," *Journal of Economic Literature* 32(1): 30–59.
A survey of Cowles Commission activities at Chicago by an insider.

Haavelmo, Trygve (1944) "The Probability Approach in Econometrics," *Econometrica* 12, supplement.

Introduced the probabilistic approach into econometrics by showing how to use the Neyman and Pearson statistical theory of hypothesis testing. While the second part is concerned with method, the first part is methodological.

Hendry, David F. (1980) "Econometrics – Alchemy or Science?," *Economica* 47(188): 387–406.

The methodological state-of-the-art article by one of the current leaders in econometrics.

Johnston, J. (1984) *Econometric Methods*, Singapore: McGraw-Hill.

A popular textbook on econometrics. Introductions to these kinds of textbooks often reveal how practitioners define their own field. See Johnston's introduction as representative.

Kydland, Finn E. and Edward C. Prescott (1990) "Business Cycles: Real Facts and a Monetary Myth," *Federal Reserve Bank of Minneapolis Quarterly Review* 14(2): 3–18.

Contains their more methodological views on empirical research.

Magnus, Jan R. and Mary S. Morgan (1999) *Methodology and Tacit Knowledge: Two Experiments in Econometrics*, Chichester: Wiley.

An interesting methodological study and unique comparison of various econometric approaches.

Marshall, Alfred (1925) "Mechanical and Biological Analogies in Economics," in A.C. Pigou (ed.), *Memorials of Alfred Marshall*, London: Macmillan.

A methodological paper by one of the most influential economists.

Morgan, Mary S. (1990) *The History of Econometric Ideas*, Cambridge: Cambridge University Press.

The standard history of econometrics of the pre-Haavelmo period.

Musgrave, Alan (1981) "Unreal Assumptions' in Economic Theory: The F-Twist Untwisted," *Kyklos* 34: 377–87.

One of the very rare philosophy of science responses to Friedman's methodology coming from outside economics. Musgrave was a student of Karl Popper.

Keynes–Tinbergen debate

Tinbergen, Jan (1939) *Statistical Testing of Business-Cycle Theories. Volume I A Method and its Application to Investment Activity; Volume II Business Cycles in the United States of America*, Geneva: League of Nations.

Keynes, John Maynard (1939) "Professor Tinbergen's Method," *The Economic Journal* 49: 558–68.

Tinbergen, Jan (1940) "On a Method of Statistical Business-Cycle Research: A Reply," *The Economic Journal* 50: 141–54.

Keynes, John Maynard (1940) "Comment," *The Economic Journal* 50: 154–6.

Cowles Commission versus Friedman

Friedman, Milton (1940) "Review," *Business Cycles in the United States of America, 1919–1932* by Jan Tinbergen, vol. II, *American Economic Review* 30: 657–60.

Friedman, Milton (1949) "The Marshallian Demand Curve," *The Journal of Political Economy* 57(6): 463–95.

Christ, Carl F. (1951) "A Test of an Econometric Model for the United States, 1921–1947," in *Conference on Business Cycles*, New York: National Bureau of Economic Research, pp. 35–107.

Friedman, Milton (1951) "Comment," in *Conference on Business Cycles*, New York: National Bureau of Economic Research, pp. 107–14.

Friedman, Milton (1953) "The Methodology of Positive Economics," in *Essays in Positive Economics*, Chicago and London: University of Chicago Press, pp. 3–43.

Measurement-without-theory debate

Koopmans, Tjalling C. (1947) "Measurement Without Theory," *Review of Economic Statistics* 29(3): 161–72.

Vining, Rutledge (1949) "Koopmans on the Choice of Variables to Be Studied and of Methods of Measurement," *The Review of Economics and Statistics* 31(2): 77–86.

Koopmans, T.C. (1949) "A Reply," *The Review of Economics and Statistics* 31(2): 86–91.

Vining, R. (1949) "A Rejoinder," *The Review of Economics and Statistics* 31(2): 91–4.

Samuelson's descriptivism debate

Samuelson, Paul (1963) "Problems of Methodology: Discussion," *American Economic Review* 53: 231–6.

Machlup, Fritz (1964) "Professor Samuelson on Theory and Realism," *American Economic Review* 54: 733–6.

Samuelson, Paul (1964) "Theory and Realism: A Reply," *American Economic Review* 54: 736–9.

Samuelson, Paul (1965). "Professor Samuelson on Theory and Realism: Reply," *American Economic Review* 55: 1164–72.

Focus 2.1 Methodologies before Friedman

Harro Maas

From the first days of its establishment as a separate discipline in the early nineteenth century, political economists have debated the methodological principles of their field. The best known and most influential of these early works were John Stuart Mill's (1806–1873) famous *On the Definition of Political Economy: And on the Method of Investigation Proper to It*, first published in 1836, and the final book of his *Logic* (1843) that was devoted to the methods of the "moral sciences," including political economy. Mill set the terms of debate for much of the nineteenth century and his influence is best seen in the writings of the Irish political economist John Elliot Cairnes (1835–1874) and in *Scope and Method of Political Economy* (1891) written by John Neville Keynes (1852–1949), the father of John Maynard Keynes.

At the turn of the nineteenth century the influence of Mill's ideas waned, partly because of the rise of marginalism in economics – an approach based on marginal utility analysis – and partly because of the vehement so-called *Methodenstreit* ("battle over method") between the German Historical School and Austrian (marginalist) economists like Carl Menger (1840–1921).

Drawing more on Austrian than on English themes, Lionel Robbins's (1898–1984) well-known textbook definition of economics as the science of choice under scarcity, formulated in *An Essay on the Nature and Significance of Economic Science* (first published 1932, and then reissued in a considerably revised edition in 1935), more or less closed off nineteenth-century methodological concerns.

Beginning with Terence Hutchison's *The Significance and Basic Postulates of Economic Theory* (1938), a logical positivist-inspired diatribe against Robbins's apparent unwillingness to put economic postulates to an empirical test, economic methodology turned to questions of empirical testing. These questions became increasingly interesting to economists (and statisticians) who considered the integration of mathematical economic theory with statistical estimation procedures to be the only true route to making economics a discipline that could match the alleged scientificity of the natural sciences. Just as economics after World War II was strongly influenced by economists in the United States, so the terms of this debate were also set in the United States.

The emergence in the 1980s of economic methodology as a separate field within economics led to a reconsideration of much of John Stuart Mill's work. It became clear that many of the themes of contemporary methodology could be re-phrased in terms of the arguments advanced by Mill. It also became clear that Mill's concerns had been very different from those expressed in the German *Methodenstreit* or Robbins's *Essay*.

For Mill, the central problem in developing any social and political philosophy was the complexity of the social world. This, along with his allegiance to the political radicalism of the utilitarianism of Jeremy Bentham (1748–1832) and the political economy of David Ricardo (1772–1823), influenced all his subsequent choices regarding how to think about political economy as a science. Mill argued that events in the social world did not allow for the isolation of individual causal factors – as could be achieved, for example, in laboratory settings in natural sciences like chemistry and mechanics. Neither was it possible to formulate regularities based on observations, as in astronomy. Mill argued that social events were influenced by so many causes that it was impossible to distinguish between those that were significant and those that were irrelevant.

For this reason for Mill it was inconceivable how an inference to a regularity (let alone a law) might be made from the inspection of a wide variety of observations. Mill formulated this problem in terms of induction and deduction.

Fortunately in Mill's view it was unnecessary for political economy to consider the complexity of social affairs. It was sufficient to focus on one single aspect: the consequences of man's striving for wealth. Mill was perfectly aware that this entailed a reductionist image of man – the depiction of what came to be referred to as *Homo economicus*, or economic man – but he felt that this simplification nevertheless enabled the political economist to formulate principles that were as robust as the laws of mechanics.

That man strove for wealth was a fact that the political economist could know with certainty (on what Mill called an *a priori* basis). We only need make a "mental experiment" about the motives of individuals in the marketplace to know this principle to be true. However, such principles were never manifested purely in the real world; they were always contaminated by many other influences that obscured their working. For this reason political economy should focus on the study of tendencies, or principles, that were true in the abstract but modified in the real world.

The principles Mill was considering were simply those of Ricardian economics: Malthus's population principle, diminishing returns to land, and the pursuit of wealth (profit). It was the task of the statesman or politician to sort out the other factors that were at work in practice as well. By adopting this approach, Mill fenced off a secure realm of scientific knowledge from practical political concerns, meaning that for much of the nineteenth century the question of the scientific status of political economy was answered.

The Victorian consensus around the merits of Mill's methodology began to crumble with the emergence of marginalism in economics. It was not just that utility analysis questioned the principles of (Ricardian) political economy; early marginalists, such as William Stanley Jevons (1835–1882) and Francis Ysidro Edgeworth (1845–1926), also questioned its methods. Jevons showed how empirical regularities could be derived from statistics, which undermined Mill's rejection of induction in economics. Edgeworth looked to the emergence of experimental research in psychology in Germany as a method that could be emulated by economists.

Separately, though these criticisms attracted little attention in Victorian England, matters were different in the German-speaking world, in which the dominant school of economics at that time was the Historical School. The adherents of the Historical School identified the same problem for political economy as Mill – dealing with the complexity of social events. However, they drew the radically different conclusion that the only way to make progress in political economy was to produce detailed historical case studies. They believed that only in this way could more general principles be derived gradually. This was, however, a very long-term project that required sustained attention from a community of devoted scholars. As it developed, the political agenda of the German Historicists became much more conservative than the traditional liberal agenda pursued by John Stuart Mill. They placed a considerable emphasis on the importance of national character, which fitted well with the German unification under Bismarck, and a strong resistance to the free trade agenda of the English (both by the Historical School and Karl Marx (1818–1883) alike referred to as "Manchestertum").

Simultaneously, the criticisms of Mill by the Austrian marginalists came from a completely different direction from those advanced by the British marginalists. In the *Methodenstreit* the marginalists of the Austrian School, building on the work of Carl Menger, argued that the German fine-grained studies in fact added nothing of significance; their principal contribution was to serve dubious ideological preconceptions. The Austrian marginalists suggested that the decisive factor in the identification of the appropriate method of political economy was the subject matter under consideration rather than the complexity of social processes. They also argued that a categorical distinction had to be made between economics and the natural sciences.

According to them, the correct purpose of economics was to study economizing behavior; in other words, how individuals tried to reach their goals by economizing on the means to obtain them. This relation between means and ends was fundamental to economics, and it was a relation that was not present in the natural sciences. A planet did not turn around the sun as the result of a conscious decision; it did so because of universal gravity.

This did not mean that means–ends relations could not be considered causal relations; however, the nature of such relationships was completely different from those found in the natural realm. It was simply a confusion of methods to try to derive meaningful generalizations in economics from historical observations – as the Historical School sought to do. What was important was to interpret the conduct of individuals in concrete situations as meaningful conduct in terms of means–ends relations. Hence, in contrast to British marginalists such as Jevons and Edgeworth, the Austrian School placed little value on empirical methods of research, believing that they made no contribution to political economy's ultimate aim: the study of economizing behavior.

In his famous *Essay* on the definition and method of economics Lionel Robbins adopted an approach that was broadly similar to that of the Austrian School. However, more clearly than the Austrians, Robbins emphasized that economics, as a science, distinguished itself from other sciences, not just because of its interest in economizing behavior, but also because it studied economizing behavior in the face of multiple ends.

For Robbins, economists were not interested in how individuals, or firms, aimed to attain a goal with the minimum of means. If that had been their aim, there would be no distinction between technical (engineering) problems and economic problems. Rather, economists were interested in how economic actors attempted to reach different goals with limited means at the same time. This was the crucial distinction between a merely technical and a genuinely economic problem.

Because not all ends could be reached simultaneously, economic actors were confronted with the problem of exercising choice under conditions of scarcity. The only necessary assumption (which Robbins defended on common sense grounds) was that economic actors were able to place their goals in a definite order – that is, they were able to rank their preferences. As a consequence, in common with the Austrians, Robbins considered economics to be a largely *a priori* science. It did not *require* statistical investigations to determine its principles, because these principles followed from its definition.

In the light of Robbins's *Essay*, economics became defined as a deductive science of first principles that were not in need of being tested empirically. Though this position sounds similar to that advanced by John Stuart Mill in the nineteenth century, the conclusions were now drawn for very different reasons. It was no longer because of the complexity of the subject, but – as had been argued by the Austrians – because of the distinctive nature of the problems faced by economics.

Focus 2.2 Measurement

The standard theory of measurement in science is the Representational Theory of Measurement (RTM), which takes measurement to be a process of assigning numbers to attributes of the empirical world in such a way that the relevant qualitative empirical relations among these attributes are reflected in the numbers themselves as well as in important properties of the numerical relation system. A numerical relation system representing an empirical relational structure is also called a model; therefore the RTM is sometimes called the Model Theory of Measurement.

One problem encountered by the RTM is that when the requirements for choosing a representation or model are not further specified, it can easily lead to an operationalist position (see the discussion of operationalism in Chapter 1), which does not tell us why one representation should be preferred to another one. As Stanley Stevens (1959) expresses it: Measurement is "the assignment of numerals to objects or events according to rule – any rule." In order to be considered an adequate representation of an empirical relational structure a model should meet certain criteria. In economics, there are two different foundational approaches to producing these criteria for assessing representations: the axiomatic and the empirical approach.

The axiomatic approach

According to the axiomatic approach, the foundations of measurement are established by axiomatization (see Focus 1.1 Axiomatization, which offers a consideration of axiomatization in rational choice and game theory). Another subject in economics in which the axiomatic approach has been influential is index theory. Axiomatic index theory originates in Irving Fisher's publications *The Purchasing Power of Money* (1911) and *The Making of Index Numbers* (1922). Fisher systematically evaluated a very large number of indices with respect to a number of different criteria. These criteria were called "tests." Fisher himself did not expect that it would be possible to devise an index number that would satisfy all of these tests. Moreover, in 1930, Ragnar Frisch proved the impossibility of maintaining a certain set of Fisher's tests simultaneously. It appeared that the tests were inconsistent with each other.

In current axiomatic index theory, axioms specify mathematical properties that are essential or desirable for an index formula. One of the problems of axiomatic index theory is the impossibility of simultaneously satisfying all axioms. In practice, however, a universally applicable solution to this problem is not necessary. The specifics of the problem at hand, including the purpose of the index and the characteristics of the data, determine the relative merits of the possible attributes of any index formula.

The empirical approach

Not all relational structures lend themselves to axiomatization, since it is very hard to axiomatize structures that consist of a very large number of relations. Though this does not mean that measurement is impossible in such cases, it is necessary that any representation should also satisfy empirical criteria in addition to theoretical requirements.

Further, economic measurements are often developed in order to inform economic policy, so representations should also satisfy criteria of applicability. For example, a national accounts system should be a consistent structure of interdependent definitions, that enables both uniform analysis and the comparison of various economic phenomena.

To understand empirical measurement approaches, let us consider the problem of measuring a property x of an economic phenomenon. Regard y_i ($i = 1, \ldots, n$) as repeated observations to be used to determine a value x. Each observation involves an observational error, ε_i. This error term, representing noise, reflects the operation of many different, sometimes unknown, background conditions, indicated by B:

$$y_i = f(x, B_i) = f(x, 0) + \varepsilon_i \qquad (i = 1, \ldots, n) \qquad (1)$$

To measure x, a model M has to be specified for which the values of the observations y_i function as input and the output estimate functions as the measurement result, $\hat{x} = M[y_i; \alpha]$, where α denotes the parameter set of the model. If one substitutes equation (1) into model M, assuming that M is a linear operator (usually the case), one can derive:

$$\hat{x} = M[f(x) + \varepsilon; \alpha] = M_x[x; \alpha] + M_\varepsilon[\varepsilon; \alpha] \qquad (2)$$

A necessary condition for the measurement of x is that a model M must entail a representation of the measurand, M_x, and a representation of the environment of the measurand, M_ε.

The performance of a model built for measuring purposes is described in terms of both its accuracy and its precision. Accuracy is defined as a statement about the closeness of the model's outcome to the true value of the measurand. Precision is a statement about the spread of the estimated measurement errors. As a result, accuracy and precision have to be dealt with in different ways. To see this, we split the measurement error into two parts:

$$\hat{\varepsilon} = \hat{x} - x = M_\varepsilon + [M_x - x] \qquad (3)$$

To show how this measurement error is to be addressed, it may be helpful to compare it with the "mean-squared error" of an estimator as defined in statistics:

$$E[\hat{\varepsilon}^2] = E[(\hat{x} - x)^2] = Var\hat{\varepsilon} + (x - E\hat{x})^2 \qquad (4)$$

The first term of the right-hand side of equation (4) is a measure of precision and the second term is called the bias of the estimator. Comparing expression (3) with expression (4), one can see that the error term M_ε is reduced, as much as possible, by reducing the spread of errors, that is by aiming at precision. The second error term $(M_x - x)$ is reduced by finding an accurate as possible representation of x. In the empirical approach this is achieved by the empirical testing of each proposed model.

Measurement is a matter of arriving at informative numbers about phenomena or objects. To attain these numbers, we have to measure – that is, we have to find appropriate mathematical mappings of a phenomenon or object. We do this kind of mathematization by modeling the phenomena in a very specific way. These aspects of measurement mean that a methodological standpoint on measurement is closely connected to standpoints on mathematization and modeling (see Focus 1.2).

Relevant readings

Boumans, Marcel (forthcoming) "Measurement in Economics," in Uskali Mäki (ed.), *Handbook of the Philosophy of Economics*, Elsevier.
A survey of measurement accounts in economics.
Campbell, Norman R. (1928) *Account of the Principles of Measurement and Calculation*, London: Longmans, Green.
The classic account of measurement, but only as applied to natural science.
Ellis, Brian (1968) *Basic Concepts of Measurement*, Cambridge: Cambridge University Press.
A sophisticated account of measurement, but only as applied to natural science.
Krantz, David H., R. Duncan Luce, Patrick Suppes and Amos Tversky (1971, 1989, 1990) *Foundations of Measurement*, 3 vols, New York: Academic Press.
The standard and most complete work of the Representational Theory of Measurement.
Stevens, S.S. (1959) "Measurement, Psychophysics, and Utility," in C.W. Churchman and P. Ratoosh (eds), *Measurement. Definitions and Theories,* " New York: Wiley.
An explicit account of Stevens's operationalist view of measurement.

Focus 2.3   Experiments

Andrej Svorencik

Imagine the following situation during a class on methodology of economics. You, and each of your classmates, receive €10 (an endowment) from the lecturer (an experimenter) and are given the task of choosing how much they are willing to keep for themselves and how much to put into (invest in) a group pot (budget). The size of your contribution will remain anonymous. The sum of the contributions will be doubled by the lecturer and distributed equally among all participants in this game (experiment).

This hypothetical situation is a classroom demonstration of a "public goods experiment" (*PGE*) that I will use as a guide to more refined actual economic experiments and the methodological challenges they pose. The key ingredient of any experiment, regardless of its disciplinary pedigree, is control. The main – but not the only – goal of experiments is to uncover causal relationships that are predicted by theory or models. This is attempted by creating a specific predetermined situation, in which relevant independent variables can be varied, and some variables fixed, so that the former's impact on the dependent variables under investigation can be observed.

Experimental economists have developed a specific set of rules for conducting experiments. In their terminology, the main parts of any experiment are environments, institutions which supply the rules governing the interactions, and performance criteria which determine outcomes or behavior.

The independent and controlled variables constitute the environment of an experiment. The PGE's environment consists, for example, of the €10 endowments, the number of students, the information received by the participants, the fact that the group pot is doubled, and the wording of the instructions. The institutions characterize the mode of interaction between participants. In the case of the PGE it is a so-called Voluntary Contributions Mechanism, in which everyone's contribution and final payoff is private.

One of the unique features of economic experiments, which distinguishes them from experiments carried out in psychology, is that the subjects receive monetary payments based on their performance. Detailed written instructions, another distinguishing feature, inform subjects about how to perform in an experiment in order to earn money (or other rewards such as coupons, course grades, lottery tickets, and so on). The key methodological assumption comes from Induced Value Theory. The key idea of Induced Value Theory is that proper use of a reward medium allows an experimenter to induce prespecified characteristics in experimental subjects, so that the subjects' innate characteristics become largely irrelevant.

Preferences are a crucial part of economic models. Specifying parameters in a model allows point predictions to be made. In order to achieve this the following conditions should hold: saliency, dominance, and nonsatiation of the payments. The first of these means that the amount of payoff has to depend on the participant's behavior. The second says that the payoff needs to dominate any cost or other values that subjects may attach to participation in the experiment. The third states that a larger payoff is preferable to a smaller payoff.

In the PGE case, an outcome in which every participant receives the highest payoff (the Pareto-efficient group optimum) occurs when everyone contributes their entire endowment to the group budget, and hence everyone's endowment is doubled. But the rational agent in game theory, *Homo economicus*, would keep their entire endowment and "free ride" on other individuals' contributions, if there are any. The Nash equilibrium of this game (which can be obtained by using backward induction) involves each individual making the least payment possible. Since the amount of money that participants receive varies between these two boundaries, it induces a ranking over these outcomes.

All the experimental controls are geared toward gaining valid inferences based on experimental data, that is, assuring the internal validity of the experiments. Experimental research also need to address the **Duhem–Quine Thesis**, which asserts that theories are tested not in isolation, but together with background assumptions (Focus 3.1). If a test, an experiment for example, does not confirm a hypothesis, one cannot logically deduce whether the fault lies with the theory or with the background assumptions.

In experimental economics, these background assumptions consist of factors such as the environment, institutions, Induced Value Theory, and so on. Moreover, one cannot be sure that these assumptions can be implemented fully in experiments. There is no simple way to address the Duhem–Quine problem, but running further experiments can help us to make reasonable choices about those assumptions that should be accepted and those that require further scrutiny. The comparison of various competing models, which is a primary strategy of experimental economics, is another way of addressing this problem.

One particularly interesting example that shows the sensitivity of experimental research to its environment is the impact of the particular wording of instructions given to subjects (the so-called "framing" effects). It has been established on a number of occasions that subjects will behave differently if they face a choice with the same expected payoffs, but with the instructions phrased one time in terms of losses and another time in terms of gains. Learning and experience of the subject of an experiment has also been known to bias experimental inferences.

So far, we have confined our discussion of experimental goals to the testing of a particular theory or the discrimination between competing theories. The PGE example also fits several of the other research goals investigated by economists, including the exploration of new phenomena, the measurement of parameters, the reasons why theories fail in the lab, and the investigation of policy-related decisions.

How would the observed behavior change in a PGE if: contributions were to be publicly announced; several rounds of the experiment were played; more students participated; different educational, vocational, or gender backgrounds were present; the endowment was €1 or €100; instead of an equal share of the pot redistribution a distribution proportional to the contribution was adopted? These and many other issues of the sensitivity of results to environmental parameters have been explored experimentally, because researchers face the challenge of applying their models to public goods phenomena in environments that cannot be reproduced in the laboratory. Behind this challenge is the problem of **external validity** or robustness – that is, how accurate models are when applied to environments that are much more complicated than the laboratory, such as complex field (real world) environments.

Experimental economics marks one of the most significant innovations in the practice of economics over the past half-century. In general, experiments are designed to throw light on aspects of the real world that are not addressed by theories. Economic theories often do not specify details regarding the institutions that need to be specified in an experiment. Moreover, theories do not distinguish between laboratory and real world settings, and how or when they should hold in both.

Since the laboratory is a simplified version of the world, experimental economists have come to believe that if a theory does not hold in the lab, then such a theory – compared to another theory that is more successful in the lab – will be less relevant to the real world and should be "returned" to the theorist for further refinement or revision. This is an ideal description of the feedback that experiments provide to link economic theory with reality. Take again the research on the PGE which reports that in a one-shot or in finitely repeated experiments the original level of provision of the public good is neither the Nash equilibrium nor the Pareto-efficient allocation, but around 50 percent of the latter. It declines with repetition.

To increase the provision, that is, to move closer to a position of Pareto efficiency, it is necessary to introduce a change of institutions, such as, for example, face-to-face communication. Some institutional and theoretical issues have thus been understood, but many new research questions require meticulous attention. This is a viable, albeit methodologically and practically challenging way to proceed.

Relevant readings

Friedman, Dan and Alessandra Cassar (2004) *Economics Lab: An Intensive Course in Experimental Economics*, London: Routledge.
    An introduction to experimentation in economics.
Guala, Francesco (2005) *The Methodology of Experimental Economics*, Cambridge: Cambridge University Press.
    A sophisticated methodological account of experiments in economics.
Kahneman, Daniel and Amos Tversky (1979) "Prospect Theory: An Analysis of Decision Under Risk," *Econometrica* 47: 263–91.
    An influential article on the problem of framing experimental tasks.
Ledyard, John (1995) "Public Goods: A Survey of Experimental Research," in *Handbook of Experimental Economics*, Princeton: Princeton University Press, pp. 111–95.
    A survey of public good experiments.

Plott, Charles and Vernon Smith (eds) (2008) *Handbook of Experimental Economics Results*, vol. 1, Amsterdam: Elsevier.

The most up-to-date survey of experimental results.

Smith, Vernon (1982) "Microeconomic Systems as an Experimental Science," *American Economic Review*, 72: 931–5.

A formal description of economic experiments and Induced Value Theory.

Smith, Vernon (1989) "Theory, Experiment and Economics," *Journal of Economic Perspectives*, 3: 154–76.

An accessible account that describes the relationship between economic theories, the lab, and the real world, and discusses various uses of experiments.

Chapter 3

Popper's Logic of Discovery

Karl Raimund Popper is widely seen as one of the twentieth century's most influential philosophers of science. He was also a social and political philosopher of considerable stature, and an influential critic of totalitarianism in all of its forms. Together with Thomas Kuhn and Imre Lakatos (whose contributions are discussed in Chapter 4), he has had a considerable influence on economic methodology.

Born in Vienna on July 28 1902, Popper's student years were in many respects the most formative years of his intellectual life. He became actively involved in left-wing politics, joined the Free Association of Socialist High-School Students, and for a time became a communist. However, he quickly became disillusioned with the doctrinaire character of the party, and soon afterwards abandoned it entirely. In his student years he also studied the psychoanalytic theories of Sigmund Freud and Alfred Adler (under whose guidance he engaged briefly in social work with deprived children), and became familiar with Einstein's scientific breakthroughs.

At this time philosophical life in Vienna was dominated by the discussions of the Vienna Circle (see Chapter 1). Although Popper was friendly with some of its members and shared their high regard for science and logic, he was never invited to join the group. He became increasingly critical of the main tenets of logical positivism, and in particular of the role of the verifiability principle in scientific methodology.

His critique of the logical positivists was published in *Logik der Forschung* in 1934 (republished in 1959 as *The Logic of Scientific Discovery*), a book which also contained the first account of his thoughts about science. The book attracted considerable attention, and in 1935 Popper was invited to lecture in England. He spent the next few years working on an explanation of the relationship between science and philosophy, but the rise of Nazism in Germany and Austria compelled him, in common with many other intellectuals who shared his Jewish origins, to leave Europe. Popper would get a position teaching philosophy at the University of Canterbury in New Zealand, where he was to remain for the duration of the Second World War.

The events of this period led Popper to focus increasingly on social and political philosophy. His resulting publications, *The Poverty of Historicism* (1957; read as a paper in 1936 and first published in the LSE journal *Economica* in 1944–45) and *The Open Society and Its Enemies* (1945), his most impassioned social works, offer a powerful defense of democratic liberalism, and a devastating critique of the principal philosophical presuppositions underpinning all forms of totalitarianism.

The Open Society and Its Enemies was the result of the application of Popper's anti-authoritarian approach to human knowledge – in which rigorous criticism is stressed and the aim of justification is abandoned – to the area of political thought. It champions the cause of democracy, which it argues to be the only form of government in which human reason can prevail and non-violent reform can take place. Popper launched a strong attack on the three thinkers he saw as the greatest enemies of democracy: Plato, Marx, and Hegel.

In 1946 Popper moved to England. He taught at the London School of Economics, before becoming a professor of logic and scientific method at the University of London in 1949. His reputation and stature as a philosopher of science and social thinker grew enormously over the following decades, and he continued to write prolifically – a number of his works, particularly the re-issued *The Logic of Scientific Discovery*, are now recognised as classics in the field.

A number of biographical factors can be seen to have had a particular influence upon the development of Popper's thought. His youthful political attachments had made him thoroughly familiar with the Marxist view of economics, class war, and history. Secondly, he was appalled by the failure of the democratic parties to stem the rising tide of fascism in his native Austria in the 1920s and 1930s, and the effective welcome extended to it by the Austrian Marxists, who had acted on the ideological grounds that fascism constituted what they believed to be a necessary dialectical step towards the implosion of capitalism and the ultimate revolutionary victory of communism. Thirdly, Popper was profoundly impressed by the differences between the allegedly "scientific" theories of Freud and Adler and the revolution effected by Einstein's theory of relativity in physics in the first two decades of the twentieth century.

As Popper saw it, the main difference between the theories put forward by Freud and Adler and Einstein's theory of relativity was that the latter when originally proposed was highly "risky," in the sense that it was possible to deduce consequences from it which were, in the light of the then dominant Newtonian physics, highly improbable. One of the astonishing implications of the general theory of relativity which Einstein presented to the Prussian Academy of Sciences in 1915 is the proposition that light is bent by gravitational bodies, though this effect is very small, and to be observed one needs a very large body, the Sun being the closest nearby candidate. Even though the predicted deflection is very small, the position of stars in the sky would be oberved to be affected by their proximity to the Sun. It was hoped that this kind of observation could be used to test Einstein's theory.

The only problem was that the Sun would have to be "edited out" of the picture; otherwise those stars closest to it would not be visible. The ideal opportunity would be in making observations during a total eclipse of the Sun. In 1916 the astronomer Arthur Stanley Eddington received Einstein's papers on the general theory (at a time when Britain and Germany were at war with one another). He was impressed by the beauty of Einstein's work, and immediately began to promote it.

Eddington laid a particular stress on the importance of testing the theory using measurements of light bending. He saw that the eclipse of May 29, 1919 would be especially suitable for this task since the Sun at the time would position itself right in front of a prominent grouping of stars known as the Hyades. The day of the eclipse itself began with heavy clouds and rain, but near the totality of the eclipse the Sun began to appear dimly through the clouds, and a number of photographic images were taken. The value of deflection obtained was 1.61 ± 0.40 arc seconds, which was sufficiently within the range that Einstein had predicted.

At a special joint meeting of the Royal Astronomical Society and the Royal Society of London on November 6, 1919 there was a discussion of these results. The chair of the meeting, the eminent professor Joseph J. Thomson (1856–1940), discoverer of the electron (for which he received the 1906 Nobel Prize in Physics), stated that: "This is the most important result obtained in connection with the theory of gravitation since Newton's day." The eclipse observation of 1919 was a significant step in the eventual acceptance of Einstein's general theory of relativity in the scientific community, and also to an increase in his fame outside that community. The London *Times* of November 7 carried a substantial article about the Royal Society meeting, headlined "Revolution in Science: New Theory of Universe."

In stark contrast to Einstein's "risky" theory, according to Popper there was nothing that could falsify psychoanalytic theories. One reason is that these theories are immune to refutation. For Popper an immunization of a theory, an **immunizing stratagem**, is an ad hoc adjustment made to it that shows the theory to still be correct despite evidence that it has been shown to be wrong. For example, one of the in-built immunization mechanism in psychoanalytic theory is the concept of denial: anything the subject says or does that appears to disprove the interpreter's theory is explained, not as evidence that the interpreter's theory is wrong, but rather in terms of the subject being "in a state of denial." Popper was also highly critical of the imprecision and generality of these theories, which renders the statements they make always true and not risky. In this latter sense, Popper came to feel, psychoanalytic theories had more in common with primitive myths than with genuine science.

Popper concluded that psychoanalysis can predict that people will *either* repress or sublimate deep emotional experiences, but not which approach they will choose. For example, both Freud and Adler were able to explain a person who pushes a child into water intending to drown it, and at the same time another who jumps into the water to save it, by repression and sublimation of the same drives (in terms of Freud) or as the overcoming of inferiority feelings (according to Adler).

Under what conditions, Popper asked, were Freud and Adler willing to concede that their theories had failed? Popper concluded that apparently the chief source of the appeal of psychoanalysis and the principal basis on which its claim to scientific status was grounded, namely its ability to accommodate and explain every possible form of human behavior, was in fact a critical weakness. By their very nature, psychoanalytic theories are not precise enough to have negative implications, and so are immunized from experimental falsification. Popper introduced the term **falsification** to indicate that a theory is disproved by empirical observations that contradict the implications of that theory.

He held that the Marxist account of history is also unscientific, although it differs in certain crucial respects from psychoanalysis. Popper's belief was that Marxism had initially been a scientific theory. Marx had postulated a theory which was genuinely predictive – that is, one that produced predictions that could be falsified. However, when these predictions were not in fact borne out, the theory was saved (that is, immunized) from falsification by the addition of a variety of *ad hoc* hypotheses which allowed it to remain compatible with the facts. The result, Popper asserted, was that a theory which was initially genuinely scientific degenerated into pseudo-scientific dogma.

These factors combined for Popper to make **falsifiability** his criterion for demarcating science from non-science: if a theory can be incompatible with possible empirical observations – that is what Popper meant by "risky" – it is scientific; conversely, a theory which is compatible with all possible observations is unscientific. This is either because, as in the case of Marxism, it has been modified to accommodate particular incompatible observations, or because, as in the case of psychoanalytic theories, it is consistent with all possible observations. In neither case was a theory "risky."

For Popper, however, the assertion that a theory is unscientific does not necessarily mean that it is unenlightening, or still less that it is meaningless. In this respect he differed strongly from the logical positivists. For it sometimes happens that a theory which is unscientific at a given point in time (because it is unfalsifiable) later becomes falsifiable, and thus scientific, perhaps as the result of technological developments or the further articulation and refinement of the theory. For example, the existence of atoms had been hypothesized by philosophers since the fifth century BC. But their existence was also very much questioned, even though from the late 18th century onwards they became increasingly important in chemical explanations with respect to the composition of matter. Einstein's article on Brownian motion, published in 1905, is considered as a definite confirmation of the existence of the atom.

The problem of demarcation

Like the logical positivists, Popper considered the central problem in the philosophy of science to be demarcation. By this he meant the distinction that could be drawn between science and what he terms "pseudo-science," under which heading he includes, amongst other disciplines, metaphysics and psychoanalysis. However, in contrast to logical positivism, Popper accepted the validity of the Humean problem of induction (see Chapter 1), and he also made the additional claim that induction is never actually used by the scientist. In this way he criticized the central logical positivist view that science can be distinguished from pseudo-science on the basis of its inductive methodology.

Popper, then, repudiates induction, rejecting the view that it is the characteristic method of scientific investigation and inference. In its place he substitutes the notion of falsifiability. It is easy, he argues, to obtain evidence in favor of virtually any theory, and he consequently holds that such "corroboration," as he terms it, should be scientifically significant only if it is the result of a genuinely "risky" prediction which might conceivably have been false. For Popper, a theory is scientific only if it is refutable by some conceivable event. Every genuine test of a scientific theory, then, is logically an attempt to refute or to falsify it, and therefore one genuine counter-instance falsifies the whole theory.

Popper's theory of demarcation, then, is based upon his perception that there is a *logical asymmetry* between verification and falsification. Thus while it is logically impossible to conclusively verify a universal proposition like "all swans are white" by reference to a large number of observed white swans, a single counter-instance, in this instance a black swan, conclusively falsifies this proposition. Therefore, for Popper, an exception, far from "proving" a rule, conclusively refutes it. Logically speaking, then, a scientific law is conclusively falsifiable but is not conclusively verifiable. Through his demarcation criterion Popper could avoid the problem of induction and so was able to keep laws to the scientific side of the demarcation line – as long as they are falsifiable of course.

In particular, Popper stresses that there is no unique way, no single method such as induction, which functions as the route to universal laws, a view which Einstein had personally endorsed with his statement that, "There is no logical path leading to these… laws. They can only be reached by intuition, based upon something like an intellectual love (*Einfühlung*) of the objects of experience" (quoted in Popper's *Logic of Scientific*

Discovery, p. 32). Scientific theories arise in many different ways, and the manner in which a particular scientist comes to formulate a particular theory may be of biographical interest, but it is of no consequence as far as the philosophy of science is concerned.

Science, in Popper's view, begins with problems rather than observations — it is, indeed, precisely in the context of grappling with a problem that the scientist makes observations in the first instance, and his observations are selectively designed to test the extent to which a given theory functions as a satisfactory solution to a given problem. Science, Popper believes, consists largely of problem-solving.

In accordance with Popper's criterion of demarcation, physics and chemistry can be classified as sciences, whereas psychoanalysis and astrology are pseudo-sciences (that is, they may well contain useful and informative truths, but until such time as they can be formulated in such a manner as to be falsifiable, they will not attain the status of scientific theories). Formally, then, Popper's theory of demarcation may be articulated as follows: taking a "basic statement" to be a particular observation-report, we may say that a theory is falsifiable, that is scientific, if it divides the class of all possible basic statements unambiguously into the following two non-empty sub-classes: first, the class of all those basic statements with which it is inconsistent (or which it rules out or prohibits), or what Popper called the class of the potential falsifiers of the theory (that is, those statements which, if true, falsify the whole theory), and secondly, the class of those basic statements which it does not contradict (or which it permits). This can be summed up in the following statement: a theory is falsifiable if the class of its potential falsifiers is not empty.

In Popper's view, every genuine scientific theory is prohibitive in the sense that it excludes particular events or occurrences. As such, it can be tested and falsified, but can never be logically verified. This is why he stresses that it should never be inferred that a theory has been verified simply because it has withstood the most rigorous testing for a long period of time. Rather we should recognise that such a theory has received a high measure of corroboration, and may be provisionally retained as the best available theory until it is finally falsified, and/or is superseded by a better theory.

The growth of knowledge

For Popper, accordingly, the growth of knowledge proceeds from problems and our attempts to solve them. These attempts involve the formulation of theories which, if they are to solve the problems present in earlier theories, must go beyond existing knowledge and therefore require a leap of the imagination.

For this reason, Popper places a particular emphasis on the role that creative imagination plays in the formulation of theory. Problems are central to Popper's account of science, and lead him to characterize scientists as "problem-solvers." Further, since the scientist begins with problems rather than with observations (or "bare facts," see Focus 4.3), Popper argues that the only logical technique which is an integral part of scientific method is that of the deductive testing of theories. In this deductive procedure conclusions are inferred from a tentative hypothesis that is produced by imagination. These conclusions are then compared with one another and also with other relevant statements to determine whether they falsify or corroborate the hypothesis.

How then does the deductive testing of theories work? Popper distinguishes four different lines along which the testing of a theory can be carried out:

First there is the logical comparison of its conclusions themselves by which the internal consistency of the theoretical system is tested.

Secondly, there is the investigation of the logical form of the theory with the object of determining whether it has the character of an empirical theory, or whether it is simply tautological.

Thirdly, there is comparison with other theories, chiefly with the aim of determining whether the theory would constitute a scientific advance should it survive our various tests. If it does not constitute such an advance, it will not be adopted. If, on the other hand, its explanatory success matches that of the existing theories, and additionally it explains some hitherto unexplained phenomenon, or solves some hitherto unsolved problems, it will be deemed to constitute an advance upon the existing theories, and will be adopted.

Thus science involves theoretical progress. However, Popper stresses that we find out whether one theory is better than another by deductively testing both theories, rather than through a process of induction. For this reason, he argues that one theory is said to be better than another if (while unfalsified) it has greater empirical content – and therefore greater predictive power – than its rival. (Perhaps the most famous illustration of this in the field of science was the replacement of Newton's theory of universal gravitation by Einstein's theory of relativity.)

This makes clear the nature of science as viewed by Popper: at any given time there will be a number of conflicting theories or conjectures, some of which will explain more than others. Those with greater explanatory power will consequently be adopted provisionally. In short, for Popper any theory X is better than a "rival" theory Y if X has greater empirical content, and hence greater predictive power, than Y.

Fourthly, there is the testing of the theory by way of empirical application of the conclusions which can be derived from it. If such predictions
are shown to be true, the theory is 'corroborated' (but never verified). If
the conclusion is shown to be false, then this is taken as a signal that the
theory cannot be completely correct (logically the theory is falsificd),
and the scientist begins his quest for a better theory. He does not, however, abandon the present theory until such time as he has a better one
to substitute for it.

More precisely, the final kind of test is as follows: certain singular statements are deduced from the new theory – these are called "predictions"
and they include a number that are readily testable, that is, that are "risky"
(in the sense of being either intuitively implausible or startlingly novel).
From these statements, a selection is made of those that are not derivable
from the current theory, and more especially those which are contradicted
by the current theory. These (and other) derived statements are then compared to the results of practical applications and experiments. If the predictions turn out to be acceptable, then the new theory has, for the time
being, passed the test, it is corroborated (and the old one falsified), and it
is adopted as a working hypothesis. However, if the predictions have been
falsified, then their falsifications also falsify the theory from which they
were logically deduced. Thus Popper does retain an element of empiricism: for him, scientific method involves making an appeal to experience.
However, unlike the logical positivists, Popper holds that experience cannot *determine* theory (that is, we cannot argue or infer from observation
to theory). Rather, experience delimits theory: it shows which theories are
false, not which theories are true.

Popper emphasized that a positive decision can only provide tem-
porary support for a theory, since it is always possible that it will be over-
thrown by subsequent negative decisions. So long as a theory withstands
detailed and severe tests, and is not superseded by another theory in the
course of scientific progress, we may say that it is corroborated by past
experience.

The general picture of Popper's philosophy of science, then, can be
summarized as follows:

1. Scientific theories are not inductively inferred from experience, nor
    is scientific experimentation carried out with a view to verifying or
    finally establishing the truth of theories; rather, all knowledge is pro-
    visional, conjectural, hypothetical.
2. We can never finally prove our scientific theories, but merely (provi-
    sionally) confirm or (conclusively) refute them.
3. Hence whenever we have to choose between a number of competing
    theories which will explain the set of phenomena under investigation,

we can only eliminate those theories which are demonstrably false, and rationally choose between the remaining, unfalsified theories.

This helps to explain Popper's emphasis on the importance of the critical spirit for science — for him, critical thinking is the very essence of rationality. For it is only through the use of critical thought that we can eliminate false theories, and determine which of the remaining theories is the best in terms of possessing the highest level of explanatory force and predictive power. He believed that just such critical thinking is missing in both later Marxism and psychoanalysis.

Probability and knowledge

In the view of many social scientists, the more probable a theory is, the more reason there is to accept it. This means that if we have to choose between two theories which are equally strong in terms of their explanatory power, and differ only in that one is probable and the other is improbable, then we should select the former.

Popper, however, rejects this approach. In his view science, or more precisely the working scientist, is interested in theories that have a high empirical content, because such theories possess a high predictive power and are consequently highly testable. But if this is true, Popper argues, then, paradoxically, the more improbable a theory is the stronger it is scientifically, because theories with a higher empirical content will have a lower probability. The more empirical content a theory (its potential falsifiers) contains, the greater the number of ways in which it may eventually turn out to be false.

Take, for example, the following statement: "It rains in Amsterdam, or it does not rain in Amsterdam." This is a highly probable (indeed certain!) statement because it is tautologically true, but it has no empirical content since it contains no potential falsifiers. Compare this with the statement "It rains in Amsterdam." This statement has a lower probability because it does not always rain in Amsterdam, but its empirical content has increased. It has one potential falsifier, namely "There is a time when it does not rain in Amsterdam."

Thus those theories which are of particular interest to the scientist are ones that have a high degree of empirical content and (consequently) a low probability which nevertheless come close to the truth. Empirical content, which is inversely proportionate to the probability, is directly proportionate to testability. Consequently, the severity of the test to which a theory can be subjected, and by means of which it may be falsified or corroborated, is all-important.

Popper was uneasy with the concept of truth itself, and in his writings he avoided asserting that a theory which is corroborated is true – for clearly if every theory is an open-ended hypothesis, as he maintains, then *ipso facto* it has to be at least potentially false. For this reason Popper restricted himself to the contention that a theory which is falsified is false and is known to be such, and that a theory which replaces a falsified theory (because it has a higher empirical content than the latter, and explains what has falsified it) is a "better theory" than its predecessor.

As may have been noted, Popper's philosophy shares similarities with Friedman's methodology (discussed in Chapter 2). Friedman's dictum, "the more significant the theory, the more unrealistic the assumptions," appears to be echoed in Popper's statement, "the more improbable a theory the more scientific it is." Both also emphasize the requirement that theories should assess their empirical value through the generation of testable predictions.

This is not coincidental. Friedman once confessed that the "only methodology philosophy I've read is Popper." Friedman had read Popper's *Conjectures and Refutations* (1963) and *The Open Society and Its Enemies* (1945). But his introduction to Popper and the influence Popper may have had on Friedman's own essay on methodology did not come from these writings (one is published much later, and the other does not even concern the philosophy of science). Friedman had met Popper in person in 1947 at Mont Pelerin, Switzerland (at a conference organized by the economist and political philosopher Friedrich Hayek to discuss the state of liberalism):

> I was very much impressed with him, and I spent a long time talking to him there. I knew about *Logik der Forschung* but it was in German; there was no English translation at that time. I can read a little bit of German, but it's beyond me really, so I never read anything in original German. I didn't read his *Logik der Forschung*, but I knew the basic ideas from my contact with him, and I have no doubt that that contact with him did have a good deal of influence on me.
>
> (Friedman interviewed by Hammond 1992: 95)

Social and political thought – the critique of historicism

Popper's personal history and background led him to develop a deep and abiding interest in social and political philosophy. However, it is worthwhile stressing that his approach to these fields is through a consideration of the nature of the social sciences, particularly history. It is in this context that he offers an account of the nature of scientific prediction, which in turn allows him a point of departure for his attack upon totalitarianism and all its intellectual supports, especially **historicism**: the view that history develops inexorably and necessarily according to certain principles or rules toward a determinate end (as, for example, in the dialectic of Hegel, which was modified and developed by Marx in his theory of historical materialism).

These beliefs lead to what Popper calls "The Historicist Doctrine of the Social Sciences," or the view that:

1. The principal task of the social sciences is to make predictions about the social and political development of mankind; and
2. The task of politics, once the key predictions have been made, is, in Marx's words, to lessen the "birth pangs" of future social and political developments.

Popper regards this view of the social sciences as both theoretically misconceived, in the sense of being based upon a natural science view of methodology which he believed to be totally wrong, and socially dangerous, in that in his view it inevitably led to totalitarianism and authoritarianism – to centralized governmental control of the individual and the attempted imposition of large-scale social planning. In countering this view Popper forcefully advances the view that what happens in history is largely the unplanned and unforeseeable result – the unintended consequence – of the actions of many individuals. Large-scale social planning according to an antecedently conceived blueprint is an inherently misconceived program – and inevitably disastrous – precisely because human actions have consequences which cannot be foreseen.

In this sense Popper is a historical indeterminist. He holds that history does not evolve in accordance with intrinsic laws or principles, that in the absence of such laws and principles unconditional prediction in the social sciences is impossible, and that there is no such thing as historical necessity.

The link between Popper's philosophy of science and his social philosophy is referred to as his doctrine of **fallibilism**. Just as we make theoretical progress in science by deliberately subjecting our theories to critical scrutiny, and abandoning those which have been falsified, so too, Popper holds, this critical spirit can – and should – be sustained in the social world.

More specifically, an "open society" can be brought about only if the individual citizen is able to critically evaluate the consequences of the implementation of government policies, which can then be abandoned or modified in the light of such scrutiny. In such a society, the rights of the individual to criticize administrative policies need to be formally safeguarded and upheld, so that undesirable policies are eliminated in a manner analogous to the elimination of falsified scientific theories, and the differences between people on social policy are resolved by critical discussion and argument rather than by force.

Looking ahead

Popper's thinking has been remarkably popular and influential by virtue of its strong emphasis on the need for a critical perspective. Yet it also effectively became a victim of its own success in that a fully critical perspective left little of science untouched, and this did not seem to reflect the views and practices of scientists. In the following chapter, then, we turn to two different responses to Popper's fallibilism: one, put forward by Thomas Kuhn, that largely abandoned Popper's assumptions and the other, by Imre Lakatos, that sought to revise them – in effect, a revolutionary strategy and a reformist strategy.

   These two approaches, however, placed less emphasis on the choices between individual theories made by the individual scientist, and increased the attention devoted to entire scientific communities engaged in research that was framed by networks of theories. This shared focus has proved to be of lasting significance in the philosophy of science and economic methodology.

Exercises

1   According to Popper, to allow for progress in science, immunizing stratagems are not allowed. Describe two different kinds of immunizing stratagems.

2   Evaluate the following statement from the perspective of Popper's philosophy: "Intense emotions are having their way with you and that could be fun or distressing depending on the context." Explain whether this is a scientific statement or not. Give Popperian arguments.

3   According to Popper, the development of science can be progressive if it takes place according to the application of a specific methodological rule. Give a description of this rule.

4   Is Popper's methodology positive or normative? Explain your answer.

5   What implication does the Duhem–Quine Thesis have for Popper's methodology?

6   Explain why Popper considered falsificationism an improvement on past methodologies.

7   An important aim of prescriptive methodologies is to demarcate science from pseudo-science. Consider the following statement from N.G. Mankiw, *Macroeconomics*, 3rd edn: "An increase in the rate of savings causes a period of high growth until the new steady state is reached."
   a.   Is this a scientific statement according to logical positivism?
   b.   Is this a scientific statement according to Popper?

8   According to Popper's theory, the empirical content of a theory can be increased by the addition of potential falsifiers. Take for example the following statement: "If the profit of an enterprise increases, its share price will increase." Add potential falisifiers to increase the empirical content of this statement.

Relevant readings

Hacohen, Malachi H. (2000) *Karl Popper – The Formative Years, 1902–1945*, Cambridge: Cambridge University Press.
    A comprehensive and detailed biography of Popper, but only of the first half of his life.
Hammond, J. Daniel (1992) "An Interview with Milton Friedman on Methodology," in *Research in the History of Economic Thought and Methodology*, ed. Warren Samuels, vol. 10, Greenwich, CT: JAI Press, pp. 91–118.
    An interview about Friedman's ideas on methodology.
Popper, Karl R. (1957) *The Poverty of Historicism*, London: Routledge.
    Popper's main critique of historicism.
Popper, Karl R. (1945) *The Open Society and Its Enemies*, London: Routledge & Kegan Paul.
    An important critique on the the ideas of Plato, Marx, and Hegel.
Popper, Karl R. (1959) *The Logic of Scientific Discovery*, London: Hutchinson.
    Popper's main text on philosophy of science.

Focus 3.1   The Duhem–Quine Thesis

Mark Blaug

The demarcation criterion based on the principle of falsifiability does not cut cleanly between scientific and non-scientific subjects – as we shall see in the next chapter. But there is a deeper problem with the criterion. It is that falsifiability is just as inconclusive and question-begging as the verifiability criterion of the logical positivists. You cannot unambiguously verify any theory but, unfortunately, you also cannot unambiguously falsify any theory. This perfectly straightforward idea is labeled the Duhem–Quine Thesis after its two contributors: Pierre Duhem (1861–1916), a nineteenth-century French physicist and historian of science, and William Van Orman Quine (1908–2000), a twentieth-century American philosopher and logician.

The idea behind their thesis is that any attempt to falsify a theory is never a matter of one contradictory fact or one refuting demonstration or one counter-example, but rather a combination of a check on the assumptions to see which one has failed and also an experimental demonstration involving a particular false measurement plus a search for disconfirming instances. So, when a theory is refuted or falsified it is always possible to blame this on other factors such as the measuring instruments, or the experimental controls, or the laboratory set-up, or the particular assumption or version of the assumption selected for purposes of refutation, etc.; the only limit on the number of excuses that can be invented when a favored theory is refuted is the inventiveness of the experimenter. Accordingly, the Popperian notion that falsification is decisive but verification is hesitant and inconclusive is simply wishful thinking; there is, in fact, little to choose between verification and falsification.

This objection to Popperianism was well known even to Popper who can in fact be seen, in *The Logic of Scientific Discovery*, to be a remarkable forerunner of the Duhem–Quine Thesis. Popper had read Duhem, and recognised that it is perfectly possible for a scientist confronted with a falsification of his theories to adopt immunizing stratagems, as he called them, to protect the theories from refutation.

He provided a list of such stratagems, including:

(i)   amending a refuted theory by weakening its implications;
(ii) making it more difficult to find contrary reproducible effects: and in general
(iii) rendering the theory less testable,

and he urged that scientists should avoid them. What is Popperianism or **falsificationism** is not just falsifiability by itself but falsifiability plus the methodological rules that forbid immunizing stratagems.

The gist of the edict to avoid immunizing stratagems is to amend theories only by increasing their empirical content, their "verisimilitude" (a lovely word), making them paradoxically easier to contradict than before. But verisimilitude, Popper was soon shown by one of his critics, is not a quantifiable magnitude; it is difficult to show that any amendment of a theory renders it more observable, more truthful. Verisimilitude remains a qualitative criterion, according to which we may judge a new version of a theory an improvement over the old version but we cannot measure that improvement.

So, we are left with a falsifiability criterion that cannot be applied conclusively to a scientific theory. Even if it is, the Duhem–Quine Thesis makes it impossible to know whether the theory has or has not been falsified.

Nevertheless, the Duhem–Quine Thesis does not completely rob Popperianism of its initial promise of solving all problems in choosing between theories. It remains true that when confronted with a theory of science, or indeed any proposition claiming to be scientific, there is nothing more enlightening than to ask: how could it be refuted by empirical evidence, at least in principle? If it cannot be so refuted because it is partly either a metaphysical proposition or a tautological one relying on its own self-defined terms, it will be better understood on its own philosophical merits. And again, when confronted with a fervently held belief or an apparently unshakeable conviction, there is nothing more enlightening than to ask: what would have to happen in the world to make one abandon this belief or conviction? If there is nothing that could possibly affect the belief, we will know at least that we are confronting not a synthetic proposition but an analytic one – in which case the gathering of evidence is simply irrelevant.

In summary, the work of Popper is a constant reminder that what we care about in science or any activity professing to be scientific is empirical evidence that either corroborates or contradicts our theoretical assertions. Of course, a skeptic might argue that we hardly need Popper to tell us that. This is true, but no philosopher says it more clearly and more insistently than Popper. And no philosopher of science is more emphatic than Popper that no scientific theory is ever final, that all scientific truths are fallible and are true only as of today, and that, in short, there is no foundation in science where the quest for truth will finally come to an end.

We have space for only a single one example – but it is very telling. One of the most famous and long-standing theories in economics is the quantity theory of money, which asserts that any increase in the supply of money will begin by affecting the level of nominal income (PY), but will eventually affect only the level of prices (P). This is what is meant by the famous proposition that "money is neutral." Here is a distinction often encountered in economics between effects in the short run and effects in the long run, with the actual length of the run being left unspecified. Although this was the common practice in the long-run history of the quantity theory of money going right back to the eighteenth century, it is belied by the pronouncements of the most recent prominent advocate of the quantity theory, Milton Friedman. Milton Friedman has always been fairly explicit about the length of the short run and the long run during which the effects of an increase in the money supply work themselves out. In his magisterial *Monetary History of the United States, 1870–1960* (1963), he and Anna Schwartz concluded:

> For most Western countries, a change in the rate of monetary growth produces a change in the rate of growth of nominal income about six to nine months later... The effect on prices like that on income and output... comes some twelve to sixteen months later, so that the total delay between a change in monetary growth and a change in the rate of inflation averages something like two years. In the short run, which may be as long as three to ten years, monetary changes affect primarily output. Over decades, on the other hand, the rate of monetary growth affects primarily prices.

So, if we want to defend the quantity theory of money, we will do well to consider only time series that span more than ten years: yet not considering data relating to a span of one to three years, however, could be regarded as an instance of a Popperian immunizing stratagem that was intended to protect the quantity theory of money against empirical refutations.

Focus 3.2   Popper's Situational Analysis

In his *The Poverty of Historicism* Karl Popper advanced the concept of **situational analysis** or situational logic. This was the approach he thought appropriate to the social sciences. He claimed that it involved a generalization of rational decision analysis as employed in economics.

Situational analysis requires that the social scientist should reconstruct the problem situation faced by the agent so as to explain the agent's choice as a response to that situation. By "the method of logical or rational construction," he explained, "I mean the method of constructing a model on the assumption of complete rationality (and perhaps also on the assumption of the possession of complete information) on the part of all individuals concerned" (p. 141).

But what are we to say in a situation in which people do not behave rationally or do not have complete information – the situation that is generally referred to today as bounded rationality? In *The Open Society and Its Enemies* Popper went on to criticize explanations of behavior that are made in terms of psychological states, shifting his emphasis from the rationality of the agent to the situation and the constraints faced by the agent. According to Popper, social science explanations ought to focus on the logic of the situation, which, he added, is the method of economic analysis.

Popper was not always clear about how situational analysis explanations were to be developed but Noretta Koertge (1975) has offered the following clarifying summary:

1. Description of the situation: agent A was in a situation of type C.
2. Analysis of the situation: in a situation of type C, the appropriate thing to do is X.
3. Rationality principle: agents always act appropriately to their situation.
4. *Explanandum*: (therefore) A did X.

Given Popper's emphasis on employing a deductive approach (see Chapter 3), this seems to provide a good illustration of how it should be applied. Indeed, it clearly resembles Carl Hempel's deductive-nomological type of explanation, which we saw depends upon employing a (covering) law to move from an *explanans* associated with initial conditions – here as in point (1) – to the *explanandum* (see Chapter 1).

However, this creates a problem for Popper, since the rationality principle is formulated as an exceptionless universal law, and Popper's falsificationism only accepts universal laws if they are falsifiable. Wade Hands thus differentiates between the methodological writings of a Popper$_n$ (*n* for natural science) and a Popper$_s$ (*s* for social science), and points out that Popper$_n$ observes the falsification principle, but Popper$_s$ ignores it by using immunizing stratagems to protect the rationality principle. What, then, was the status of the rationality principle for Popper?

When asked to comment on this question in 1985, Popper insisted one can never reject the rationality principle, and that it is not empirically refutable. But if the rationality principle is unfalsifiable, then for him, given his adherence to the logical positivists' rejection of synthetic *a priori* statements, it is either an analytic statement and true by definition or a piece of metaphysics; yet it clearly is not true by definition. But Popper made the matter even more confusing. Paradoxically, though he asserted that the rationality principle is unfalsifiable, he also said he believed there were good reasons to think that it is false! Actually, his view was that it is "actually false but a good approximation to the truth." Thus the rationality principle is false and not empirically refutable. But he continued to maintain it ought to be treated as essential to social science and is fundamental to economic analysis.

There have been two main responses to this dilemma on the part of economic methodologists. Bruce Caldwell notes that there is no problem here for most economists, who find the method of situational analysis conducive to their explanations of economic behavior. Thus they abandon

Popper's falsificationism to preserve the rationality principle, and put aside the question of whether it is a piece of metaphysics. We might say that they adopt Imre Lakatos's methodology of scientific research programs, and assign the rationality principle to the hard core of the neoclassical research program made up of principles that cannot be abandoned without abandoning the entire program (see Chapter 4). Roy Weintraub advances this interpretation of the general equilibrium research program by distinguishing what it includes in the hard core from what it includes in the "protective belt" of testable theories.

A second, more recent response to Popper's dilemma on the part of economic methodologists is to state that the rationality principle is indeed empirically refutable, and ought to be abandoned (or appropriately modified, as in the case of theories of bounded rationality) if it is not supported by observational evidence. This response recalls the empiricist and anti-metaphysics emphasis of the logical positivists (though without adopting their view of allowable types of statements in science), and recognizes the new role that experimentation has come to play in economics in recent decades – especially where experimental economics addresses the rationality principle (see Focus 2.3). In a recent book, Francesco Guala (2005) exhibits this methodological view in his account of how experimental methods have changed the practice of economics.

Hands's division of Popper's thinking into a Popper$_n$ and a Popper$_s$ recalls another issue that runs through this book: are the forms of explanation in the social sciences essentially similar to or different from those of the natural sciences? Popper was willing to abandon his falsificationism for the social sciences – if they adopted the rationality principle – and accept the charge that he had adopted an immunizing stratagem, precisely what he had condemned in natural science. But Lakatos (whose work will be discussed in Chapter 4) was surely right when saying that natural sciences also operate with hard core principles which do not get challenged, and so in this respect there does not seem to be an important difference between social science and natural science. At the same time, both kinds of science appear from time to time to undergo "revolutions" that involve the rejection of even hard core principles. None of this, however, tells us much about the differences between social science and natural science.

Relevant readings

Caldwell, Bruce (1991) "Clarifying Popper," *Journal of Economic Literature* 29: 1–33.
    An informative discussion of the development of Popper's later thinking.
Guala, Francesco (2005) *The Methodology of Experimental Economics*, Cambridge: Cambridge University Press.
    A very good account of experimental practice in economics.

Hands, Wade (1985) "Karl Popper and Economic Methodology: A New Look," *Economics and Philosophy* 1: 83–99.

Hands' identification of the inconsistency in Popper's thinking.

Koertge, Noretta (1975) "Popper's Metaphysical Research Program for the Human Sciences," *Inquiry* 18: 437–62.

An influential reconstruction of Popper's situational analysis view.

Popper, Karl (1985) "The Rationality Principle," in D. Miller (ed.), *Popper Selections*, Princeton: Princeton University Press.

Popper's attempt to address the inconsistencies in his thinking about rationality.

Weintraub, E. Roy (1985) *General Equilibrium Analysis*, Cambridge: Cambridge University Press.

An application of Lakatosian thinking to general equilibrium analysis.

Focus 3.3 Testing

In writing about testing, economists draw on several distinct traditions, and it is not always apparent to which tradition – or combination of traditions – they are referring at any particular time. In the literature relating to economic methodology, one can distinguish (at least) the following types:

(1) *Testing as confirmation.* This is the logical positivist idea of testing (Chapter 1), involving the gathering of as much evidence as possible to support a hypothesis. Only if a hypothesis is sufficiently confirmed should it be accepted. Whether or not a hypothesis is sufficiently confirmed is often decided by a relevant measure of statistical significance. One way to do this kind of testing is to measure the hypothesized relationship by, for example, estimating its coefficients. The statistics then will also provide information about the statistical significance of these estimates, which can be considered as degrees of confirmation. A theory can be tested by validating its assumptions or by assessing its consequences. The latter approach was suggested by Friedman, who proposed validating a theory by its predictive performance (Chapter 2).

(2) *Testing as falsification.* This is a Popperian view. Popper advocates confrontations between theories and facts to discover errors (Chapter 3). The aim is to be as rigorous as possible in testing one's theory in an attempt to knock it down – that is, to falsify it. Every test a theory survives is considered a corroboration of that theory.

(3) *Statistical hypothesis testing.* Of these the Neyman–Pearson test is perhaps the best known. This often takes the form of deciding between a null hypothesis and an alternative hypothesis based on the performance of a particular statistic. This kind of testing does not show whether a hypothesis is true, but only whether or not it should be rejected.

(4) *Characteristics testing.* Characteristics testing involves matching particular features in an empirical model to specific characteristics in

selected data sets. An early example of this kind of testing in economics is Irma and Frank Adelman's (1959) computer simulation of the Klein–Goldberger (1955) macroeconomic model of the United States economy. They showed that this model, when shocked by disturbances, generates cycles with the same characteristics as the business cycles observed in the United States economy. Indeed, the Klein–Goldberger model cycles were remarkably similar to those described as being characteristic of the United States economy by the National Bureau of Economic Research (NBER). From this they concluded that the Klein–Goldberger model was "not very far wrong."

(5) *Calibration.*   The term calibration was first introduced into macro-economics by Kydland and Prescott in their paradigmatic new-classical equilibrium/real-business-cycle paper (1982). Generally, calibration is seen as a method of estimation that works by simulating a model with ranges of parameters and then selecting elements from these ranges which best match properties of the simulated data with those of historical data. Calibration, however, is also used as a method for testing a model when a model's data-output moments are compared with those of historical time series. Seen in this way, calibration is a specific case of characteristics testing. But by deliberately giving the label calibration to this type of testing, Kydland and Prescott emphasized that they see models as having a very specific func-tion – namely, they function as measuring instruments. A thermometer is tested by putting it in ice water to verify whether it shows 0° Celsius. Likewise, a model economy is tested by verifying whether it mimics the actual economy with respect to characteristics associated with long-term growth. These characteristics are the so-called "stylized facts" of economic growth, and thus function as benchmarks. These stylized facts include:

1.   Real output grows at a more or less constant rate.
2.   The stock of real capital grows at a more or less constant rate greater than the rate of growth of the labor input.
3.   The growth rates of real output and the stock of capital tend to be about the same.
4.   The rate of profit on capital has a horizontal trend.

(6) *Turing testing.*   A Turing test is generally described as follows: reports based on the output of a quantitative model and on measurements of the real system are presented to a team of experts; when they are unable to distinguish between the model output and the system output, the model is said to be valid. An economic example of this kind of test is Robert Lucas's (1977) interpret-ation of the way the Adelmans tested the Klein–Goldberger model (4):

> The Adelmans posed, in a precise way, the question of whether an
> observer armed with the methods of Burns and Mitchell (1946) could

distinguish between a collection of economic series generated artificially by a computer programmed to follow the Klein–Goldberger equations and the analogous series generated by an actual economy.

Alan Turing (1912–1954) was a British mathematician, and an early pioneer in the field of computing science. In 1950, in the article "Computing machinery and intelligence," Turing asked the question "Can machines think?" He did not offer a direct answer to this question: rather he discussed what he termed the "imitation game."

This "game" involves two people – one of them an interrogator – and a machine. The interrogator stays in one room, with the other person and the machine in a second room, and is allowed to put questions to both (via a teleprinter). The object of the game for the interrogator is to determine which of the respondents is the human being and which is the machine. If the interrogator decides wrongly – or is unable to make a decision – the machine can be considered to be intelligent. It is crucial in this question-and-answer game that the questions asked are ones to which the answer is approximately known. Likewise, Lucas (1980) considered models to be "imitations of reality" which are tested by putting questions to them of which we are "fairly certain" about the answers: "The more dimensions on which the model mimics answers actual economies give to simple questions, the more we trust its answers to harder questions."

Relevant readings

Adelman, Irma and Frank L. Adelman (1959) "The Dynamic Properties of the Klein–Goldberger Model," *Econometrica* 27: 596–625.
  One of the first computer simulations of a macroeconomic model to investigate its dynamic properties.
Keuzenkamp, Hugo A. and Jan R. Magnus (eds) (1995) *The Significance of Testing in Econometrics*. Special issue of *Journal of Econometrics*, 67(1).
  A collection of articles by econometricians and philosophers of science to discuss the purpose and intended consequences of testing in econometrics.
Kydland, F.E. and E.C. Prescott (1982) "Time to Build and Aggregate Fluctuations," *Econometrica* 50: 1345–70.
  The paradigm new-classical equilibrium/real-business-cycle paper introducing calibration.
Lucas, Robert E. (1977) "Understanding Business Cycles," in K. Brunner and A.H. Meltzer (eds), *Stabilization of the Domestic and International Economy*, Amsterdam: North-Holland, pp. 7–29.
  One of the few methodological articles to explain Lucas's new approach.
Lucas, Robert E. (1980) "Method and Problems in Business Cycle Theory," *Journal of Money, Credit, and Banking* 12(4): 696–715.
  Another of the few methodological articles to explain Lucas's new approach.
Turing, Alan (1950) "Computing Machinery and Intelligence," *Mind* 59: 433–60.
  Turing's classic article in which he introduces and discusses his test.

Chapter 4

Kuhn and Lakatos

This chapter looks at two responses to the work of Karl Popper. The first, developed by Thomas Kuhn, is a strategy for going well beyond the logical positivist origins of Popper's thinking. It was in effect an attempt to change the whole approach to the philosophy of science. The second, found in the work of Imre Lakatos, is a strategy for taking the best of logical positivist thinking, and trying to combine it with an understanding of scientists' actual practices. The two approaches represent not just reactions to Popper but also an awareness of changes in science and scientific institutions in the post-World War II period.

Thomas Kuhn

Thomas Samuel Kuhn (1922–1996) is perhaps the twentieth century's most influential philosopher of science. His *The Structure of Scientific Revolutions* is one of the most cited academic books of all time, mainly because of its central concept of "paradigm." His contribution to the philosophy of science was a move away from several key positivist doctrines. However, it also led to a new style of philosophy of science that brought it much closer to the history of science and scientific practice.

Kuhn began his academic life in physics. He then switched his interest to the history of science. As his career developed, he moved on to study philosophy of science, while retaining a strong interest in the history of physics. Graduating from Harvard in 1943 he spent the remainder of the war years in research related to radar, first at Harvard and then in Europe. He gained his master's degree in physics in 1946, and his doctorate in 1949.

Between 1947 and 1956, Kuhn taught a class in science for humanities undergraduates at Harvard. The course consisted largely of historical case studies, and was Kuhn's first opportunity for detailed study of historical scientific texts. His initial bewilderment on reading the scientific work of Aristotle was to prove a formative experience, as he made clear in an autobiographical preface to his book *The Essential Tension*:

> My own enlightenment began in 1947, when I was asked to interrupt
> my current physics project for a time in order to prepare a set of lectures

on the origins of seventeenth-century mechanics. For that purpose, I needed first to discover what the predecessors of Galileo and Newton had known about the subject, and preliminary inquiries soon led me to the discussion of motion in Aristotle's *Physica* and to some later works descended from it. [...] When dealing with subjects other than physics, Aristotle had been an acute and naturalistic observer. In such fields as biology or political behavior, his interpretations of phenomena had often been, in addition, both penetrating and deep. How could his characteristic talents have failed him so when applied to motion? How could he have said about it so many apparently absurd things? And, above all, why had his views been taken so seriously for so long a time by so many successors? The more I read, the more puzzled I became. Aristotle could, of course, have been wrong – I had no doubt that he was – but was it conceivable that his errors had been so blatant?

(Kuhn 1977: xi)

There are a number of different ways of reading a text, and those that are most accessible to a modern reader are often inappropriate when applied to the writings of the past. What Kuhn's reading of Aristotle revealed to him was that there had been a global change in the way scientists viewed nature and applied language to it, one that could not properly be described as constituted by cumulative additions to knowledge (the logical positivist's view of scientific development) or by the mere piecemeal correction of mistakes (Popper's view of the growth of science). It was this global change that Kuhn termed a "paradigm shift," a term he compared with the psychologcal phrase "*gestalt* switch."

In 1961 Kuhn became a full professor at the University of California at Berkeley, having moved there in 1956 to take up a post in history of science, though in the philosophy department, which enabled him to further develop his interest in the philosophy of science. Shortly thereafter in 1962 Kuhn published *The Structure of Scientific Revolutions* in the series "International Encyclopedia of Unified Science," edited by Otto Neurath, Rudolf Carnap, and Charles Morris, an outlet of the logical positivism movement.

The structure of scientific development

The central argument of Kuhn's book can be laid out as follows:

The development of science is driven in "normal" periods of science by adherence to a **paradigm**.

The function of a paradigm is to supply puzzles for scientists to solve and to provide the tools for their solution, an activity called **normal science**.

A crisis in science arises when confidence is lost in the ability of the paradigm to solve particularly worrying puzzles called **anomalies**.

The crisis is followed by a **scientific revolution** if the existing paradigm is superseded by a rival.

Kuhn claimed that science guided by one paradigm would be "incommensurable" with science developed under a different paradigm, meaning that it is impossible to make certain kinds of comparisons between theories. This **incommensurability thesis** rules out certain kinds of comparisons between the two theories and consequently rejects some traditional views of scientific development, including significantly both the view that science builds on the knowledge contained within earlier theories, and the view that later theories are closer approximations to the truth than earlier theories. Most of Kuhn's subsequent work in the area of philosophy was spent in articulating and developing the ideas outlined in *The Structure of Scientific Revolutions*.

Although *The Structure of Scientific Revolutions* did in due course create the interest among philosophers that Kuhn had intended, its initial reception was hostile. Since the following of rules (of logic, of scientific method, etc.) was regarded as the *sine qua non* of rationality, Kuhn's claim that scientists do not employ rules in reaching their decisions appeared tantamount to the claim that science is irrational.

[margin note: indespensible and essential action]

This assertion was highlighted by Kuhn's rejection of the distinction between discovery and justification (see Chapter 1) and his emphasis on incommensurability (discussed below). The negative response from philosophers was made worse by Kuhn's insistence on the important role that the history of science played in developments in the philosophy of science. This is stated baldly in the opening sentence of his book: "History, if viewed as a repository for more than anecdote or chronology, could produce a decisive transformation in the image of science by which we are now possessed" (p. 1). Also significant and novel in his approach was Kuhn's appeal to psychological literature and examples (such as linking theory-change with *gestalt*-switch).

In 1964 Kuhn left Berkeley to take up the position of Professor of Philosophy and History of Science at Princeton University. The following year saw an important event that helped raise Kuhn's profile among philosophers. An International Colloquium in the Philosophy of Science was held at Bedford College, London, which was intended to include a debate between Kuhn and two other philosophers – Paul Feyerabend and Imre Lakatos. In the event, Feyerabend and Lakatos did not attend and the papers delivered at the meeting devoted considerable time to Kuhn's work. In addition, a discussion between Kuhn and Popper – in which their viewpoints were compared and contrasted – increased the focus on Kuhn's writings. These papers, along with contributions from Feyerabend and Lakatos, were published in *Criticism and the Growth of Knowledge* (1970), edited by Lakatos and Alan Musgrave. The same year saw the publication of the second edition of *The Structure of Scientific Revolutions*, which included an important postscript in which Kuhn clarified his notion of paradigm, which had been the subject of some confusion. At the London Colloquium, Margaret Masterman (1910–1986) had shown that the term "paradigm" was used in at least 22 different ways!

A collection of Kuhn's essays in the philosophy and history of science was published in 1977 with the title *The Essential Tension*, taken from one of Kuhn's earliest essays in which he emphasizes the importance of tradition in science. In 1983 he moved to MIT. Throughout the 1980s and 1990s Kuhn continued to work on a variety of topics related to both the history and philosophy of science, including further development of his concept of incommensurability.

Scientific Revolutions

In *The Structure of Scientific Revolutions* Kuhn gives a highly original account of the development of science. This involved the introduction into philosophy of science of a number of new concepts, including normal science, paradigm, incommensurability, and revolution, which are considered below.

Normal science

Normal science is the label Kuhn gives to research that is based firmly upon previous scientific achievements. These are the foundations that some particular scientific community has acknowledged as supplying the basis for its further practice. Today such achievements are set out, although seldom in their original form, in science textbooks. These textbooks lay out the body of accepted theory, illustrate many or all of its successful applications, and compare these applications with exemplary observations and experiments.

Alongside these textbooks, the famous classics of science fulfill a similar function – for a time these and many other works serve implicitly to define the legitimate problems and methods of a research field for succeeding generations of practitioners. An example of such a classic in economics is Samuelson's *Foundations of Economic Analysis*. These classics share two essential characteristics:

1. Their achievement was sufficiently unprecedented to draw a group of adherents away from competing modes of scientific activity.
2. At the same time, they are sufficiently open-ended to supply all sorts of unsolved problems for the new generation of practitioners.

Kuhn referred to these works as paradigms. In choosing this term, he meant to show how such accepted examples of scientific practice provide models which lead to the creation of specific traditions of scientific research. The term was borrowed from a grammar where "paradigm" means "model," "pattern," or "example." For example, "*amo, amas, amat*" is a paradigm because it displays the pattern to be used in conjugating a large number of other Latin verbs. In this sense, a paradigm functions by permitting the replication of examples, any one of which could in principle serve to replace it. In a science, however, a paradigm is rarely an object for replication. Instead, like an accepted judicial decision in the common law, it is an object for further articulation and specification under new or more stringent conditions.

According to Kuhn, the principal outcome of the study of paradigms is to prepare students for membership in a particular scientific community. Scientists whose research is based on shared paradigms are committed to the same rules and standards for scientific practice. That commitment – and the apparent consensus it produces – are among the prerequisites for normal science, that is, for the genesis and continuation of a particular research tradition.

Paradigms achieve their status within a science because they are more successful than their competitors in solving a few problems that practitioners have come to recognize as being acute. To be more successful is not, however, to be either completely successful with a single problem or especially successful with any large number of them. Initially, the success of a paradigm is largely a promise of success discoverable in selected and still incomplete examples. Normal science consists in the actualization of that promise, and an actualization achieved by extending the knowledge of those facts that the paradigm displays as particularly revealing, by increasing the extent of the match between those facts and the paradigm's predictions, and by further articulating the paradigm itself.

These "mopping-up" operations, as Kuhn calls them, are what engage most scientists throughout their careers. They constitute the basis of normal science. That appears to be an attempt to force nature into the pre-formed and relatively inflexible box that is supplied by the paradigm. It is no part of normal science to unearth new sorts of phenomena; indeed, those that do not fit into the box are often not seen at all. Nor do scientists normally aim to create new theories, and they are often intolerant of those created by others. Instead, normal-scientific research is directed to the articulation of those phenomena and theories that are already supplied by the paradigm.

To clarify this "mopping-up" characteristic, Kuhn describes normal science as essentially a puzzle-solving exercise. Though this term suggests that normal science is not an especially heroic activity, its main purpose is to convey the nature of the scientific enterprise. Like someone solving crossword puzzles, chess puzzles, or jigsaws, the "normal scientist" expects to have a reasonable chance of success. The chances will depend mainly on the puzzle-solver's own ability, and whether the puzzle itself – and the way in which it should be solved – have a substantial degree of familiarity. In general, a puzzle-solver will not be entering completely uncharted territory. Because its puzzles and their solutions are familiar and relatively straightforward, normal science can expect to accumulate a growing stock of puzzle-solutions.

In addition to testing ingenuity or skill in finding solutions, puzzles like jigsaws or crosswords share other characteristics with the problems of normal science. One of these is that it is not a criterion of goodness in a puzzle that its outcome should be intrinsically interesting or important. On the contrary, really pressing problems – such as, for example, finding a cure for AIDS or the design of a lasting peace (Kuhn's own example) – are often not puzzles at all, because they may have no solution. Though intrinsic value is no criterion for a good puzzle, the assured existence of a solution is.

When it adopts a paradigm, a scientific community acquires a criterion for choosing those problems that can be assumed to have solutions. To a large degree these are the only problems that the community will admit as scientific, or encourage its members to address. Other problems are rejected – for being metaphysical, for being the concern of another discipline, or sometimes for being just too problematic to be worth the effort. This means that a paradigm may exclude those socially important problems that are not reducible to the puzzle form, because they cannot be stated in terms of the conceptual and instrumental tools supplied by the paradigm. One of the reasons why normal science seems to progress so rapidly is that its practitioners concentrate on problems that they can be prevented from solving only through their own lack of ingenuity. As such, normal science, the puzzle-solving activity, is a highly cumulative enterprise, and has proved eminently successful in achieving its aim – the steady extension of the scope and precision of scientific knowledge.

Another characteristic common to both puzzles and the problems encountered in normal science is that puzzles involve more than simply an arrival at a solution. They also involve rules that limit both the nature of acceptable solutions and the steps taken to obtain them. This can be understood if we consider the jigsaw example: In order to solve it correctly, all the pieces must be used, their plain sides must be turned down, and they must be interlocked without forcing them together until no spaces remain to be filled. These are among the rules that govern jigsaw-puzzle solutions. Similar restrictions would apply to the solution of crossword puzzles, riddles, and chess problems.

Kuhn's description of normal science amounts to a rejection of the romantic image of science, with its notion of the individual genius triumphing over nature. In characterizing science as mainly a puzzle-solving activity, he provided a more realistic picture of science, especially as it developed after World War II.

A similar, but more dramatic description of postwar science is given by the mathematician Norbert Wiener (1894–1964) in his autobiography *I Am a Mathematician* (1956: 359–60):

> I am lucky to have been born and to have grown up before the First World War, at a period at which the vigor and *élan* of international scholarship had not yet been swamped by forty years of catastrophes. I am particularly lucky that it has not been necessary for me to remain for any considerable period a cog in a modern scientific factory, doing what I was told, accepting the problems given by my superiors, and holding my own brain only *in commendam* as a medieval vassal held his fiefs. If I had been born into this latter day feudal system of the intellect, it is my opinion that I would have amounted to little. From the bottom of my heart I pity the present generation of scientists, many of whom, whether they wish it or not, are doomed by the "spirit of the age" to be intellectual lackeys and clock punchers.

Crisis and revolution

The development of a novel scientific theory begins with the recognition of an anomaly, that is, with the recognition that nature has somehow violated the paradigm-induced expectations that govern normal science. It then continues with a more or less extended exploration of the area of the anomaly. And it closes only when the paradigm theory has been adjusted in such a way that the anomalous has become the expected.

In science, novel approaches emerge only with difficulty, manifested by resistance, against a background provided by expectation. Initially, scientists only observe what they expect to observe – even under circumstances where an anomaly is later revealed. Gradually, however, there comes an awareness that something is wrong. That awareness of the anomaly opens up a period of re-examination in which conceptual categories are adjusted until that which was initially anomalous has become the anticipated.

Thus in the first instance an anomaly is considered to be a puzzle. If this problem cannot be solved immediately, scientists are willing to wait, particularly if there are many other problems in other parts of their field. It follows that if an anomaly is to bring about a crisis, it must become more than just a puzzle, since difficulties are always encountered in solving a theory's puzzles. Failure to achieve the solution of a puzzle will usually discredit the scientist rather than the theory.

The transition to a crisis starts when an anomaly begins to seem more than just another of the puzzles of normal science. The anomaly itself now becomes generally recognized as such by the profession. Increasing numbers of the field's most eminent scientists devote more and more time to attempting to solve it. If it continues to resist solution, many will come to view its resolution as *the* key problem of their discipline. For them, the field will no longer look quite the same. This is due, at least partly, to their fixation on a new point of scientific scrutiny. But an even more important source for change is the divergent nature of the numerous partial solutions that will be produced by the concerted attention being paid to the problem.

The earliest attempts to address the problem will have followed the paradigm rules quite closely. But with continuing resistance, an increasing number of approaches involve some minor – or even not so minor – adjustments of the paradigm. No two of these will be quite alike, each will be achieve at least partial success, but none of them will be accepted as paradigmatic by the group. Through this proliferation of divergent adjustments (more and more frequently they will come to be described as *ad hoc*), the rules of normal science become increasingly blurred. Though there still is a paradigm, few practitioners are in very much agreement about what it would consist of. Even formerly standard solutions to long-solved problem are now likely to be called into question. Thus, a crisis is the product of an increasing failure of normal problem-solving activity.

Kuhn, however, emphasized that severe and prolonged anomalies are not the same as Popperian kinds of falsifications that refute a theory (Chapter 3). Though the field's scientists may begin to lose faith and consider alternatives, they are unlikely to renounce the paradigm that has led them into crisis. Once it has achieved the status of a paradigm, a scientific theory is declared invalid only if an alternative candidate emerges to take its place. No process disclosed by the historical study of scientific development, according to Kuhn, resembles the methodology of falsification that relies on direct comparison with nature.

This does not mean that scientists do not reject scientific theories, or that experience and experiment are not essential to the process by which they do so. But it does mean, however, that the act of judgment that leads scientists to reject a previously accepted theory is always based upon more than a comparison of that theory with the world. The decision to reject one paradigm is always simultaneously the decision to accept another, and the judgment that leads to it involves the comparison of both paradigms with nature *and* also with each other. "To reject one paradigm without simultaneously substituting another is to reject science itself" (p. 79).

All crises, then, begin with the blurring of a paradigm and the consequent loosening of the rules for normal research. And all crises are resolved in one of three ways:

1. Normal science ultimately proves able to handle the crisis-provoking problem in spite of the despair on the part of those who have seen it as the end of an existing paradigm.

2. On other occasions the problem resists even apparently radical new approaches. Then scientists may conclude that no solution will be forthcoming in the present state of their field. The problem is labeled and set aside for a future generation with more developed tools.
3. Or, finally, a crisis may end with emergence of a new candidate paradigm and with the ensuing battle over its acceptance.

The transition from a paradigm in crisis to a new paradigm which leads to a new tradition of normal science is far from a gradual process, to be achieved by a rearticulation or extension of the old paradigm. Rather, it involves a reconstruction of the field from a new set of fundamentals, a reconstruction that changes the field's most elementary theoretical principles along with its methods and applications. There will also be a decisive difference in the modes of solution. When the transition is complete, the profession will have changed its view of the field, its methods, and its goals.

Kuhn liked to compare this aspect of paradigm shift with a change in a visual *gestalt* as in the case of the image that is seen as first a rabbit, and then as a duck, or vice versa (see Figure 4.1). Kuhn also warns us, however, that this parallel can be misleading. Scientists do not see something *as* something else; instead, they simply see it. In addition, the scientist does not preserve the *gestalt* subject's freedom to switch back and forth between ways of seeing. Nevertheless, the switch of *gestalt* is a useful elementary prototype for what occurs in full-scale paradigm shift.

Figure 4.1   *Duck–Rabbit*

Transformations such as these, though usually more gradual and almost always irreversible, are common concomitants of scientific training. Only after a number of such transformations of vision does the student become an inhabitant of the scientist's world, seeing what the scientist sees and responding as the scientist does. The world that the student then enters is not fixed once and for all by the nature of the environment, on the one hand, and by science, on the other. Rather, it is determined jointly by the environment and the particular normal-scientific tradition that the student has been trained to pursue. Therefore, at times when the normal-scientific tradition changes, scientists' perception of their environment must be re-educated – in some familiar situations they must learn to see a new *gestalt*. After they have done so the world of their research will seem, here and there, incommensurable with the one inhabited before.

This also explains why scientists who develop the fundamental principles of a new paradigm are often either very young or comparatively new to the field. This is because they have little commitment to prior practice or to the traditional rules of normal science.

The resulting transition to a new paradigm – a paradigm shift – can rightly be labeled a "scientific revolution." Scientific revolutions are noncumulative developmental episodes in which an old paradigm is replaced by an incompatible new one.

Kuhn described a paradigm shift as a revolution because it shares specific parallels with political revolutions. Political revolutions are inaugurated by a growing sense, often limited to only a small number of the political community, that the existing institutions no longer address the problems faced by a society. Similarly, scientific revolutions are inaugurated by a growing sense, again often restricted to a small part of the scientific community, that an existing paradigm has ceased to offer a satisfactory explanation of all observed phenomena. In both cases, the sense that malfunction can lead to a crisis is a prerequisite to revolution.

The parallel, however, has a second and more profound aspect upon which the significance of the first depends. Political revolutions aim to change political institutions in ways that are prohibited by those very institutions. The success of political revolutions necessitiates, therefore, the partial relinquishment of one set of institutions in favor of another, and in the interim, society is not fully governed by any single set of institutions. Initially, it is the crisis alone that undermines the role of political institutions as we have already seen it weaken the role of paradigms. Increasing numbers of individuals become progressively estranged from political life, and act more and more in the margins of it.

As the crisis deepens, many of these individuals commit themselves to some concrete proposal to reconstruct society within a new institutional framework. At this point society is divided into competing camps or parties, one seeking to defend the old institutional constellation, the others seeking to institute new ones. Once such a polarization has occurred, any recourse to politics will fail. Because the groups differ about the institutional matrix within which political change is to be achieved and evaluated, and because they do not acknowledge any shared supra-institutional framework for the adjudication of revolutionary differences, the parties to a revolutionary conflict must finally resort to the techniques of mass persuasion, often including force and violence. Though revolutions have played a vital role in the evolution of political institutions, that role depends upon their being partially extra-political or extra-institutional events.

The historical study of paradigm change reveals very similar characteristics in the evolution of the sciences. Like the choice between competing political institutions, that between competing paradigms proves to be a choice between incompatible modes of community life. Because it has that character, the choice is not – and cannot be – determined solely by the evaluative procedures characteristic of normal science, for these depend in part upon a particular paradigm – and in these circumstances it is the very paradigm that is at issue. When competing paradigms enter into a debate about paradigm choice, their role is necessarily circular. Each of the rival groups uses its own paradigm to argue their case. As in political revolutions, so in paradigm choice – there is no standard higher than the assent of the relevant community.

The historical reconstruction of theory change in terms of paradigms and revolutions that is provided by Kuhn is clearly different from the philosopher's views of change in terms of testing and verification or falsification that has been explored in the earlier chapters.

According to Kuhn, a scientist is a solver of puzzles, rather than a tester of paradigms. Though the researcher may, during the search for the solution of a particular puzzle, try out a number of alternative approaches – rejecting those that fail to yield the desired result – this does not amount to a testing of the paradigm itself. These actions can be likened to the actions of the chess player who, having identified a problem, tries out various alternative moves to try and solve it. These trial attempts, whether by the chess player or by the scientist, are trials only of themselves – they do not attempt to overturn the rules of the game. They are possible only so long as the paradigm itself is taken for granted.

Therefore, paradigm-testing occurs only when the persistent failure to solve a significant puzzle has given rise to a crisis. And even then it occurs only after the sense of crisis has evoked an alternative candidate for paradigm. In the sciences the testing situation never consists, as puzzle-solving does, simply in the comparison of a single paradigm with nature. Instead, testing occurs within the context of the competition between two rival paradigms for the allegiance of the scientific community.

As we saw in Chapter 3, Popper emphasizes the importance of falsification, that is, of the test, because its negative outcome necessitates the rejection of an established theory. Clearly, the role attributed to falsification is similar to that of anomalous observations, that is, observations that – by leading to a crisis – prepare the ground for a new theory. Nevertheless, anomalous observations cannot be seen as identical to falsifying ones. As has been emphasized above, no theory will ever solve all the puzzles with which it is confronted at a given time; nor are the solutions already achieved always perfect ones. On the contrary, it is the very incompleteness and imperfection of the existing data–theory fit that at any time defines many of the puzzles that characterize normal science. If any and every failure of fit were to be grounds for the rejection of a theory, all theories ought to be rejected at all times.

In this respect, it is interesting to relate an anecdote concerning Popper's exemplary scientist of falsificationism, Einstein, and his theory of relativity. One of Einstein's students, Ilse Rosenthal-Schneider (1891–1990), reported the following conversation with Einstein:

> Once when I was with Einstein in order to read with him a work that contained many objections against his theory … he suddenly interrupted the discussion of the book, reached for a telegram that was lying on the windowsill, and handed it to me with the words, "Here, this will perhaps interest you." It was Eddington's cable with the results of measurement of the eclipse expedition [1919]. When I was giving expression to my joy that the results coincided with his calculations, he said quite unmoved, "But I knew that the theory is correct;" and when I asked, what if there had been no confirmation of his prediction, he countered: "Then I would have been sorry for the dear Lord – the theory is correct."
>
> (Holton 1973: 254–5)

Clearly, in this instance the falsification of Einstein's theory did not mean that he would abandon it.

Incommensurability

There are a number of reasons why the proponents of competing paradigms *must* fail to understand each other's viewpoints completely, which are described in terms of the incommensurability of the pre- and post-revolutionary normal-scientific traditions. In the first place, the proponents of competing paradigms often disagree about the list of problems that are to be resolved by any candidate for paradigm. Both their standards and their definitions of science are not the same.

However, this process involves more than simply an incommensurability of standards. New paradigms often incorporate much of the vocabulary and apparatus of the paradigm that they are replacing. But they will usually establish new relationships between these elements. The inevitable result is that there will be misunderstandings between the two competing schools.

The third – and most fundamental – aspect of the incommensurability of competing paradigms is that the two groups of scientists actually see different things when they are looking from the same point in the same direction.

This is not to say that they can see anything they please. Both groups are looking at the same world, and what they look at does not change from one perspective to the next. But they see different things, and they see them in different relations to one another. Take, for example, the duck–rabbit *gestalt*-switch. One group will see the rabbit, the other will see the duck. Before they can hope to communicate fully, one group or the other must experience the conversion that we have been calling a paradigm shift.

In mathematics, incommensurability means that a number cannot be expressed as a whole number or a ratio of two whole numbers. A well-known example of incommensurability is the square root of 2. There exists a story about Pythagoras that goes with this mathematical fact, which shows in another way what resistance means when dealing with an anomaly. According to Pythagoras, rational numbers (whole numbers and ratios of whole numbers) can explain all natural phenomena. A student of Pythagoras was toying with the square root of 2 attempting to find an equivalent ratio. He may have arrived at this anomalous number by employing Pythagoras' well-known theorem. Take both legs of the right triangle to be one, and then the hypotenuse is the squared root of 2. Eventually he came to realize that no such ratio exists. The student must have been overjoyed by his discovery, but his master was not. Pythagoras had defined the universe in terms of rational numbers, and the existence of irrational numbers brought his ideal into question. Pythagoras was unwilling to accept that he was wrong, but at the same time he was unable to destroy the student's argument by the power of logic. To his eternal shame he sentenced the student to death by drowning.

Disciplinary matrix

One central problem with Kuhn's use of the term "paradigm" in his *Structure* is that he uses the term in two different senses:

- On the one hand, it stands for the entire constellation of beliefs, values, techniques, and so on, shared by the members of a given scientific community.
- On the other, it denotes one sort of element in that constellation, the concrete puzzle-solutions which, employed as models or examples, can replace explicit rules as a basis for the solution of the remaining puzzles of normal science.

tools to solve problems in normal science

The first sense of the term given here makes it very hard to disentangle it from the notion of a scientific community. A paradigm is what the members of a scientific community share; conversely, a scientific community consists of scientists who share a paradigm.

In a postscript added to the 1970 edition of his *Structure* Kuhn admits that if he were to rewrite the book, he would open it with an examination of the community structure of science. A scientific community consists of the practitioners of a scientific specialty. They share similar educations and professional training; in the process they have studied the same technical literature and drawn many of the same conclusions. Usually, the boundaries of that standard literature will mark the limits of a scientific subject matter, and each community ordinarily has its own literature and subject matter. The members of a scientific community see themselves – and are seen by others – as uniquely responsible for the pursuit of a set of shared goals, including the training of their successors.

In the pre-paradigm period, a number of scientific schools compete for the domination of a given field. Later, in the wake of some significant scientific achievement, the number of schools is reduced greatly, often to just one, and this leads to a more focussed mode of scientific practice. It should be emphasized at this point that Kuhn was discussing the situation in relation to the natural sciences rather than the social sciences. He thought the latter had not yet developed sufficiently to be governed by a single paradigm.

Both normal science and revolutions are community-based activities. In their analysis, one must first unravel the changing community structure of the sciences over time. From this perspective, a paradigm governs not a subject matter but rather a group of practitioners. The study of any paradigm-directed or paradigm-shattering research must begin by locating the responsible group or groups. Having isolated a particular community, one may then ask: what do its members share that accounts for the common foundation of their professional judgments? For this purpose Kuhn introduced the term **disciplinary matrix**: "disciplinary," because it refers to the practitioners' common possession of a particular discipline; "matrix," because it is composed of ordered elements of various sorts, each requiring further specification.

The four different elements in the disciplinary matrix are as follows:

Symbolic generalizations

These are expressions, deployed without question or dissent by group members, which can readily be represented in logical or mathematical form, for example max $U(x)$. They are the formal or the readily formalizable elements of the disciplinary matrix. Absent the general acceptance of expressions such as these, there would be no points at which group members could apply the powerful techniques of logical and mathematical manipulation in their puzzle-solving enterprise. These generalizations sometimes resemble laws of nature, but their function is to define some of the symbols they deploy.

The metaphysical parts of the paradigms

These are the shared commitments to beliefs in particular models, including their heuristic value. All models have similar functions. They supply the group with preferred or permissible analogies and metaphors (see Focus 6.1). By doing so they help to determine what will be accepted as an explanation and as a puzzle-solution; conversely, they assist in the determination of the roster of unsolved puzzles and in the evaluation of the importance of each.

Values

Usually, these are shared more widely among different communities than either symbolic generalizations or models, and they do much to determine the scientific community's self-image. Though they are present in the background at all times, their particular importance emerges when the members of a particular community must identify a crisis, or, later, choose between incompatible ways of practicing their disciplines. According to Kuhn, probably the most deeply held values are related to predictions: they should be accurate; quantitative predictions are preferable to qualitative ones; whatever the margin of permissible error, it should be consistently satisfied in a given field; and so on. There are also, however, values to be used in the judgment of whole theories: they must, first and foremost, permit puzzle-formulation and solution; where possible they should be simple, self-consistent, plausible, and compatible with other theories currently deployed. Other sorts of values also exist – for example, science should (or need not) be socially useful. The role of values and value judgments in economics is discussed more fully in the final chapter of the book.

Paradigm

The fourth and final sort of element in the disciplinary matrix is "paradigm" – used here in its original sense of an exemplar, the concrete solutions to problems that students encounter from the beginning of their scientific education, whether in laboratories, in examinations, or in their science textbooks. These shared exemplars can be supplemented by some of the technical problem-solutions found in the periodical literature that scientists encounter during their post-education research careers.

In explaining how these elements combine to form a discipline, Kuhn offers the following description of what is entailed by disciplining or training. It is a common experience for students to report that they have read through a chapter of their textbook, and have understood it perfectly, but they have nevertheless had difficulty in solving a number of the problems set at the end of the chapter. Usually, those difficulties can be overcome when the students discover, either with or without guidance, similarities with problems they have encountered earlier in their studies. Having recognised the resemblance, and grasped the analogy between two or more distinct problems, students can then interrelate symbols and attach them in ways that have proved effective in the past.

The generalization, say max $U(x)$, has functioned as a tool, informing the student about what similarities to look for, signaling the *gestalt* in which problems are to be seen. The resulting ability to see the similarities between a variety of problems, as subjects for max $U(x)$ or some other symbolic generalization, is the main thing students acquire by doing exemplary problems, whether with a pencil and paper or in a well-designed laboratory. They have learned to view problems with the same *gestalt* as other members of their specialists' group, and they have assimilated a group-licensed way of seeing. Scientists solve puzzles by modeling them on previous puzzle-solutions.

Imre Lakatos

Imre Lakatos (1922–1974), born Imre Lipschitz into a Hungarian Jewish family, spent the war years at the University of Debrecen, graduating in 1944 with a degree in mathematics, physics, and philosophy. To avoid the Nazi persecution of Jews he changed his name to Imre Molnár, and so would survive while others of Jewish descent were deported to the gas chambers in German concentration camps, including his mother and grandmother who died in Auschwitz. After the war ended Lakatos, who had become an active communist, changed his name again, not back to the Jewish Lipschitz but rather, in keeping with his political views, to the Hungarian working-class name of Lakatos. In 1947 Lakatos obtained a post in the Hungarian Ministry of Education. However, his political prominence soon got him into trouble. In 1950 he was arrested and served three years in a Stalinist prison.

Following his release, Lakatos found himself unemployed and penniless. In 1954, the mathematician Alfréd Rényi (1921–1970) secured him a job translating mathematics works in the Mathematical Research Institute of the Hungarian Academy of Science. After the 1956 Hungarian Uprising and its violent suppression by Soviet forces, he escaped to Vienna, eventually found his way to England, and began to study for a doctorate in philosophy at the University of Cambridge. Lakatos's work was influenced by the work of Popper and also that of the mathematician George Pólya (1887–1985), and he went on to write his doctoral thesis *Essays in the Logic of Mathematical Discovery*, which was submitted in 1961. In 1960

Lakatos was appointed to the London School of Economics, where he later became a Professor of Logic; he taught there until his death.

A sophisticated falsificationism

Lakatos's main criticism of Kuhn's account of paradigm shifts is that it is irrational. He describes it as a "mystical conversion which is not and cannot be governed by rules of reason and which falls totally within the realm of the (*social*) *psychology of discovery*. Scientific change is a kind of religious change" (Lakatos 1970: 93).

In defense of Popper's rational account of scientific growth, Lakatos introduces a more "sophisticated" account of scientific development – the methodology of scientific research programs – that was not based on "naive falsificationism." This naive falsificationism is Popper's original falsificationism as outlined in his *Logic of Discovery* (see Chapter 3). Lakatos's proposed "sophisticated falsificationism" integrates Popper's rationalism with Kuhn's account of normal science.

Sophisticated falsificationism differs from naive falsificationism in terms of both its rules of acceptance (or demarcation criterion) and its rules of falsification. For the naive falsificationist, any theory that is falsifiable is acceptable or scientific, whereas for the sophisticated falsificationist a theory is acceptable or scientific only if it has corroborated excess empirical content over its predecessor, that is, only if it leads to the discovery of **novel facts**, that is, facts that are improbable in existing theory. For the naive falsificationist a theory is falsified by an observational statement which conflicts with it, whereas for the sophisticated falsificationist a theory T is falsified if and only if another theory T' has been proposed with the following characteristics: (1) T' predicts novel facts, that is, facts that are improbable in the light of, or even forbidden, by T; (2) T' explains the previous success of T, that is, all the unrefuted content of T is included in the content of T'; and (3) some of the excess content of T' is corroborated.

In proposing his "more sophisticated" account of falsificationism, Lakatos took account of the Duhem–Quine Thesis (see Focus 3.1) that any theory can be saved from refutation by suitable adjustments in the background knowledge in which it is embedded, for example by a change in some auxiliary hypothesis or by a suitable reinterpretation of its terms. To maintain rationality one needs standards to determine the theoretical adjustments by which one is allowed to maintain a theory. The problem is how to demarcate between scientific and pseudo-scientific adjustments – that is, between rational and irrational changes of theory.

According to both Popper and Lakatos, saving a theory through the use of auxiliary hypotheses is only permissible when it satisfies certain well-defined conditions representing scientific progress. For them, scientific progress means an increase in the level of empirical content. But then any theory has to be assessed together with its auxiliary hypotheses, initial conditions, etc., and, especially, together with its predecessors so that we may see by what sort of change it was brought about. As a result, in each instance we have to assess a series of theories rather than a single, isolated theory.

To assess a series of theories, Lakatos defined two kinds of progress. Let us take a series of theories, $T1$, $T2$, $T3$, ..., where each subsequent theory results from the successive addition of auxiliary clauses and/or from reinterpretations of some of the terms of the previous theories in order to accommodate some anomaly. Let us assume also that each theory has at least as much content as the unrefuted content of its predecessor. Such a series of theories is "theoretically progressive" if each new theory predicts some novel – that is, hitherto unexpected – fact. A theoretically progressive series of theories is also said to be "empirically progressive" if each new theory leads to the actual discovery of some new fact. By contrast, a series of theories is "degenerating" if it is not progressive, either theoretically or empirically. So, progress is measured by the degree to which a series of theories leads us to the discovery of novel facts. A theory in the series is falsified when it is superseded by a theory with higher corroborated content. There is no falsification before the emergence of a better theory.

So, one of the crucial features of Lakatos's falsificationism is its replacement of the concept of theory by the concept of series of theories. It is a succession of theories, rather than one given theory, which is to be assessed as either scientific or pseudo-scientific. Lakatos emphasized that in the growth of science the most important of such series of theories are characterized by a certain continuity which connects their members. This continuity evolves from a genuine "research program" outlined at the start, which is comparable to Kuhn's concept of normal science. This research program consists of methodological rules: some tell us what paths of research to avoid, the "negative heuristic," and others tell us what paths to pursue, the "positive heuristic."

All **scientific research programs** are characterized in terms of their **hard core**. The negative heuristic of the program forbids us to attack this hard core. Instead, we must use our ingenuity to articulate or even invent auxiliary hypotheses, which form a "protective belt" around this core, and we must redirect the attack to these. It is this protective belt of auxiliary hypotheses which has to bear the brunt of tests and which is subject to adjustment and re-adjustment, or even completely replaced, to defend the thus-hardened core. An example of an element of the hard core in the standard microeconomic research program is the weak axiom of revealed preference. Research programs, besides their negative heuristic, are also characterized by their positive heuristic. The positive heuristic consists of suggestions and hints about how to modify the "refutable" protective belt.

These concepts of research programs and progress provide the basis for transforming a paradigm shift from a "religious change" into a rational one. Thus, the selection of the most progressive research program becomes a rational one. This means that an empirically progressive research program is to be preferred to a theoretically progressive research program, but that the latter is in turn preferable to a degenerating research program.

One problem remains, however. Proving empirical progress can take an indefinite period of time. One can always defend a research program by claiming that its predicted "novel" facts will be empirically proven at some unspecified point in the future. It should be recalled that it took four years before Einstein's general relativity theory was verified by the readings produced by Eddington (see p. 73).

Looking ahead

If Popper was a transitional figure in the development of philosophy of science who sought to make rational improvements to the thinking of the logical positivists, Kuhn and Lakatos substantially changed its direction and character by emphasizing the historical character of science and the social nature of scientific communities – considerations that were altogether foreign to the logical positivists. As will be seen in the following chapter, this latter direction was sustained in developments that came after Kuhn and Lakatos through the application of, first, new sociological approaches and, second, economic approaches to scientific communities. It would be wrong to state, however, that the logical positivist foundations of the twentieth-century philosophy of science were abandoned altogether. Rather, what emerged was a division between kinds of approaches, with many remaining committed to essentially rationalist views of science and others adopting more historically and socially based views. We turn first, then, to the sociology of scientific knowledge, which will be the subject of the following chapter.

Exercises

1   Give a description of an anomaly. Give an account of Kuhn's view of the role of anomalies in normal science.
2   Give Kuhn's explanation why two different paradigms are incommensurable.
3   Why did Kuhn speak of revolutions in science?
4   Within a period of normal science, scientific progress is possible, according to Kuhn. Describe what progress within such a period of normal science entails.

5   Imre Lakatos's Methodology of Scientific Research Programs con-
    sists of two heuristics for how to deal with anomalies. Give a short
    description of both heuristics.
6   Describe Lakatos's proposal to evaluate different research programs.
7   According to Lakatos, one can compare different research programs.
    Nevertheless, one cannot decide definitely in favor of the most pro-
    gressive program. Why not?
8   Kuhn's theory of paradigms has significantly contested the idea that
    science is a rational process.
    a.   Explain how Kuhn's theory might contest the idea that a para-
         digm shift is rational.
    b.   Explains how Lakatos idea of scientific progress in its turn con-
         tested the supposed irrationality of a paradigm shift.

Relevant readings

Glass, J.C. and W. Johnson (1989) *Economics: Progression, Stagnation or
    Degeneration*, Ames, IA: Iowa State University Press.
    An introductory-level application of Popperian, Kuhnian, and especially
        Lakatosian approaches to economics.
Holton, Gerald (1988) *Thematic Origins of Scientific Thought: Kepler to Einstein*,
    revised edn, Cambridge, MA: Harvard University Press.
    Historical case studies of physicists meant as an empirical input to philosophy
        of science.
Kuhn, Thomas S. (1970) *The Structure of Scientific Revolutions*, 2nd enlarged
    edition. International Encyclopedia of Unified Science, vol. 2, no. 2, Chicago
    and London: The University of Chicago Press.
    Kuhn's most influential work in which he introduced the concepts of normal
        science, paradigm, incommensurability, and revolution. The title is mislead-
        ing, because the book argues that scientific revolutions have no structure.
Kuhn, Thomas S. (1977) *The Essential Tension: Selected Studies in Scientific
    Tradition and Change*, Chicago and London: The University of Chicago
    Press.
    A collection of Kuhn's most important articles published before and after his
        Structure.
Lakatos, Imre and Alan Musgrave (eds.) (1970) *Criticism and the Growth of
    Knowledge*, Cambridge: Cambridge University Press.
    Proceedings of the colloquium in which Kuhn's *Structure* was discussed by the
        leading philosophers of science, including Popper. It contains Lakatos's ori-
        ginal article on his Methodology of Scientific Research Programs.

Focus 4.1   Research Programs in Economics

Mark Blaug

The term "scientific research programs" (SRP) is used by Imre Lakatos to describe what previous philosophers of science had called a "theory." Lakatos used this word to emphasize both the fallibility and also the dynamic, forward-looking character of scientific theories, and also the notion that scientific theories constitute a program that allows their advocates to improve and perfect the theory they are defending. In addition, he denied that it was ever possible to judge an isolated theory; what could be judged and appraised were clusters of more or less interconnected theories, and it was these clusters that he labeled "scientific research programs."

As time passes research programs inevitably encounter falsifications – a lesson that Lakatos had learned from Kuhn – and the issue for scientific progress was how it dealt with such falsifications. According to Lakatos, a SRP contains a "hard core" of purely metaphysical beliefs that unite the protagonists of the SRP and which cannot be rejected without abandoning the entire research program. This hard core is surrounded by what Lakatos sarcastically called a "protective belt" of testable theories, which can – and indeed must – be amended as the program encounters falsifications or what Kuhn terms "anomalies" – parts of the theory that do not stand up to examination in the light of further evidence.

These amendments may be what Popper called "content increasing or content decreasing," or what Lakatos more pointedly called "progressive or degenerating problem shifts." A SRP is said to be "theoretically progressive" if successive formulations of a program contain excess empirical content over its predecessors, which must mean that it predicts novel, hitherto unsuspected facts. It is "empirically progressive" if this excess empirical content is corroborated. However, if the SRP is only amended to accommodate whatever new facts become available, or if it fails to discover "novel facts," it is considered to be "degenerating."

These are relative, rather than absolute distinctions. Further, they are applicable not at a given point of time but over a period of time. The forward-looking character of a research strategy, as distinct from an isolated theory, defies instant appraisal. For Lakatos, therefore, a SRP is not "scientific" once and for all; rather it may cease to be scientific as time passes, slipping from a "progressive" state to a "degenerating" state.

So far the discussion has been abstract, involving a number of definitions. However, it comes to life as we consider a SRP in economics, such as so-called neoclassical or orthodox economics. For example, the very foundation of orthodox economics is a metaphysical belief that the private interests that are encouraged by a free enterprise economy also serve the social interests of society by maximizing the gross national product and, ultimately, the living standards of the population. This is a metaphysical belief because it cannot be proven like a theorem in geometry, and further it cannot be conclusively demonstrated just by pointing your finger at history or the world outside your window. It is often referred to in terms of the short-hand reference to "the invisible hand" of the market that harmonizes private and social interests through the action of competition.

This hard core is surrounded by a variety of theories about the concrete working out of competition – for example, that it encourages firms to maximize profits by equating marginal revenue and marginal costs. This requires the assumption that demand curves are negatively inclined, meaning that an increase of supply will cause the price of whatever commodity we are talking about to fall, and to rise for a decrease of supply. Likewise, it requires the assumption that supply curves are positively inclined, meaning that an increase of demand causes price to increase and a decrease in demand causes it to fall.

These are assumptions, but it is clearly possible to test them using empirical evidence. If they are found to be false, this requires a revision of the "invisible hand" theorem. They may be capable of being accommodated by suitable revision, but only the track record of the research program in the face of possible refutations will establish whether it is a "progressive" or "degenerating" SRP. Here is not the place to review this track record. The point is that the question of whether a SRP is "progressive" or "degenerating" has no "once-and-for-all" answer.

On the best available evidence, most economists are agreed that almost all demand curves are negatively inclined, but this is a decision reached on the basis of empirical evidence rather than theory. It is an inductive inference, pure and simple. And the same thing is true of the generally agreed upon belief that virtually all supply curves are positively inclined.

A number of other theories also flourish in the "protective belt" of neoclassical theory, including human capital theory to explain the earnings differences between individuals, the Heckscher–Ohlin theory of international trade to explain the commodity composition of international trade, and the marginal productivity theory of distribution to account for the relative shares of wages and rents. All of these are individual SRPs, but in combination they form a cluster of interconnected theories that constitute the main neoclassical SRP.

Focus 4.2   Scientific Revolutions in Economics?

Both Kuhn's discussion of paradigms and Lakatos's accounts of research programs were concerned with science rather than economics. However, in his attempt to discover the difference between communities of social scientists and of natural scientists Kuhn began to recognize the key role that was played by paradigms in both sorts of disciplines. Spending 1958–59 at the Center for Advanced Studies in the Behavioral Sciences at Stanford University, he was "struck by the number and extent of the overt disagreements between social scientists about the nature of legitimate scientific problems and methods" (Kuhn 1970: viii) – in other words the lack of what he would call a unifying paradigm.

Nonetheless, historians of economics are in general agreement that the history of economics can be viewed as a succession of dominant approaches, where economics in each historical period is given a broad label: classical political economy (1776–1890), neoclassical economics (1890–1936), Keynesian economics (1936–1970s), and new classical economics (1970s–date).

Further, these periods are often identified with publications of the "founders" of each approach: *The Wealth of Nations* (1776) by Adam Smith, *Principles of Economics* (1890) by Alfred Marshall, *The General Theory* (1936) by John Maynard Keynes, and a collection of articles by Robert Lucas and Thomas Sargent published as *Rational Expectations and Econometric Practice* (1981). Some historians have referred to such shifts as revolutions: they speak in terms of the marginalist revolution, the Keynesian revolution, and the rational expectations revolution; other historians, however, believe that the use of the term revolutions is too strong, because it overlooks the simultaneous existence of rival approaches.

Though it is not easy to state conclusively the reasons that lay behind these shifts, it can be argued that the global economic depression of the 1930s represented an anomaly for neoclassical economics, and that, similarly, the phenomenon of stagflation in the 1970s was an anomaly for Keynesian economics. Further, Kuhn's idea that it takes a new generation of researchers to build a new paradigm is often in evidence. Consider, for example, Robert Lucas's account of the rise of new classical economics:

> I guess when we first got going it was kind of exciting because the people who were interested in this rational expectations model were a tiny minority at first. We were pretty confident of what we were doing, but we were regarded as very far out by other people. I had a lot of fun going to Yale and other places to talk in these chaotic seminars where I stand up and people throw darts at me [laughter]. It was a lot of fun. But now the stuff is much more widely accepted. A whole new generation of people has gotten into these models, so they're not quite as exotic.
>
> (Lucas in conversation with Klamer 1984: 34)

So despite his own doubts about social science, Kuhn's thinking about paradigms and scientific revolutions can be applied to economics.

There are, however, good reasons to think that Lakatos's framework offers a better characterization of the history of economics. Most importantly, Lakatos's methodology of scientific research programs allows for the existence of multiple scientific research programs within a discipline, and this appears to offer a more accurate picture of the history of economics.

It is true that the history of economics has often been characterized by dominant schools of thought (though there are also historical periods which are more pluralistic and during which there is no dominant approach). For example, contemporary economics is still strongly influenced by neoclassical economics, but there are also a number of active heterodox approaches (such as institutional economics, post-Keynesian economics, Marxist economics, feminist economics, critical realism, and social economics) and also a number of new non-neoclassical approaches (such as behavioral economics, experimental economics, complex adaptive systems theory, and neuroeconomics). Kuhn might have suggested that economics is simply in a pre-paradigmatic stage of development, but this view is difficult to square with its history of development in terms of "dominant" approaches.

These issues of paradigms and revolutions are the concern not only of historians but also of economic methodologists, because they are central to the issue of whether or not economics can be considered a science. For example, the existence of several simultaneous paradigms within one discipline was, for Kuhn, reason to suggest that the discipline is still in a pre-paradigmatic phase, which means implicitly that the discipline in question is not yet a science.

Indeed, this idea of a unifying framework as one of the main characteristics of a science is also shared by economists like Jan Tinbergen. When the stagflation of the 1970s caused extensive debate among different groups of economists – monetarists, supply-siders, anti-regulation economists, and Keynesians – Tinbergen called for the development of a synthesis on the grounds that this was the essence of scientific work: "If we, economists, continue to oppose each other, we fail in our duty as scientists." It may be that this call for a synthesis was prompted by his background in physics.

One of the key conclusions of Lakatos's methodology of scientific research programs (MSRP) is that since research programs can change in ways that is either progressive or degenerating, we can judge them by the standards of progress in science. This would mean, of course, that the concept of scientific progress proposed by both the logical positivists and Karl Popper offers a meaningful way to think about science.

But is it? In an attempt to address this question, in 1989 leading economic methodologists, historians of economics, and economists organized a conference on the island of Capri. Its intention was to investigate whether Lakatos's MSRP has shown itself to be an appropriate framework for analyzing if economics has made progress as a science – and if so, in what sense. However, Lakatos's framework turned out to be much more problematic than was expected for two specific reasons:

1. The first was the recognition that there was no simple and unambiguous way of stating once and for all what the precise and fixed content of the hard core of any SRP in economics was in the sense of what would command the universal assent of all its adherents.

2. The second, deeper problem was the difficulty of using any empirical yardstick to measure scientific progress. Lakatos's insistence on the importance of novel facts in the appraisal of rival SRPs turned out to be rather complicated for a social science, such as economics, in which it is difficult to identify novel facts. Thus it was not clear what would constitute theoretical progress in economics, and much harder to pinpoint when empirical progress has been achieved.

One of the principal consequences of the 1989 conference was an increased interest among economic methodologists in the subject of scientific practices in economics – how economists actually carry out their research – as an alternative to a rule-based methodological approach. This signaled two important departures from the MSRP framework: (i) a move toward the increased use of case studies; and (ii) a substitution of descriptive for rule-based prescriptive analysis. It also reflected the influence of the sociology of scientific knowledge's "naturalistic turn" approach on methodologists. For example, greater attention was now being devoted to topics such as how economists model the world (see Focus 1.2). Here questions of scientific revolutions and progress were at best secondary concerns and increasingly fell off the research agendas of economic methodologists. But who knows what will happen when the next Keynes or Lucas emerges?

Relevant readings

de Marchi, Neil and Mark Blaug (eds) (1991) *Appraising Economic Theories: Studies in the Methodology of Research Programs*, Aldershot: Edward Elgar.
　　The proceedings of the Capri conference where the applicability of Lakatos's methodology to economics was discussed.
Klamer, Arjo (1984) *Conversations with Economists: New Classical Economists and Opponents Speak Out on the Current Controversy in Macroeconomics*, Totowa: Rowman and Littlefield.
　　Klamer's path-breaking set of interviews about the emergence of new classical economics.

Focus 4.3　Facts

In the preceding discussion we have treated facts and observations as equivalent types of empirical evidence. But not every observation report counts as a fact. To understand this distinction we will first take a closer look at observation.

The received view of science (Chapter 1) assumes a sharp distinction between observation statements and theoretical statements.

Observation statements (what the logical positivists call protocol sentences) contain no theoretical terms. Since observation statements contain only words defined in terms of observation and a logical vocabulary, observation statements are claims whose truth or falsity can be determined by observation alone with no appeal to theory.

The philosopher of science Norwood Russell Hanson (1924–1967), however, showed that observations are theory-laden. To illustrate **theory-ladenness** it is helpful to consider again the duck–rabbit figure in Chapter 4 (p. 101). Normal retinas receive similar impressions from this figure, but do we all see the same thing? Some will see a rabbit, others will see a duck. This difference in seeing is caused by our different ways of organizing the sense impression, that is, by the particular *gestalt* ("unified whole") we each bring to observation. The way we organize a visual experience is based on what we already know, so our observation will be shaped by prior knowledge. In the case of such common notions as a duck and a rabbit, little theory may be involved. But take Duhem's example about a visit to a laboratory (quoted in Hanson 1958):

> Enter a laboratory; approach the table crowded with an assortment of apparatus, an electric cell, silk-covered copper wire, small cups of mercury, spools, a mirror mounted on an iron bar; the experimenter is inserting into small openings the metal ends of ebony-headed pins; the iron oscillators, and the mirror attached to it throws a luminous band upon a celluloid scale; the forward–backward motion of this spot enables the physicist to observe the minute oscillations of the iron bar. But ask him what he is doing. Will he answer 'I am studying the oscillations of an iron bar which carries a mirror'? No, he will say that he is measuring the electric resistance of the spools. If you are astonished, if you ask him what his words mean, what relation they have with the phenomena he has been observing and which you have noted at the same time as he, he will answer that your question requires a long explanation and that you should take a course in electricity.

Thus the visitor must learn some physics before he can see what the physicist sees. In science, then, phenomena are only seen in the light of a theory.

Acknowledging that observations are theory-laden, however, also means that in order to acquire the status of a scientific fact they must meet certain requirements. Take, for example, my holiday experience near Loch Ness in Scotland: enjoying my daily evening walk alone along this beautiful lake, I suddenly saw an enormous head on a long neck coming out of the water, looking around, seeing me watching and then quickly diving back into the water.

Could one say on the basis of this observation that it is a fact that the Loch Ness Monster exists? No, because it is not clear at this point whether my observation was caused by a misinterpretation of what met my eyes. Moreover, such an interpretation should not be only a personal judgment, but should be shared by others. I have to ask "Do you see what I see?" to help decide whether what I saw is to be explained by something about me (being tired I really needed this holiday) or by knowledge of the presumed object. This requirement is called intersubjectivity. I must try to reach agreement with others regarding my interpretation of what I saw.

In science, however, it is irrelevant whether I can persuade my friends or relatives; it must be the peers of the relevant discipline(s) dealing with the phenomenon I believe I have seen. Who these peers are who I have to convince is determined by the object or phenomenon I have observed. They must be acknowledged as experts in the relevant research fields and disciplines. In the case of the Loch Ness Monster, the experts would include paleontologists, zoologists, and biologists who specialize in the wildlife to be found in Scottish Highland lakes. If they agree on my interpretation, that the Monster exists is a fact; if not, it is a fact that the Monster does not exist.

To attain intersubjective acceptance of an observation in a laboratory, reproducibility is the standard requirement. Reproducibility concerns closeness of agreement between results obtained by experiments on the same object or process carried out under changed conditions. These changed conditions may include: principle, method, observer, instrument, reference, location, conditions of use, and time. If an experimental result cannot be reproduced, the result is not accepted as a fact.

One classic example of non-reproducibility is the "discovery of cold fusion" in 1989. This term refers to a postulated nuclear fusion process thought to explain an anomalous heat production of a magnitude that would defy explanation except in terms of nuclear processes. This discovery raised hope of a cheap and abundant source of energy. Initial enthusiasm turned to skepticism, however, after other laboratories failed to reproduce the phenomenon. A review panel organized by the US Department of Energy found that the evidence for the discovery of a new nuclear process was not persuasive. As a result, the existence of cold fusion is not considered to be a fact.

Many important scientific observations have taken place on particular occasions whose recurrence is incidental to their scientific significance. Of particular importance in the advance of behavioral science are special events such as clinical outbursts, disasters, and financial crises, as well as regularly occurring ones such as elections. Of course, when such events happen again we can observe them again, but we cannot repeat the observations at will. And the recurrences can be expected to differ in ways relevant to the purposes of the observation.

To attain intersubjectivity, an alternative requirement but one rather similar to reproducibility is then more appropriate for these non-laboratory observations, namely **triangulation** (Chapter 6). This term indicates that more than one method has been used to validate an observation. The idea is that we can have more trust in a certain result when different methods are found to be congruent and yield comparable data. These different methods may include interviews, surveys, and statistics. Bringing together different kinds of evidence based on different sources, acquired by different methods, is a way to make your peers see what you have seen, and so create a new scientific fact.

Relevant readings

Hanson, Norwood Russell (1958) *Patterns of Discovery*, Cambridge: Cambridge University Press.
> A classic in the philosophy of science, not only for his treatment of theory-ladenness, but also for his account of the context of discovery.

Jick, Todd D. (1979) "Mixing Qualitative and Quantitative Methods: Triangulation in Action," *Administrative Science Quarterly* 24: 602–11.
> A survey article on triangulation.

Kaplan, Abraham (1964) *The Conduct of Inquiry: Methodology for Behavioral Science*, Scranton, NJ: Chandler.
> An early work on the methodology of empirical research, including experiments, in social science.

Chapter 5

The Sociology of Scientific Knowledge

Much of the recent history of philosophy and economic methodology relates a further move away from an *a priori* rule-based reasoning in terms of methodological principles set forth in an abstract and logical way so as to achieve a more descriptive type of methodology that models itself directly on the empirical practices of modern science. This development is sometimes referred to as a "naturalistic turn" because science is said to be concerned with the natural world, and this should be reflected in the philosophy of science.

Further, since science proceeds in an *a posteriori* manner by a process of reasoning from facts and evidence to conclusions rather than by starting from abstract principles, and then considering how evidence can be explained, Wade Hands associates the "naturalistic turn" with a new view of the theory of knowledge – or epistemology – that is labeled "naturalized epistemology." With a "naturalized epistemology" philosophy takes its cue from the practices of modern science in establishing what counts as knowledge.

Within this general development, there are a number of distinct approaches. In this chapter we focus on two that are especially appropriate to the social sciences, which Hands has labeled "the sociological turn" and "the economic turn."

The main idea behind each of these approaches is that reasoning about what counts as knowledge should be modeled on the practices of modern social science, rather than on the methods and concepts of abstract philosophical reasoning. Thus when we consider the way in which sociology has been used to explain science and knowledge, this is referred to as the **sociology of scientific knowledge** (SSK) and when we consider how economics has been used to explain science and knowledge, this is termed the **economics of scientific knowledge** (ESK).

The sociology of scientific knowledge (SSK)

Traditionally, the philosophy of science as influenced by logical positivism has focused on the justification of the rules of proper scientific method for all sciences, dealing with matters such as logic, inference, truth, the role

121

of assumptions, and the use of evidence. These were seen as constituting the justified rational grounds according to which scientific theories should be accepted or rejected, or the basis on which they should be modified in order to reconstruct the reasoning of scientists along rational lines.

In this respect, traditional philosophy of science can be viewed as prescriptive: it relies on rules that prescribe rational judgments about what counts as knowledge. Here we should recall Reichenbach's distinction between the context of discovery and the context of justification (see p. 12). A prescriptive philosophy of science is concerned with the rational justification of knowledge. It is not concerned with how theories may be discovered, but only with whether or not they are rationally justifiable.

SSK rejects Reichenbach's distinction, and holds that knowledge is determined according to what theories and concepts are established and accepted according to the social, political, and professional interests of scientists. In other words, it is these interests that determine what scientists come to regard as knowledge, rather than a set of abstract *a priori* standards regarding what *ought* to be regarded as true.

According to SSK, science can – and for some should – be seen as being "socially constructed." This means that the acceptance of a scientific theory is dependent upon its compatibility with the social interests of the scientific community rather than its success in terms of explaining the state of the world. Consequently, whereas traditional philosophy of science considers what is true or false in theories of science, the focus of SSK is on what is true or false regarding scientists' behavior.

SSK also rejects the received view of science according to which there is a privileged realm of correct scientific reasoning, including mathematics, logic and probabilistic reasoning. For SSK there is no such privileged realm of scientific reasoning, since determining what counts as a justified inference is a matter of scientists' beliefs. Further, scientists' beliefs reflect factors that are specific to their lives as working scientists.

SSK reflects the influence of Kuhn's work on scientific paradigms and scientific revolutions in two key respects:

1. As we saw, Kuhn's view of scientific paradigms was that they constituted frameworks which caused scientists unconsciously to "see" things from a particular perspective or paradigm, leading them then to make certain fundamental assumptions. Thus scientists typically believe many things without being entirely aware that they believe them, or what the implications are of holding such beliefs. One significant example is the evolution paradigm in biology, which is a presumption in most of the work in that science, but which is not questioned by most working biologists.
2. Scientists' attachments to particular paradigms are usually influenced by aspects of the scientific community within which they have received

their original training: where they originally studied, who they were trained (or mentored) by, and where they were later employed. Thus scientists hold on to many of their most fundamental assumptions, because they come from a certain scientific background and have worked within a particular scientific community where those assumptions are taken to be true. This can be seen, for example, in the influence of the Chicago School of neoclassical economics, whose students and staff share the assumptions that markets work competitively and that individuals are generally rational, and have been increasingly influential in guiding the direction of global economic policy since the 1970s.

One famous example of SSK research is found in Steven Shapin and Simon's Schaffer's *Leviathan and the Air Pump*, which offers an account of the seventeenth-century dispute in Britain over the value of experiments in science. The English philosopher Thomas Hobbes (1588–1679) rejected the value of experimentation, and argued that science ought to progress by deduction from first principles, as in the case of Euclid's geometry. By contrast, Robert Boyle (1627–1691) – often regarded as the founder of modern experimental science – carried out experiments using an air pump to create a near vacuum, and used the results to argue in favor of the experimental method.

Shapin and Schaffer point out that the dispute between Hobbes and Boyle also involved wider social issues. It took place at the time of the English Civil War, and both Hobbes and Boyle also wrote about the problem of social order. For Hobbes, what could be established deductively compelled assent, and since he believed the legitimacy of royal power ("the leviathan" as he termed it) could be demonstrated, dissent was an unjustified cause of social unrest. In contrast, Boyle believed that since knowledge was acquired experimentally, it was often piecemeal and incomplete, and thus dissent was justified – because it reflected an inevitable diversity of opinion. Shapin and Schaffer's argument, then, was that often "solutions to the problem of knowledge are embedded within practical solutions to the problem of social order" (p. 15). These cannot be disentangled easily, and thus our view of what knowledge is always reflects a variety of social interests. Let us look, then, at two of the main SSK approaches.

The Edinburgh Strong Programme and the laboratory studies approach

The first influential SSK statement is known as the **Edinburgh School Strong Programme**, and was advanced by Barry Barnes and David Bloor. Because this sociological study of science program makes the radical assertion that *all* scientific knowledge is socially constructed, it is labeled "the strong" program. To study science from this position they advanced a "naturalistic" approach to the production of scientific knowledge. Scientists themselves are part of the social world, and thus their beliefs and behavior are to be examined in the same way that sociologists or anthropologists examine other aspects of the social world, such as religion, social groups, organizations, institutions, and ethnicity. In order to study science as a social construct Barnes and Bloor formulated four methodological or organizing principles:

1. *Causality*: focus on the causal conditions of scientists' beliefs;
2. *Impartiality*: be impartial between true and false beliefs;
3. *Symmetry*: the same type of cause explains both true and false beliefs;
4. *Reflexivity*: the same kind of explanation also applies to SSK.

To study whether beliefs are true or false would mean that it is necessary to study science in terms of its relation to nature – precisely what is being rejected in this approach. The beliefs and theories held by scientists are to be learned from the study of how professional training, job opportunities, and sources of funding act as causal factors in determining their beliefs. Further, understanding how scientists come to hold the beliefs they do is independent of whether those beliefs are true or false; indeed, the same causal factors offer equal explanations for both true and false beliefs.

The fourth principle, **reflexivity**, acknowledges that SSK itself is subject to the same principles it applies to the scientists that sociologists of scientific knowledge study, thus implying an SSK of SSK. That is, the same sorts of causal factors that affect scientists also impact the explanations provided by sociologists of scientific knowledge. (Note that this also applies to the text that you are reading. Its authors would also be understood to be products of particular histories of professional training and paths of career development that – from the perspective of SSK – influence their views with respect to what is involved in investigating philosophy of science and methodology of economics. In other words, from the perspective of SSK a text such as this one must also be understood reflexively.) We return to this issue in Chapter 7 in connection with the issue of methodological value judgments in economics.

A second, more "microsociological" form of SSK is the **laboratory studies approach** associated with Karin Knorr Cetina, Bruno Latour, Steven Woolgar, Harry Collins, and others. In this work the emphasis rests on the daily practices of scientists in their laboratories and workplaces, and on how what they do in these locations influences the development of their theories. The standpoint that laboratory studies researchers take is often referred to as the naive perspective; they must act as if they have no preconceptions about the causal patterns being observed in the laboratory or workplace, in order to avoid reproducing scientists' own beliefs about their practices.

This approach is explained as involving an ethnomethodological approach or an approach similar to that adopted in cultural anthropology to study previously unknown people. For example, in a study of chemistry laboratories the types of experiments that can be carried out, and thus the types of theories that will be developed, are dependent upon the level of available technology. But it will also be important to take into account the meetings in which laboratory scientists discuss their results – how often they take place, who chairs the discussion, how results are presented, and so on – and also the physical organization of the workspace – is it an open space or is it separated into working areas. Even the location of the coffee machine may be relevant!

Similarly, in experimental research in economics (Focus 2.3) most experiments are carried out in university laboratories using students as subjects who communicate by computer, because students are easily available and are willing to participate for the small rewards that experimenters can offer, and because computers have become a standard tool in laboratories. Of course, students' life experiences and their willingness to accept small rewards may mean that they are not really representative of the general public. Nevertheless economists frame their scientific results in general terms because that is how the laboratory setting leads them to understand their results.

One leading version of the laboratory studies approach is Michael Callon's actor network theory. He sees science as being produced in networks in alliances between human and non-human agents whose "fusion" or combination stabilize certain scientific models of explanation. The particular networks or fields in which scientists operate make a commonality of interest possible, and laboratories or work groups that achieve this then can become influential for some period of time.

According to this view, science is seen as a process rather than as an orderly progression to an increasing set of settled truths. It is socially constructed and embedded in the lives of changing groups of scientists, and a "scientific" approach to science requires we attend to the practices of groups of scientists, and how these groups change and evolve, in connection with broad systemic factors affecting the general interests of scientists. Focus 5.1 offers a discussion of the changing relations between different groups of economists in recent economics.

Relativism, realism, and values

Social constructivism is the idea that scientific knowledge is constructed according to the social mechanisms and protocols that scientists use in the course of their work. Rather than supposing that scientists "discover" scientific truths as if they could be uncovered by inspecting the world in an experimental process, what scientists are seen to be doing in this process is actively creating what is later regarded as knowledge. More generally, then, social constructivism sees truth itself as a creation rather than something that is inherent to the world's nature. These conclusions raise a number of important philosophical or methodological issues that are the subject of continued debate.

First there is the issue of **relativism**, which is the view that truth and knowledge are not objective and unchanging features of the "real" world. Rather, they vary according to historical and social context. Often relativism is identified as the central manifesto of the Edinburgh Strong Programme, and is characterized as "the interest thesis."

Their key argument is that scientific disputes reflect contending social interests that are only settled by the resolution of conflicts between scientists. They are never decided by reference to independent sets of facts or independent reality. This relativism is in stark contrast to the more traditional view associated with the strand in philosophy of science that runs from the logical positivists through Popper and Lakatos and seeks to show how scientific reasoning conforms to ideal standards of philosophical reasoning.

Many philosophers, however, view relativism as flawed, since its central claim to be a correct interpretation of the world implies that it is *in itself* an objective characterization – something that contradicts the very notion of relativism. In other words, it is a self-defeating view.

While this criticism is very persuasive, there is also much to be gained from the SSK arguments outlined above. They alert us to the importance of the historical and social contexts in which science develops, and thus suggest that science is not objective – at least in the traditional sense.

It should be noted that this debate applies directly to the status of SSK as a scientific program through the application of Barnes and Bloor's reflexivity principle. Since the reflexivity principle states that the explanations SSK provides for the behavior of scientists apply reflexively to the very behavior of sociologists of scientific knowledge, and if the explanations that SSK scientists provide reflect their own motives and interests, there is no obvious reason to take these explanations as being objective in any substantial sense, since motives and interests are always specific to a particular social and historical context. Alternatively, it can be argued that SSK theories and conclusions are "objective relative to the SSK scientific community" – a particular group of historical individuals who occupy a place in the scientific/university community in the same way as the scientists they study. This would mean, not that "anything goes" (see Focus 6.2), but that in this instance the standards of objectivity are tied to the practices of scientific communities.

Second, there is the issue of **realism**, often defined as the view that the world is the way it is independent of human beliefs about its nature, though there are many different views of what this entails (see Focus 6.3). As suggested above, realists hold that the world is there to be "discovered" or "found" through scientists' efforts. More generally, the traditional – and still widely popular – view of science is of a long march of progress through which we obtain an increasingly realistic view of the nature of the world. SSK, however, brings this ideal clearly into question for two main reasons: On the one hand, as just stated, it raises the specter of relativism, with all of the associated difficulties. On the other hand, and more practically, SSK creates doubts about the way science is carried out.

Science, of course, is one of the most respected of all human activities. Indeed, it is held in high regard precisely because it is seen as operating above the sorts of local and partisan activities in human life that are associated with the political and social spheres. Scientists are often admired precisely because they are seen as being able to overcome social and historical contexts to achieve scientific knowledge that is regarded as being both true and universal (see Focus 7.2). Thus SSK brings into question not only the very status of science in human society, but also one of human society's most important self-images. Nonetheless, realism remains an important conviction of many philosophers of science and economic methodologists, despite the large volume of work in the SSK tradition that provides plausible accounts of how scientific knowledge is produced.

Third, there is the issue of value neutrality. The idea of a "naturalistic" approach to scientific knowledge, as understood by Barnes and Bloor, is that of an essentially descriptive representation of a given subject matter. In other words, just as scientists should not allow their own values to influence their scientific work, SSK researchers should not bring their values into their examination of the work of scientists.

However, it is by no means clear that it would ever be possible to create a purely descriptive, value-neutral science. While scientists and SSK researchers may be able to avoid explicit value judgments and policy prescriptions in their explanations and analyses, it is less clear that they would be able to avoid the use of value-laden concepts which may reflect implicit value judgments and policy prescriptions (for more on this matter, see Chapter 7).

For example, an SSK researcher conducting a study of health economists in the United States might conclude that the way in which the health economics community is organized tends to produce a type of research which ignores, for example, the fact that many people lack health insurance (because the community of academic health economists is concerned primarily with explaining how health care insurance is delivered through market structures). Though the SSK researcher may carry out this study without consciously injecting value judgments or policy prescriptions about the need for health economists to investigate the lack of health insurance, the very question of asking whether or not health economists overlook this issue seems to imply that it is a matter that *ought* to be investigated. Here, the concept that is value-laden is "lack of health insurance." Thus, the choice of the SSK researcher's concepts and topics for investigation is not necessarily always value-neutral, and may often implicitly convey a policy recommendation, in this case possibly about the need for society – and health economists – to address the lack of health insurance as a social problem.

We postpone any further discussion of the issue of value neutrality until the final chapter of this book. At this point it is simply important to acknowledge that the idea of a "naturalistic" approach to scientific knowledge is biased toward one view of the character of science. Barnes and Bloor reason that as scientists investigate the natural world, they are also simultaneously a part of the natural world, so that their beliefs can be examined just as one would examine any other part of the natural world.

Yet the world of plants, stars, animals, and rocks is natural in a completely different way from the social world of scientists. It may be that the latter can be investigated in many of the same ways as the former, but the comparison of natural science and social science makes it clear that there are important differences between the two. One significant difference in this respect is that the social world includes values which influence the behavior of individuals and organizations. SSK (and ESK, to be discussed in the next section) tend to overlook these matters.

The economics of scientific knowledge (ESK)

The economics of scientific knowledge performs essentially the same function as the sociology of scientific knowledge, though it does so by using economic rather than sociological concepts to explain scientists' motives and interests. This makes it a competing approach to SSK, since economists have long held views about human behavior that compete with those held by sociologists.

However, ESK is a more recent phenomenon than SSK because economists have only recently applied their understanding of human behavior to explain scientists as economic agents. Thus ESK represents both a refinement of SSK – in offering one particular view of human behavior – and also an alternative to SSK – in assuming that scientists are driven primarily by self-interest rather than broader social interests, such as a desire to advance the views of particular scientific communities.

Before examining ESK, it may be useful to give a brief introduction to the **economics of science** (ES). This will show how ESK has evolved from earlier thinking about economics and science. The development of

ES is associated with the work of the sociologist Robert K. Merton (1910–2003). Merton was interested in identifying the social preconditions for good science of any kind, that is, the norms and conventions which science possesses that distinguished it from other cultural forms and social institutions. There were four such preconditions that he saw as key scientific values:

1. *Universalism*: claims to truth are evaluated in terms of universal or impersonal criteria, and not on the basis of race, class, gender, religion, or nationality.
2. *Organized skepticism*: all ideas must be tested and are subject to rigorous, structured community scrutiny.
3. *Disinterestedness*: scientists are rewarded for acting in ways that outwardly appear to be selfless.
4. *Communism (communalism)*: the common ownership of scientific discoveries, according to which scientists give up intellectual property rights in exchange for recognition and esteem.

For an example of the expression of these values, refer back to the Constitution of the Econometric Society as quoted in Chapter 2 (see p. 32). Merton traced these scientific values back to the rise of Protestantism in the seventeenth century, but in contrast to the (later) arguments developed in SSK, he did not view them as being historically specific. Rather, they were cross-cultural and permanent features of modern science that only happened to have a particular origin in history. Thus Merton believed that the content of science was still to be explained in traditional terms as an objective pursuit of truth. His view has come to be seen as the basis for an ES in that it influenced many countries' economic policies in relation to science, where the economic dimensions of these policies involved funding support for scientists who clearly demonstrated commitment to these four scientific values.

In economists' subsequent development of the ES approach, national science policies that have provided funding support for scientists were justified through the use of the standard tools of welfare economics, including the concepts of externalities and public goods, to determine the optimal levels of scientific research in different fields. Consider how this can be applied to basic and applied kinds of scientific research. Since it is typically unclear what applications might ultimately be generated by basic or "pure" research, it can be argued that it lacks investment returns, and is under-produced in competitive markets.

At the same time, since basic research generates much of the knowledge that is used in applied research, it creates positive externalities for the latter approach. This is an example of market failure, and the policy implication is that governments should subsidize basic research. Once this initial decision has been made, the government must decide what areas of research to support. Here the ES approach calls for the use of cost–benefit analysis to evaluate which scientific requests for funding should be supported. Finally, government can also grant patents to scientists who generate new innovations (in either basic or applied research). This monopoly right enables scientists to earn private returns on their investments in basic research, which might otherwise be exploited by others.

In contrast to ES, ESK (sometimes labeled the "new economics of science") follows the path of SSK. It assumes not only that one needs to understand the preconditions of science, now in economic terms – that is, in terms of the government funding that would support the scientific values Merton identified – but that the content of science itself – that is, its ideas, theories, and concepts – needs to be understood as the result of the pursuit of individual economic (rather than sociological) interests. Scientists, that is, are utility-maximizing individuals, and science needs to be modeled as a market process, employing standard economic strategies such as game theory, bounded rationality, information theory, and transactions costs.

One of the earliest examples of ESK analysis was provided by the economists Partha Dasgupta and Paul David. They began by putting forward the idea that science is a particular form of social organization that is characterized by its capacity to produce reliable knowledge, termed it "open science," and cited today's universities and public agencies devoted to science as paradigmatic institutions. Drawing on Merton's communism principle, they argued that a crucial feature of this form of social organization was that it ensured that scientific results were quickly and readily available to many people (in contrast to the science organized in proprietary and military terms which restricts access to scientific results). Their most significant departure from the older ES approach was in the way that they characterized the behavior of individual scientists.

The "open science" system is successful because its reward system creates incentives for individual scientists to pursue their self-interest. In a system in which scientific results are quickly and readily made available to many people, those individuals who earn priority for scientific discoveries gain reputation, material rewards, and further opportunities for research. Dasgupta and David also drew on Merton and his principle of organized skepticism in that, because scientists' research is subject to critical examination, individual scientists acting self-interestedly need to exhibit care and caution before releasing their work to others. At the same time, since there is no advantage to being the *second* discover of something new, scientists pushed themselves to produce the most reliable results as quickly as possible. Thus, according to Dasgupta and David, an open science system is incentive-compatible with a reputational reward system based on successful claims to priority.

It should be noted that the content of science – in the form of the ideas and concepts generated in such a process – must be influenced by the type of social organization described by Dasgupta and David. In a system that emphasizes individual reputation, scientific progress becomes a matter of "breakthroughs" since these are more easily associated with individual achievements. By contrast, were science viewed as a more gradual process in which particular contributions are understood to depend upon the larger developmental frameworks within which they are embedded, there would be less reason to regard individuals' particular contributions as outstanding or deserving of particular acclaim. Indeed, this latter view of science – one more characteristic of the SSK point of view – is probably a more accurate reflection of the long history of the development of science. The difficulty, then, is that in countries developing science funding systems that emphasize particular scientists' contributions, those contributions may end up being packaged in ways that exaggerate their achievements. Moreover, as many such "breakthroughs" in popular science histories are identified with the names of the scientists responsible for them (for example, Newton's law of gravity or Einstein's theory of special relativity), developments in science are also misleadingly tangled up with individual biographies.

These problems can be made worse when public support for science is driven by the idea of competitive "tournaments" (for example, Nobel Prizes), leading people to see scientists as competing in "winner-take-all" games. Indeed it may be that the best science policy for governments is to rely less on the support of "stars" and more on the expansion of the broad base of research institutions.

Another issue is the problem of "lock-in" effects. Consider for a moment how some so-called "breakthroughs" may have undesirable consequences. In a famous historical study, David characterizes many scientific innovations as having 'lock-in' effects where a particular innovation in technology closes off the possibility of others which are ultimately more efficient. One example is the organization of the letters on the original typewriter keyboard; what he labels the QWERTY system (after the order of the letters on the top left side of the keyboard). When the mechanical typewriter was invented, the keys often jammed, because people's dexterity exceeded the capacity of the machine, and they typed too quickly. So the original keyboard was intentionally organized with a physically awkward arrangement of the keys to make it difficult for people to type too quickly. Now we use electronic rather than mechanical keyboards, but we have not rearranged the letters on keyboards to take advantage of human dexterity. The QWERTY organization is inefficient, but this technology exhibits 'lock-in' in that we have so widely come to rely upon it. This then shows the importance of seeing science as an historical system of social organization.

Another influential ESK analysis is to be found in the work of the philosopher Philip Kitcher, who seeks to maintain elements of the traditional view of science that has been associated with the goal of understanding knowledge as reliable in the sense of being "true justified belief." However, he also acknowledges the significance of Kuhn's thinking and SSK when he allows that what counts as "justified" is determined according to social standards of belief. The latter idea is developed in terms of social processes and the development of institutions that are likely to increase the ratio of reliable beliefs to the total number of beliefs in a society. At this point, Kitcher introduces an economic conception of the processes and institutions of society. He states that the ratio of reliable beliefs to the total number of beliefs in a society is likely to be higher when the cognitive labor of scientists is well organized, where in particular this is a matter of achieving a socially optimal division of cognitive labor.

Kitcher's modeling of the organization of science as a division of cognitive labor resembles early economic thinking about the division of labor in whole economies, dating all the way back to Adam Smith's *Wealth of Nations*. Smith had combined the division of labor concept with the idea that individuals occupying different locations in a division will necessarily pursue their own restricted self-interest. At the same time, Smith saw this system as producing the greatest possible economic output by virtue of the "invisible hand" of the market, or the idea that an unintended consequence of the pursuit of self-interest generates a social optimum.

Kitcher's ideas share much with Dasgupta and David. He uses economic concepts to explain the workings of a science social system in terms of individual (or economic) motives. And, also in common with Dasgupta and David, Kitcher's view of scientists as cognitive workers in a large-scale division of labor explains the content of science in terms of the kinds of ideas and concepts that individually motivated scientists are likely to produce in such a system of organization.

Of course, there are other ways in which science systems can be and have been organized in history that call on different types of motives and interests on the part of scientists. Thus the general conclusion that emerges here is that the kinds of knowledge produced by science are not only historically and socially specific, as argued in SSK, but also specific to particular types of social organization and behavioral systems. This conclusion departs significantly from the traditional philosophy of science view, and in particular its realist, anti-relativist emphasis, which sees knowledge as objective and independent of all social forms, types of science organization, and behavioral structures.

ESK faces the same three problems (relativism, realism, and value neutrality) described above in our discussion of SSK. But another type of problem emerges now that we have discussed two different strategies that draw on social science to propose a "naturalistic" approach to scientific knowledge – one drawing on sociology and the other on economics. If it is assumed that the "naturalistic" approach is a good one, which of the two approaches should we choose? Is one field a better choice than the other?

The individual preference for an SSK or ESK approach seems to be a matter of whether one has received training in sociology or economics. This appears to be, however, an arbitrary and accidental basis for determining how one should understand scientific knowledge. And moreover, as we will see, there are other approaches that are also based on the idea of a "naturalistic turn," which serve only to compound the problem.

Looking ahead

In Chapter 6 we will discuss another approach to the philosophy of science and economic methodology that shares many of the social constructivist assumptions of SSK and ESK, yet offers another distinct entry point and a new set of strategies for explaining science. This is the rhetoric approach, which adds a cultural emphasis to the sociological (SSK) and economic (ESK) emphases that we have encountered in this chapter.

The rhetoric approach, associated by Hands with the idea of "pragmatic turn," considers how scientists and economists persuade one another of their conclusions through the ways in which they use language and discourse – as well as through the ways in which these discursive practices are embedded in their scientific communities. The rhetoric approach is associated in turn with views of science that pay greater attention to the relationships between history and intellectual culture, particularly as expressed in postmodernist critiques of science. This allows us to touch upon the important methodological issue of pluralism, which will serve as an introduction to the final chapter.

Exercises

1 Give a short description of Merton's four defining norms of science.
2 How does SSK depart from the philosophy of science and economic methodology from which it arose?
3 What is SSK – and how does it differ from ESK? Give an example of each type of explanation.
4 What is the difference between ESK and the economics of science (ES)? Explain the difference by describing the ESK David–Dasgupta model and the ES welfare arguments used by governments to support funding of science.
5 Say what the laboratory studies approach involves, explain how it is like anthropology, and say why the approach is often called social constructivist.

6   Describe the Edinburgh School Strong Programme.
7   Explain why there cannot be a distinction between the context of discovery and the context of justification, according to SSK.
8   The website of Eurostat includes the following mission statement:

Eurostat's mission is to provide the European Union with a high-quality statistical information service.

Eurostat is the Statistical Office of the European Communities situated in Luxembourg. Its task is to provide the European Union with statistics at European level that enable comparisons between countries and regions. This is a key task. Democratic societies do not function properly without a solid basis of reliable and objective statistics. On one hand, decision-makers at EU level, in Member States, in local government and in business need statistics to make those decisions. On the other hand, the public and media need statistics for an accurate picture of contemporary society and to evaluate the performance of politicians and others. Of course, national statistics are still important for national purposes in Member States whereas EU statistics are essential for decisions and evaluation at European level.
    Statistics can answer many questions. Is society heading in the direction promised by politicians? Is unemployment up or down? Are there more CO_2 emissions compared to ten years ago? How many women go to work? How is your country's economy performing compared to other EU Member States? International statistics are a way of getting to know your neighbours in Member States and countries outside the EU. They are an important, objective and down-to-earth way of measuring how we all live

Which norms of good science, as formulated by Merton, can be identified in this mission statement?

Relevant readings

Barnes, Barry (1974) *Scientific Knowledge and Sociological Theory*, London: Routledge & Kegan Paul.
    An early statement of the Strong Programme.
Barnes, Barry (1977) *Interests and the Growth of Knowledge*, London: Routledge & Kegan Paul.
    Another important statement of the Strong Programme.
Bloor, David (1991) *Knowledge and Social Imagery*, 2nd edn, Chicago: University of Chicago Press.
    An authoritative statement of the Strong Programme.
Collins, Harry (1985) *Changing Order: Replication and Induction in Scientific Practice*, Beverly Hills, CA: Sage.
    A microsociological examination of scientific practice.

David, Paul (1985) "Clio and the Economics of QWERTY," *American Economic Review* 75(2): 332–7.

The article that popularized the idea of "lock-in" in technology choice.

Dasgupta, Partha and David, Paul (1994) "Toward A New Economics of Science," *Research Policy* 23: 487–521.

Dasgupta and David's "open science" model.

Davis, John and Klaes, Matthias (2003) "Reflexivity: Curse or Cure?," *Journal of Economic Methodology* 10(3): 329–52.

A discussion of multiple forms of reflexivity in economic methodology.

Kitcher, Philip (1993) *The Advancement of Science: Science Without Legend, Objectivity Without Illusions*, Oxford: Oxford University Press.

Kitcher's modeling of the organization of science as a division of cognitive labor.

Knorr Cetina, Karin (1981) *The Manufacture of Knowledge: An Essay on the Constructivist and Contextual Nature of Science*, New York: Pergamon.

A general defense of social constructivism.

Latour, Bruno and Steven Woolgar (1979) *Laboratory Life: The Construction of Scientific Facts*, Beverly Hills, CA: Sage.

The paradigm-setting laboratory studies approach.

Merton, Robert (1973) *The Sociology of Science: Theoretical and Empirical Investigations*, Chicago: University of Chicago Press.

Merton's influential statement of the values that underlie good science.

Shapin, Steven and Simon Schaffer (1985) *Leviathan and the Air Pump*, Princeton, NJ: Princeton University Press.

Shapin and Schaffer's influential account of the role of social context in the seventeenth century science debates between Bacon and Hobbes.

Focus 5.1   Economics as a Discipline

According to Lakatos, scientific research programs consist of a hard core of purely metaphysical beliefs that cannot be abandoned without also abandoning the entire research program. These are surrounded by what he labeled a "protective belt" of testable theories, which are capable of being revised and amended as the program encounters falsifications – or what Kuhn terms anomalies.

This core–periphery model for particular research programs can also be applied to entire sciences or disciplines that are made up of many different research programs. This means that some research programs occupy the discipline's core, and are identified with what is regarded as conventional or orthodox in the discipline. Others occupy the discipline's periphery, and are seen as the unconventional or heterodox elements of the discipline.

Different sciences or disciplines then encounter one another on their peripheries where their respective unconventional or heterodox research programs share certain assumptions and theories, sometimes creating entirely new fields of study (such as, for example, bio-engineering and economic sociology), while retaining their separate identities as distinct sciences in connection with their core orthodoxies.

In economics, neoclassicism has been orthodox in western economics for most of the postwar period, while research programs such as Institutionalism and Marxism have been heterodox. In the last two decades, however, a number of new unconventional research programs have emerged in economics to challenge the neoclassical orthodoxy. These include, among others, behavioral economics, experimental economics, evolutionary economics, capability theory, complexity theory, and neuroeconomics. Economists now generally refer to the dominant strand in economics as "mainstream" rather than orthodox, because neoclassicism is no longer the only research program competing to determine the hard core of economics.

For example, game theory, while sharing many assumptions with neoclassicism, such as that individuals are rational maximizing agents, has become part of mainstream training since the 1980s, though it also abandons the competitive markets price-equilibration framework of partial and general equilibrium theory to focus on strategic interaction in games, many of which have non-optimal outcomes, such as the prisoner's dilemma. Mainstream economists now draw increasingly on elements of many of the other new research programs in economics, replacing neoclassicism's former exclusive dominance of the core of the dicipline. This shows how in recent decades economics has become increasingly diverse and heterogenous (though not necessarily more pluralistic).

It remains to be seen, of course, whether one (or some combination) of the new research programs in economics will in future become orthodox, and ultimately produce a new homogenous hard core in economics. In the history of economics, there have been particular periods when one research program has been dominant, and other periods when different research programs have been in competition with one another. For example, the classical political economy of Smith and Ricardo was the dominant school in nineteenth-century Britain. By contrast, the *Methodenstreit* in nineteenth-century Germany was a historical period characterized by competition between different research programs.

One view of the growth of knowledge is that it involves the emergence of new types of knowledge that are made possible by the combination of different sciences, as in the emergence of bio-engineering. Sciences that have experienced long periods of well-defined orthodoxy can begin to exhibit diminishing returns to their dominant research programs, whether or not there are an increasing number of anomalies in Kuhn's sense. Then, the combination of assumptions and theories from different disciplines can produce a new research program that produces new types of knowledge, much like a paradigm shift.

The stimulus for a new research program of this sort will often come from one science. Thus, "economics imperialism," a term referring to the application of neoclassical economic reasoning and rationality theory to other sciences, has produced new disciplines – these have included the economics of the family and the economics of law. Alternatively, "reverse economics imperialism" involves the application to economics of reasoning that has been developed in other sciences. This can be seen, for example, in behavioral economics, which has seen the application of psychology to the theory of decision-making in economics.

When there is a change in the dominant research programs in a particular field or science, this will often have a transformative effect on its identity. For instance, when classical political economy was replaced by neoclassical economics, there was a marked change in the nature of economics, reflected in its main concerns, concepts, and theories. The earlier focus on growth and distribution in connection with social classes was replaced by a focus on marginalist reasoning and price determination in markets in connection with individual decision-making. Interestingly, many of the more recent research programs in economics have their origins in other sciences. This is likely to have an influence on the future direction of orthodox economics. Consider the recent combination of behavioral economics reasoning (with its origins in psychology), experimental economics (origins in experimental practices in many sciences), and game theory (origins in mathematics). Economists involved in this type of research are interested in what may be learned from experiments in which the psychological characteristics of individuals affect their strategic interaction. The type of economic explanations produced by this research has only a very limited resemblance to neoclassical *a priori* reasoning about rationality and competition in competitive markets.

Lakatos developed his core–periphery explanation of scientific research programs in order to be able to classify different research programs as being either progressive or degenerating (see p. 110). No such analysis is available, however, when we consider *entire* sciences or disciplines as being structured in core–periphery terms with conventional or orthodox research programs at the core and unconventional or heterodox research programs on the periphery.

Indeed as a research program can be unconventional or heterodox at one point in time and conventional or orthodox at another, what goes on in a research program on the periphery of economics cannot be classified as either progressive or degenerating as it may become a core research program in the future.

According to the perspective of the sociology of scientific knowledge, Lakatos had paid insufficient attention to the dynamics of research programs. He had tried to judge the character of research programs solely in static terms of testability and evidence, neglecting their relative and changing standing in the field to which they belong. Research programs also need to be judged in terms of how well they represent the scientists' concerns about the leading issues in their subject matter at any point in time.

This can be illustrated quite clearly in the case of economics. At different points in time economists have held different views regarding the key issues to be addressed by their work. In the 1930s Keynes was influential because economists at that time were concerned principally with the problems of high unemployment and depression. But the status of Keynesianism as a research program in economics declined in influence when those problems became less urgent. Thus, it is as difficult to talk about progressive or degenerating research programs in economics as it is in other sciences. Knowledge is better assessed according to conditions under which it is produced, and according to the understanding of scientists themselves.

Focus 5.2   Case Study Research

A widely used textbook (Yin 2003) defines **case study research** as an empirical inquiry that investigates a phenomenon within its real-life context, a circumstance in which the boundaries between phenomenon and context are not clearly evident. This emphasis on studying the phenomenon within its context is what distinguishes a case study from an experiment (see the discussion in Focus 2.3).

An experiment is carried out under conditions in which an investigator can manipulate behavior directly, precisely, and systematically. This occurs either in a laboratory setting, in which an experiment may focus on one or two isolated variables, and it is assumed that the laboratory environment controls all the remaining variables; or in a field setting, where the term "field experiment" is used to cover research in which investigators treat groups of people in different ways. Because of this difference, experiments are seen as the exemplary method of research in natural science, and case study research as the typical social science method.

To draw a sharper contrast between these two research methods, let us consider the following example.

A biologist who has an interest in the behavior of lions will find that one way of studying them is to watch their undisturbed behavior in their natural environment. This involves hiding in the bushes, keeping silent for hours, and making a detailed record of their activities. In such a manner, one hopes to find specific patterns in their behavior which may give better insights into their nature.

The choice of lions was a deliberate one, because Francis Bacon (1561–1626) had used their study as an example to justify a new research method – the experimental method. He argued that not only must we observe nature in the raw, but that we must also "twist the lion's tail," that is, manipulate our world in order to learn its secrets. A scientist must question nature, torture her by experiment, and wring from her answers to these questions. One of the paradoxes of science is that by placing nature in "unnatural" situations we will learn many of her secrets. For example, at CERN (Conseil Européen pour la Recherche Nucléaire) near Geneva, the world's largest physical particle laboratory, nature is accelerated to such an extent that her fundamental building blocks are revealed. This paradoxical method has worked very successfully for particles, but will it have a similar effect when applied to the study of human beings and organizations?

While an experiment investigates a phenomenon in an artificial, designed environment, a case study is designed specifically to allow the study of the phenomenon in its natural environment. The advantage of conducting research in a designed environment is that the results can, in principle, be validated through being reproduced on a number of occasions (see Focus 4.3). The disadvantage is that it may be difficult to transfer the validity of these results to a context outside the artificial setting. This is known as the problem of external validity. By contrast, because case study results are obtained in a natural setting, they do not face this problem of external validity. Because each case is usually unique, however, it is difficult to generalize from one case to another. For this reason, case studies are said to face a problem of general validity.

Because experiments and case studies are carried out in very different environments, the validity of their respective results are demonstrated in different ways. Richard Butler compares the demonstration of case study results with storytelling to indicate that a different set of procedures must be followed to persuade an audience of the validity of its results, that is, to acquire intersubjectivity (see Focus 4.3 and McCloskey's emphasis on storytelling in Chapter 6). He suggests that the presentation of a story involves more heterogeneous elements than are present in an experiment, and needs to be delivered in a natural language that describes and interprets the actions of individuals within a plot, over time, with the emphasis being placed upon descriptions of process. In contrast to this, the set of procedures in experiments are much more homogenous and standardized. The language is technical, and only accessible to people trained in the relevant discipline.

The disadvantage of an observation report worded in natural language is that the terms it uses are less objective and less precise than the scientific language of a specific discipline. On the other hand, a natural language has a much richer vocabulary for describing processes and situations, and is therefore more appropriate for relating people's real-life experiences, as many good novels actually do. To clarify this we will take as an example the set of measurement scales below and discuss which concepts can be ascribed to each scale.

	Nominal	*Ordinal*	*Ratio*	*Absolute*
Description	Codes assigned to attributes as labels	Ranking of attributes	Ratio between two magnitudes of the same kind	Ratio between a magnitude and its standard unit
Examples	Gender, ethnicity, marital status	Movie ratings, happiness	Annual income, price level	Length in meters, weight in kilos

Every category attributed appropriately to a specific scale can also be attributed to the scale to the left of it, but the reverse does not apply. Not every category in the nominal column can be ranked; for example it would be absurd to rank gender. Going from the ordinal scale to the ratio scale means that the ranking is made more specific by attributing numbers. To put happiness, however, on a ratio scale is absurd, because that would imply a statement like "Today I am three times happier than yesterday." Going from the ratio scale to the absolute scale means that for the relevant attribute a standard must be defined. Moving the price level to the absolute scale means that one has to define a standard price level, though it is hard to imagine what this could be.

Having to deal with a more heterogeneous set of rules than in the case of experiments means that intersubjectivity is attained differently. Triangulation of the results to show convergence is the most recommended approach in case study research (Focus 4.3 and Chapter 6).

Relevant readings

Butler, Richard (1997) "Stories and Experiments in Social Inquiry," *Organization Studies* 18(6): 927–48.
A methodological comparison of experiments and case studies.
Hacking, Ian (1983) *Representing and Intervening: Introductory Topics in the Philosophy of Natural Science*, Cambridge: Cambridge University Press.
A modern classic in philosophy of science on experiments.
Yin, Robert K. (2003) *Case Study Research: Design and Methods*, 3rd edn, Thousand Oaks, CA: Sage.
A popular textbook on case study research.

Focus 5.3   Feminist Philosophy of Science and Feminist Political Economy

In addressing how science is socially constructed, we concentrate on how the acceptability of a theory is dictated by its compatibility with the social interests of the scientific community. The fact that through history most scientists have been men, that women have been generally excluded from scientific communities, and that their work in science has often been disregarded means that scientific theories, particularly in the social sciences where social interests are more immediately at issue, are vulnerable to the charge that they one-sidedly reflect men's interests and concerns – what Charlotte Perkins Gilman has labeled an "androcentric bias." In an attempt to address this **gender perspective**, in recent years feminist philosophers and economists have examined the role played by gender in science and economics, and their response has been in terms of three main epistemological and methodological approaches: feminist empiricism, feminist standpoint theory, and feminist postmodernism.

Feminist empiricism

This is the view that the problem of gender bias lies not with the scientific method itself, but rather with the actions of those scientists who fail to follow it correctly. It is a realist approach in the sense that it assumes a flawed and incomplete understanding of the world can, in principle, be replaced by one that reveals the objective nature of the world, and it is also empiricist in supposing that women's experience is needed to correct and widen the scope of science as traditionally developed from the male point of view. Further, science is not produced by isolated individuals. It is produced by individuals working in communities that shape theories and observation; good science thus depends on there being multiple scientific communities that can balance and complement one another.

Feminist standpoint theory

This approach holds that the goal of feminist empiricism is unattainable. According to this theory, the values of privileged groups always dictated what should be investigated – though this may go unstated or even be denied – and values at odds with these (which reflect social differences with respect to race, ethnicity, class, and sexual orientation, as well as gender) are invariably excluded. In place of the ideal of value neutrality, Sandra Harding thus recommends the goal of "strong objectivity" as a goal whereby science advances by uncovering the implicit cultural assumptions of dominant groups that are knowledge-distorting and prevent scientists from producing "faithful" accounts of the real world.

Feminist postmodernism

The third approach – feminist postmodernism – rejects both of these approaches, because it denies the existence of universally knowable and objective reality, seeing this as unattainable. Accordingly, scientists are always socially situated, truth is a constructed category, and women and men have multiple identities – of race, class, gender, etc. Nonetheless, postmodernist feminists do have something in common with both feminist empiricists and feminist standpoint theorists: they share a commitment to epistemological pluralism (see Chapter 6), which is also seen to be central to the practice of feminist political economy.

Feminist political economy

Feminist political economy, like other approaches to political economy and in contrast to mainstream economics, investigates the economy in terms of power relationships. Indeed, feminist political economy investigates the role that power plays in women's lives with respect to class, race, ethnicity, and sexual orientation, while emphasizing that it also plays a primary role with respect to gender. The concept of power used in this instance goes beyond the conventional concept of market power in economics, which ignores the wider power relationships in society. By this standard, feminist political economy and other political economy approaches are interdisciplinary forms of investigation. In its emphasis on power, feminist political economy often also relies on historical methods of analysis as a means of explaining the origins and evolution of power relationships. Further, as feminist political economy regards economics as value-laden (see Chapter 7), it emphasizes the need to make investigators' values explicit.

One of the most significant contributions made by feminist political economy is their detailed study of the economics of the household. Most early models of the household associated with neoclassical human capital analysis ignore the gendered character of power relationships in households, treat the division of labor in non-gendered terms, and explain economic behavior as a set of rational responses to differences in family members' respective endowments. However, as is argued by Nancy Folbre (1994) and other feminist economists, such an approach misrepresents why family divisions of labor specifically leave women with disproportionate responsibility for non-market domestic labor, and also eliminates any analysis of non-self-interested forms of activity such as caring labor. Accordingly, one strategy for a political economic approach is instead to begin with the gendered character of power relationships in the household, and then to explain both what behavior this generates and also the resulting distribution of resources.

Feminist political economy has also carried out important research into the feminization of poverty, especially in the developing world. Much traditional development economics has emphasized issues such as the growth of per capita income, desired investment, and countries' international competitiveness. Progress can be made toward the achievement of each of these goals without any attention being paid to issues regarding the internal redistribution of well-being among individuals and groups. Yet if the well-being of women, families, and communities is instead taken as an entry point for empirical investigation, evidence may also be collected that shows that growth in these economy-wide measures is often accompanied by their increasing disadvantage. One remarkable measure of this is Amartya Sen's (1998 Nobel Prize laureate, "for his contributions to welfare economics") estimate that since the 1980s more than 100 million women have suffered premature mortality because of the systematic denial of life-sustaining resources.

There are many different methods of investigation in feminist political economy, reflecting its diverse commitments in the social sciences, the history of economic thought, politics, social practices, and social affiliations. Feminist political economy is therefore pluralist on a number of different levels: in the three main epistemological and methodological approaches that make up the contemporary feminist philosophy of science, in the range of its methods of investigation, and in the multiple orientations and communities that are drawn upon by its practitioners.

Relevant readings

Barker, Drucilla and Edith Kuiper (eds) (2003) *Towards a Feminist Philosophy of Economics*, London: Routledge.
  A leading collection of articles on feminist philosophy, primarily by women economists.
Elson, Diane (ed.) (1991) *Male Bias in the Development Process*, Manchester: Manchester University Press.
  A collection of articles on feminist political economy of development.
Ferber, Marianne and Julie Nelson (eds) (2003) *Feminist Economics Today: Beyond Economic Man*, Chicago: University of Chicago Press.
  An early (re-issued) influential feminist critique of standard economics.

Folbre, Nancy (1994) *Who Pays for the Kids?*, London: Routledge.
    An analysis of conflicting burdens on women and introduction to the problem
        of care in market economies.
Gilman, Charlotte Perkins (1911) *The Man-Made World or, Our Androcentric
    Culture*, New York: Charlton Company.
    A pioneer feminst critique of the androcentric perspective.
Harding, Sandra (1991) *Whose Science? Whose Knowledge? Thinking From
    Women's Lives*, Ithaca, NY: Cornell University Press.
    A leading statement of feminist epistemology.
Olson, Paulette and Zohreh Emami (2002) *Engendering Economics: Conversations
    with Women Economists in the United States*, London: Routledge.
    A collection of interviews with 11 US postwar women economists.
Sen, Amartya (1990) "More Than 100 Million Women Are Missing," *New York
    Review of Books* 37(20): 61–6.
    Sen's original statement regarding the premature mortality of women.

Chapter 6

Rhetoric, Postmodernism, and Pluralism

This chapter examines several of the most recent currents in philosophy of science and economic methodology, extending many of the ideas that lie behind the sociology of scientific knowledge (SSK) and the economics of scientific knowledge (ESK), but also developing new views about the status and nature of science and knowledge. Interestingly, for those concerned primarily with economic methodology rather than philosophy of science in general, one of these, the **rhetoric approach**, like ESK, has been developed primarily by economists and economic methodologists in connection with their thinking about economics and the practices of economists.

At the same time, however, the rhetoric approach draws on thinking about science and knowledge that has its origins outside economics and indeed outside science – drawing on reflections upon history, literature, and culture. Thus the rhetoric approach as developed by economists has created an opening for a new non-science-based type of reasoning about both economics and science in general that draws on quite different motivations from those observed in SSK and ESK.

One umbrella label that has been applied to much of this new non-science-based reasoning is **postmodernism**. In recent years, postmodernist views have come to play an increasing role in thinking related to both philosophy of science and also economic methodology. A further important development in this connection concerns **pluralism**, the view that multiple competing positions can obtain at the same time. These new currents are examined below in terms of their similarities to – and differences from – the rhetoric approach.

The rhetoric approach

The rhetoric approach has its earliest roots in the classical rhetoric of the ancient Greeks, who understood it to be concerned with the forms and methods of argument and communication.

The contemporary rhetoric approach is similarly concerned with the forms and methods of argument and communication, but it now also applies to the practices of science, whereas the ancient Greeks applied it to statecraft and public ceremony. In addition, the contemporary approach to rhetoric often employs a somewhat more modern vocabulary to describe its focus, namely, it seeks to explain the *discourse* – or discursive practices – of economists and scientists, to reflect that, where the ancient Greeks were concerned primarily with oration and speech-making, the main concern of the contemporary approach to rhetoric relates to dialogues between economists or between scientists. That is, dialogue is discourse, or, more plainly, it is simply conversation between economists or between scientists. Accordingly, the rhetoric approach is now sometimes labeled discourse analysis.

Classical rhetoric, as the study of the means of persuasion, identifies three different dimensions:

- *Logos* (word): the internal consistency of the message – the clarity of the claim, the logic behind its reasons, and the effectiveness of its supporting evidence.
- *Pathos* (experience): the appeal to the audience's emotions, sympathies, and imagination.
- *Ethos* (character): the trustworthiness or credibility of the writer or speaker.

Philosophers of science – ranging from the logical positivists to Popper – have generally only taken account of *logos*, regarding the other two dimensions as being subjective and therefore alien to science. Only gradually did later philosophers (for example, Kuhn) become aware that science is more than *logos*. After more than two thousand years, this resulted in philosophers renewing their interest in the study of rhetoric and how it could be applied to the understanding of science.

The rhetoric approach also extends ideas developed in connection with SSK and ESK in that it examines the ways in which economists and sciences influence one another.

As we saw in the previous chapter, SSK and ESK examine the motives and interests of scientists and economists to understand how they develop theories and models. But they understand motives and interests sociologically (in the case of SSK) and in terms of self-interest (ESK).

The rhetoric approach builds on these approaches by introducing a psychological aspect. It does this by emphasizing the classical rhetoric concept of persuasion.

1. First, the rhetoric approach considers the social framework of a scientific community in terms of how it disseminates its ideas and arguments. For example, within the scientific community an important role is played by the scientific journal paper in terms of the sharing and transferring of ideas, results, and arguments.

2. Second, the rhetoric approach considers how individual economists or scientists are persuaded within the framework of those structures of communication that are relied upon by a scientific community. For example, a paper in a scientific journal will typically include a list of acknowledgements to those individuals who have commented on the paper prior to its publication. Readers of scientific papers are more likely to be persuaded by the ideas, results, and arguments contained within the paper if they find prestigious names in the acknowledgements list. (In rhetoric this device is technically known as "the argument from authority.")

The most important contributor to the rhetoric approach in economics – indeed the person who is primarily responsible for bringing it to the attention of economists – is Deirdre McCloskey, whose work has two main aims:

- On the one hand, in keeping with the spirit of SSK, she wants economic methodologists to pay closer attention to the ways in which economists actually reason and seek to persuade one another of their views. This includes considering their use of mathematics and statistics (for example, through the inclusion of mathematical proofs in scholarly papers or placing an emphasis on significance tests in empirical research).
- On the other hand, she wants to advance a clear critique of the positivism that she sees as dominating economists' understanding of science and proper method in economics.

Positivism (which McCloskey often equates with modernism) is the view that science develops through careful attention to logic and evidence, and sets aside scientists' actual practices regarding how they reach their conclusions. Positivism, according to McCloskey, is characterized by the following rules:

1. Prediction (and control) is the goal of science.
2. Only the observable implications (or predictions) of a theory are significant for its truth.
3. Observability entails objective, reproducible experiments.
4. If (and only if) an experimental implication of a theory proves false is the theory proved false.
5. Objectivity is to be treasured; subjective "observation" (introspection) is not scientific knowledge.
6. Kelvin's Dictum: "When you cannot express it in numbers, your knowledge is of a meagre and unsatisfactory kind."
7. Introspection, metaphysical belief, aesthetics, and the like may well figure in the discovery of an hypothesis but cannot contribute to its justification.

8. It is the business of methodology to demarcate scientific reasoning from non-scientific reasoning, and the positive from the normative.
9. A scientific explanation of an event brings the event under a covering law.
10. Scientists, for instance economic scientists, have nothing to say as scientists about values, whether of morality or art.
11. Hume's Fork: "When we run over libraries ..."

Thus for McCloskey, seeing how economics is practiced in the "real" world goes hand in hand with dispelling what she regards as false views of economic science.

McCloskey's 1986 book, *The Rhetoric of Economics*, which introduced the term "rhetoric" in economic methodology, also signaled an important departure from the naturalistic emphasis of SSK and ESK by arguing that economics uses literary methods as its principal rhetorical device. In this respect the key tools are analogy and metaphor (Focus 6.1).

Analogy persuades by interpreting economic statements in terms of more familiar and intuitive forms of language. For example, though game theory involves complex, highly structured accounts of strategic interactions between individuals, referring to it as a "game" has long provided students with strong intuitions about what it involves. Indeed, much of game theory instruction is constructed from a small group of classic games with seemingly familiar labels (the prisoner's dilemma, the battle of the sexes, the game of chicken, the ultimatum game, etc.), which form basic models for the investigation of the structure of these games and variations upon them.

Metaphor is similar to analogy, but has an additional dimension in that it helps in enhancing the understanding of economic concepts by comparing them to concepts whose source content is forgotten or less important. The most famous example in economics is Adam Smith's "invisible hand." What it represents in contemporary economics is a process that produces equilibrium across many interdependent markets. But rather than using this sort of technical characterization, economists have relied on the paradoxical, but intriguing idea of an unseen hand at work. Another more provocative metaphor is Chicago School economist Gary Becker's labeling children durable goods (1992 Nobel Prize, "for having extended the domain of microeconomic analysis to a wide range of human behaviour and interaction, including nonmarket behaviour"). Of course, children are not commodities or goods in any proper sense of the word. But Becker's metaphor conveys the key underlying notion he wanted to communicate, namely, that parents often regard expenditure on their children in much the same way as they see other, more traditional forms of investment.

McCloskey's 1990 book, *If You're So Smart: The Narrative of Economic Expertise*, moved beyond such literary or rhetorical devices to characterize the discourse among economists as storytelling. On the surface, of course, economic theorizing and modeling appear to have little in common with storytelling. But McCloskey noticed an important dimension to economists' practice of theorizing and modeling: models were often introduced to audiences through the use of informal descriptions of agents' behavior that took on many of the aspects of a story, and that these stories then provided an intuitive justification for the models' technical details.

One famous example of economics "storytelling" is the "lemons" model used by George Akerlof (2001 Nobel Prize with Michael Spence and Joseph E. Stiglitz, "for their analyses of markets with asymmetric information") to explain markets with asymmetric information, where the story was about the interaction between buyers and sellers of used cars – "lemons." Another famous example is Adam Smith's explanation of specialization in production by his pin factory story. These and other stories then become the means by which economists could quickly refer to different models and theories.

In addition, McCloskey argued that economists focus only on a handful of "standard" stories, and that the economics community had maintained a long history of interest in many of these stories, much as parables, legends, and fables have long occupied the audiences of traditional storytellers. All this suggests that theorizing and modeling is an adjunct to a good economics story, rather than being the main focus of the economists' work. At the same time, the holistic character of stories lends credibility to models which are theoretically complex.

This storytelling aspect of models was also made explicit by Allan Gibbard and Hal Varian in their account of economic models. They defined a model as a story with a specific structure, where the structure is given by the logical and mathematical form of a set of assumptions of the model. Interestingly, they make a distinction between two kinds of models: (i) models as approximations; and (ii) models as caricatures, where a caricature involves deliberate distortion to illuminate an aspect of economic life.

McCloskey's critique of positivism, then, should be seen in this light – a critique she has often expressed in terms of the slogan that in economics we should be talking in terms of methodology with a small "m" rather than a large "M." There are two important principles in this critique, both of which also point us toward postmodernism and pluralism.

The first principle is that it is a mistake to see knowledge as something that has "foundations." Thus, positivism in connection with epistemology (or the theory of knowledge) is the doctrine that we build up our knowledge of phenomena by inferring the truth of statements about them from what we know to be obviously true. These latter things – such as the evidence of our senses and propositions that are logically true – constitute the foundations for our knowledge of phenomena. In this sense, then, knowledge is a structure, in which the floors are built on top of the foundations. McCloskey, however, follows many philosophers by expressing doubts that any knowledge claims can ever be regarded as certain. In other words, there appear to be no foundations for knowledge. From the perspective of the rhetoric approach, then, any "foundations" we might appear to have for knowledge change according to how economists succeed in persuading one another. Thus it is a mistake to see knowledge as a structure in the first place. (Note that the idea of knowledge being like a building is itself a metaphor.)

The second important principle in McCloskey's critique of positivism is the notion of pluralism. This term can be understood in a number of different ways, but in the context of the rhetoric approach it is best understood to be a matter of how we understand the concept of meaning. Traditionally, philosophers of language have believed that language has meaning in a singuar way; that is, expressions in our language have one correct meaning, which we seek to grasp. For example, the meaning of a name has been explained as being just that to which it refers, so that the meaning of the word "Amsterdam" is simply Amsterdam itself. However, since the later work of Ludwig Wittgenstein (1889–1951) philosophers of language have widely held the belief that the meaning of language is determined by how we use language in different contexts. Thus, since the contexts and ways in which we use language change continually, so too do the meanings of terms and expressions in language.

McCloskey takes this view, arguing that meaning is plural, rather than singular. In the context of economic methodology this means that there can be different understandings of what economists believe constitutes knowledge. For example, the term "competitive market" can have different meanings depending on matters such as the type of analysis, subject of application, and policy context. Pluralism, then, combines the idea that knowledge does not have foundations with a recognition of the multi-faceted character of the language we use in constructing knowledge.

The rhetoric approach also includes some other important concepts and ideas. These go beyond the idea of rhetoric as a means of persuasion to expand its interpretation specifically as a type of social practice. McCloskey thus argued that economics ought to be viewed as a "conversation" between economists. Though conversation is usually thought as something carried out face to face, in the context of economics it can be seen as a more extended type of communication including the main forms by which economists communicate or "speak" to one another.

Two of the most significant of these channels of communication are journal articles or "scientific" papers and conference presentations. Journal articles are the highly polished products of working papers that have been revised as a result of comments by colleagues, audiences at presentations, and usually anonymous reviewers at journals. It is likely therefore that many people will have read and commented on a paper before it is published. In effect, the author will have been conducting a "conversation" with all of these people. Conference presentations are occasions when working papers are delivered to interested audiences, usually accompanied by a discussant's comments and questions from the audience. Such presentations are an important way of introducing new people into the conversation, and often lead to the development of new networks through which papers are privately circulated on their way, ultimately, to publication.

In more recent work, McCloskey has emphasized the normative dimensions of conversation. Ordinary conversation, of course, exhibits various norms and conventions, ranging from simple rules of etiquette (not interrupting another person when they are talking) to practical conventions for communication (using familiar language) or even more serious principles of ethics (ensuring that everyone is equally able to participate in a conversation). McCloskey characterizes conversation that respects these different types of normative principles as civil conversation, meaning that it reflects an open, liberal type of interaction that we might expect of civilized people. Applying this approach to an analysis of the conversations between economists, however, suggests that the science of economics should focus not only on the outcomes or results of these conversations but also the process of investigation that is carried out in the discipline of economics. This proceeds more smoothly when conversations between economists are civil, and embed the norms and conventions of good conversation.

A further aspect of the economics conversation is the publication of interviews with economists in which they discuss their work and also their views about the nature of the discipline. Arjo Klamer has made a substantial contribution to the development of this form of conversation in his interviews with a number of New Classical Economists and their critics, and interviews with economists are now commonplace.

Subsequently, Klamer and David Colander also interviewed students to determine attitudes about economics and the teaching of economics on the part of people who are "new" to the conversation. Interviews combine aspects of storytelling and case study methods (Focus 5.2). They provide evidence about how economists make decisions regarding their reseach strategies that often go beyond their views about appropriate methods. In this sense, then, a conversation produces a more realistic and informative view of how economics is carried out. Like the case study, the interview operates in a real-life context, and in this respect is a rich if challenging source for increasing their understanding of how economists carry out their work.

Finally, the rhetoric approach also views training and education in economics as a special type of communication based on multiple conversations over a course of study. In this respect a particularly important role is played by textbooks, which generally contain standardized content that represents what is believed to be known in a field. Disputes and controversies are generally excluded from textbooks so that students are not under the impression that their content merely records current beliefs. Essentially, the communicative function of textbooks is to deliver what Kuhn regarded as those exemplars that embody a field's "normal science." Similarly, training and education is built around standardized curricula and subject content – the intention is to develop the same understanding in students as is held by their instructors and professors. In this sense training and education is another kind of conversation, in this instance meant to ensure a highly structured type of communication.

Postmodernism

Postmodernism is a broad cross-disciplinary movement in the arts, literature, history, and science that questions many of the basic assumptions and principles that have been part of western culture and society since the time of the eighteenth-century Enlightenment. The main source of postmodernism is the 1960s French poststructuralism associated with philosophers such as Michel Foucault (1926–1984), Jacques Derrida (1930–2004), Jacques Lacan (1901–1981), and Louis Althusser (1918–1990). An earlier structuralist movement in such fields as linguistics, anthropology, and cultural studies had seen social explanation as a matter of uncovering deep causal structures in language and thought. However, the poststructuralists rejected a number of key structuralist assumptions. Jack Amariglio lists these as:

1. There is a single scientific method;
2. Knowledge has foundations;
3. Meaning can ultimately be determined with certainty;
4. History possesses a pattern, such as progress;
5. The self is a coherent unity;
6. Things and beings have essential natures;
7. Master narratives or universalizing accounts are possible;
8. Causal determination has a privileged role in explanation;
9. Things can be represented in language and discourse.

The breadth of this critique led subsequent commentators to suggest that it involved more than just a re-thinking of structuralism. It was more in the nature of a re-thinking of some of the most fundamental assumptions about modern society, including, indeed, the very idea that society could even be seen as "modern." This critique of modernism had far-reaching implications for traditional views of the nature of science and literature, and in embracing this larger set of concerns poststructuralism came to be known as postmodernism.

The rhetoric approach, though it preceded postmodernist thinking in the field of economic methodology, emerged subsequently to the debates over postmodernism that were occurring outside the economics disciplines. McCloskey, in fact, was influenced by postmodernism, and many of the themes of the rhetoric approach recall postmodernist arguments. Thus, of the nine points listed above, McCloskey emphasized (1) and (2) in her critique of positivism, (3) in her focus on persuasion and conversation, (7) in her emphasis on there being many stories told in economics, and (9) in her challenges to realism. But just as postmodernism has been developed outside of economics, so its influence in economics has gone beyond the rhetoric approach in the form of a number of critiques of the some of the most well-known concepts in economics. Broadly speaking, these concepts are ones postmodernists characterize as modernist. Their general argument is that these concepts represent ideal, unifying or "essentializing" conceptions which mask disorder and difference in the phenomena they represent.

Consider the equilibrium concept, which can be said to presuppose principles (6) and (8). First, the postmodern critique of principle (6) states that things do not have essential natures. In traditional terms, the equilibrium concept implies that for a given set of exogenous factors, an economic system will gravitate to a unique settled state. In effect, the equilibrium position of an economic system captures the essential nature of that system. But much recent economics research has demonstrated that multiple equilibria and unstable equilibria are outcomes that are entirely possible in rather ordinary circumstances. Of course, it would not be correct to say that this recent research in economics has been stimulated by economists' awareness of postmodernist ideas. Rather what might be asserted is that postmodernists have correctly diagnosed a general problem in modernist thinking that economists have unearthed independently in connection with the equilibrium concept. This kind of correspondence has suggested to many, however, that postmodernist arguments might merit more attention.

Second, the postmodernist rejection of principle (8) states that causal determination does not hold a privileged place in explanations of the world. This idea is presupposed by the reliance on equilibrium reasoning in economics in that the movement of an economic system into an equilibrium state is the result of a systematic set of causal forces that are associated with the demand and supply sides of the market. But one way to consider the problems in equilibrium theory in recent economics is to say that causal forces do not play the important role that they are customarily believed to play. Recent theorizing in economics in terms of complex adaptive systems theory attempts to explain this by showing that causal forces can sometimes function in arbitrary ways, as for example when the outcomes in economic systems are highly sensitive to small changes in initial conditions, which may be random and lack causal explanation. Some argue that the recent financial crisis should be understood in this way.

Also consider the rationality concept in economics, which – presupposing the presence of rational decision-makers – bears on principle (5) above. In effect, postmodernists argue that there is nothing that holds the individual together as a single self; they regard the idea of the individual as a single unity as a modernist fiction. Again, it would be incorrect to argue that recent thinking in economics is based on an awareness of this postmodernist tenet, and better to say economists have, in some instances, arrived at a surprisingly similar view. Thus one of the main conclusions of some recent work in behavioral economics is that individuals have time-inconsistent preferences and show "present-bias" in their choices. This means that individuals' choices today are not consistent with their choices tomorrow, which effectively means individuals effectively have multiple selves!

What, then, are the general implications of postmodernism for economic methodology? As we have seen, one major concern throughout the history of economic methodology has been to decide when theories can be judged scientific. Two of the most influential demarcationist accounts are to be found in the work of Karl Popper and Imre Lakatos (discussed above in Chapters 3 and 4, respectively), and their views provide criteria or rules for deciding when science can be demarcated from pseudo-science. However, postmodernists reject many of the ideas that underlie the idea of demarcation, particularly as associated with principle (7), the idea that science consists of a single narrative. Thus, postmodernists argue that attempting to distinguish between science and pseudo-science is a hopeless project. Put differently, there are no meta-criteria for knowledge, and indeed the term 'knowledge' with all its connotations as being something objective and certain is questionable.

In summary, postmodernism is the most radical view we have examined thus far. Some conclude, accordingly, that postmodernism is a fundamentally skeptical, even nihilistic doctrine, which has nothing positive to offer. Expressed in terms of the debate between realism and relativism, postmodernism is both relativist and anti-realist. The dilemma that we then face is how to take seriously those particular postmodernist arguments which, taken separately, have some plausibility, and yet avoid their most damaging view regarding the state of science and knowledge. In an attempt to achieve this balance methodologists of economics have formulated a response to this challenge, pluralism, which is the subject of the next section.

Pluralism

In philosophy of science and economic methodology the main discussion of pluralism has concerned the nature of knowledge, and for this reason pluralism is often termed **epistemological pluralism**. This is the view that there exist multiple kinds and forms of knowledge, which may be incommensurable or inconsistent with one another, but none of which can be shown to be superior to or reducible to the other. In effect, there is no independent standard that might be applied to judge between different views of what constitutes knowledge. Indeed, just as there can be multiple kinds and forms of knowledge, so equally there can be many different kinds and forms of independent standards. For example, while the science of chemistry depends to a significant extent on the science of physics, chemists do not believe that all knowledge of chemical relationships can be explained in terms of the principles of physics. Thus, an epistemological pluralist would state that chemistry and physics constitute two different kinds or forms of knowledge, neither of which is fully reducible to the other.

Epistemological pluralism is sometimes confused with relativism. Relativism, however, assumes that there are *no* standards for truth and knowledge, whereas epistemological pluralism, by contrast, assumes that there are a number of different, competing standards. That these different standards cannot be reconciled does not imply that they are not objective within the domains to which they apply. Thus, to take the example discussed above, chemistry is believed to provide knowledge about chemical relationships, and physics is believed to provide knowledge about the principles of physics.

In opposition to epistemological pluralism is the view that knowledge of all types of things ultimately takes only one basic form. Implicit in this idea is the assumption that different types of knowledge can be "reduced" to this one basic form of knowledge – a view known as **reductionism**. A version of reductionism in economics is the claim that macroeconomics needs to have microfoundations, and should thereby be reduced to microeconomics. However, were one to argue that not only do macroeconomic relationships depend on microeconomic ones, but also microeconomic relationships depends on macroeconomic ones, one would be abandoning reductionism in favor of an epistemologically pluralist understanding of the two parts of economics.

This means that whether or not one is an epistemological pluralist depends in part on one's understanding of the possible diversity in types of explanations. But there is a further rationale for epistemological pluralism that is rooted in the classical concept of a division of labor. That is, one might be risk averse with repect to investing in research in science, thus arguing for diversification strategies that depend upon there being a division of labor between scientists, groups of which work on different kinds of science problems or work on the same problems in different ways. It might ultimately be that many of these different working groups would fail to produce valuable outcomes, but the problem is that we have a high degree of uncertainty about which of the working groups will be successful. Thus, many different kinds of research strategies ought to be promoted simultaneously in the hope that some of them will be successful (see Focus 6.2

for a discussion of Paul Feyerabend's "theoretical pluralism"). One example is the practice of the Bank of England in regard to forecasts and policy decisions. In an attempt to reduce the level of risk, the Bank draws on a range of partial models in addition to its core model, in order to plot different possible scenarios under various hypothetical conditions. Thus, it emphasizes the importance of relying on a plurality of modeling strategies, comparing them according to their degrees of success.

One variant of this view is associated with the idea of triangulation, or the idea that the best way to produce reliable results in science is to come at problems from quite different points of view using different methods and perhaps data, and then focus on those results upon which these different points of view separately arrive (see Focus 5.2 for a discussion of triangulation). In effect, different methods of investigation constitute a check on one another, and that the same conclusion can be arrived at in a number of different ways gives us more confidence in that conclusion.

The position that one ought to be an epistemological pluralist is termed **methodological pluralism**. According to Warren Samuels, this is the view that absent "meta-criteria by which one methodology can be shown unequivocally to be superior to all others, analyses should not be rejected solely on the basis of methodological considerations." From this it follows that reductionism is wrong and that there are inescapably different kinds of knowledge implying the methodological policy recommendation that we ought to promote different kinds of knowledge in order to advance science as a whole. This understanding also suggests that knowledge is as much a process as a specific set of conclusions that scientists produce, since it implies a regular revision of what people believe counts as knowledge. Some methodological pluralists link this process view of knowledge to SSK social constructivist ideas that treat knowledge as something that is constructed. However, a process view can also be seen to be consistent with the traditional realist view that science aims to achieve an increasingly better picture of the way the world "really" is – independent of the theories we hold about its nature.

Looking ahead

We have now reached the end of our chronological/conceptual account of the philosophy of science and economic methodology that began with our discussion of the logical positivism of the 1930s. The history we have surveyed contains many competing strategies of explanation whose differences and disagreements may leave the student wondering which way to turn. There is no simple answer to this problem, and our goal has been simply to place the student in the same position that practitioners in economics and the sciences find themselves when they seek to methodologically and philosophically judge the results and process of economics and science, and determine for themselves how they believe they ought to proceed in their own research. If there is one clear lesson in all this, then, it is that there is no easy road forward for science. Indeed, there continues to be a lively debate about the very nature of science that is unlikely to end in the foreseeable future. Following the great certainty of the logical positivists that they knew what science is and also, significantly, what it is not, our understanding of science has only become more complex and nuanced. We believe students ought to understand something about the nature of this debate, and trust that having studied it they will be in a better position to make reasoned decisions about how they will carry out their own work.

That the student is left with so much discretion about how to think about science and economics leads to the subject of our final chapter: value judgments in economics. Values are often the anchors we rely upon to settle difficult issues. They may be methodological and ethical. In the previous chapters of this book we have hinted at the role they have played in many of the views discussed. In the final chapter, we break out of our chronological frame to focus directly on values and value judgments, particularly as they relate to economics. If there are pieces missing from the puzzle we have asked you to assemble in the previous chapters, we hope you may find some of the pieces in this last chapter. Scientists and economists live in a world of values. Though values and value judgments are not the only determinants of how they understand and practice science, it will be made clear that they certainly exert a considerable influence.

Exercises

1   What is the rhetoric approach to economic methodology, and how does it differ from falsificationism?
2   Explain how a metaphor might be important in the rhetoric approach. Give an example.
3   In what ways is economic practice like a conversation?
4   What are the implications of postmodernism for economic methodology?
5   What is the main idea behind methodological pluralism? Explain how methodological pluralism supports the existence of different schools of thought in economics.
6   Consider the following quotation from Adam Smith's *Wealth of Nations* (1789: IV.ii.9):

> By preferring the support of domestick to that of foreign industry, [the merchant] intends only his own security; and by directing that industry in such a manner as its produce may be of the greatest

value, he intends only his own gain, and he is in this, as in many other cases, led by an invisible hand to promote an end which was no part of his intention. Nor is it always the worse for the society that it was no part of it. By pursuing his own interest he frequently promotes that of the society more effectually than when he really intends to promote it.

This is the only location in the *Wealth of Nations* where the metaphor "invisible hand" appears. Its interpretation depends on whose hand it is that is invisible. Discuss different examples to show how its interpretation can change.

7   In art, an exemplary modernist artist is Piet Mondrian. Locate a selection of his paintings, and describe a key feature of modernism in art which is similar to modernism in science.

8   Discuss which rules of positivism, as characterized by McCloskey, apply to Friedman's methodology.

Relevant readings

Amariglio, Jack (1998) "Poststructuralism," in J. Davis, W. Hands, and U. Mäki (eds), *The Handbook of Economic Methodology*, Aldershot: Edward Elgar.
  An economist's introduction to the origins and thinking of postmodernism.
Bank of England (1999) *Economic Models at the Bank of England*, London: Bank of England.
  A statement of the Bank's policy regarding its procedures.
Colander, David, and Klamer, Arjo (1987) "The Making of an Economist," *Journal of Economic Perspectives* 1: 95–113.
  Colander and Klamer's initial study of graduate education in economics.
Downward, Paul and Andrew Mearman (2007) "Retroduction as Mixed-Methods Triangulation: Reorienting Economics in Social Science," *Cambridge Journal of Economics* 31: 77–99.
  An examination of different methods of triangulation applied to Tony Lawson's critical realist thinking.
Gibbard, Allan and Hal R. Varian (1978) "Economic Models," *The Journal of Philosophy* 75(11): 664–77.
  An economist's view of economic models which became well known for its view of models as stories.
Klamer, Arjo (1984) *Conversations with Economists: New Classical Economists and Opponents Speak Out on the Current Controversy in Macroeconomics*, Totowa, NJ: Rowman and Littlefield.
  Klamer's path-breaking set of interviews about the emergence of new classical economics.
McCloskey, D. (1983) "The Rhetoric of Economics," *Journal of Economic Literature*, 21: 481–517.
  The shorter version of McCloskey's 1986 book.

McCloskey, D. (1986) *The Rhetoric of Economics*, Madison: University of Wisconsin Press.

McCloskey's main statement of the rhetoric approach.

McCloskey, D. (1990) *If You're So Smart: The Narrative of Economic Expertise*, Chicago: University of Chicago Press.

McCloskey's discussion of storytelling as a form of conversation.

Samuels, Warren (1998) "Methodological Pluralism," in J. Davis, W. Hands, and U. Mäki (eds), *The Handbook of Economic Methodology*, Aldershot: Edward Elgar.

A summary statement of methodological pluralism as a position.

Samuels, Warren (ed.) (1990) *Economics as Discourse*, Dordrecht: Kluwer.

An influential collection of papers emphasizing discursive practices in economics.

Focus 6.1   Analogy and Metaphor

Two of the most important ideas in the rhetoric approach are analogy and metaphor. These play a particularly important role in philosophy of science and economic methodology because they involve a form of reasoning and explanation that cannot be accommodated readily under the umbrella of deductive rationality. On the one hand, they involve a kind of special inference; on the other, they point us toward the role of communication in the development of scientific explanation.

Making an analogy involves transferring a conceptual content from one subject, termed the source, to another subject, termed the target, so as to re-characterize the meaning of the latter. Analogies are used extensively in language and science (see Focus 1.2 on models and for Nagel's distinction between substantive and formal analogies), and play an important role in producing explanations and generating new understanding.

The persuasiveness of analogies rests on the perception of likeness and an implicit argument that the target subject can and should somehow be understood in terms of the conceptual content of the source subject. The perception of likeness involves a form of abstraction whereby a pattern or structure in the content of the source subject is said to be homomorphic with the content of the target subject. Thus the nineteenth-century physicist James Clerk Maxwell, in what he called his "physical analogy" approach to a unified representation of electric and magnetic action, argued explicitly for analogy understood in terms of a similarity of relations, not of the actual things substantially related.

The power of the argument for making a particular analogy depends on the transferability of this pattern or structure, and also on the success of the target subject's re-characterization in whatever context it is employed. For example, human capital theory results from transferring the structure of financial investment relationships to a representation of the nature of training and education in labor markets. The proponents of the analogy defend the analogy by asserting that training and education have the same structure as a financial investment; the success of the analogy is then explained in terms of the widespread use of human capital reasoning in labor market contexts. Successful analogies are claimed to generate new knowledge, which is said to result when new content is given to the meaning of education and training when formulated in terms of investment and capital. Critics of proposed analogies deny the creation of such new knowledge: they reject the re-characterization of the target subject matter. In effect, they label it a "pseudo-knowledge."

Metaphor is the result of a successful analogy, indeed one so successful that its source content is forgotten – or rather becomes relatively unimportant. For example, game theory has as its source content the variety of parlor games or games played in the home (card games, board games, etc.)

that were studied as forms of interactive exchange by John von Neumann (for von Neumann the inspiration for game theory was poker) and other mathematicians. Present-day game theory is the study of a variety of stylized types of interaction that are treated as representative of different forms of interaction in economic life. In this case, the metaphor is "dead" and its metaphorical content has come to be seen as simply the label of the target subject. Other successful metaphors preserve some of their source content, but in a relatively unimportant way. Thus the term "invisible hand" refers to free markets, while the "invisible hand" idea itself suggests the absence of government involvement or a "hands-off" approach to markets. One measure of how a metaphor becomes distant from its source content is its loss of being surprising, shocking, odd, objectionable, or paradoxical. For example, many originally thought the human capital metaphor that children are durable goods was offensive and objectionable, but it now rarely invites comment from economists.

Because they are special kinds of inference, analogy and metaphor cannot be understood within the standard understanding of deductive rationality. Deductive rationality proceeds from axioms or assumptions whose formal representation is meant to eliminate ambiguity, and everything deduced from those axioms or assumptions is implicit in them. In contrast, analogy and metaphor directly violate this by substituting likeness relationships between unlike contents in order to propound a special kind of inference. Indeed, one of the most important properties of analogy and metaphor is novelty in the explanation of the target subject made possible by the attribution of source subject contents to the target.

In this respect, analogy and metaphor are forms of inductive reasoning. Induction proceeds from the review of particular instances to the general case or rule: "one thing is like another, and they are both like a third thing, and so we say they are all alike in respect x." But analogy and metaphor are different from this standard form of inductive argument in that they treat purportedly unlike things as having similarities. Children are not commodities, as is suggested by the durable goods metaphor, but to the extent that the concepts of investment and capital are seen as transferrable to families raising children, this unlikeness is replaced by likeness. We may say that what distinguishes these two types of inductive inference is that the standard form does not produce novel understanding, but only generalizes, whereas analogy and metaphor produce novel understanding.

Deirdre McCloskey emphasizes another important feature of analogy and metaphor: that they presuppose processes of communication between scientists. Communication distinguishes a sender and receiver, and allows for multiple back-and-forth exchanges. Scientific explanations are seen to result from such exchanges, and presuppose communities of practitioners who develop their explanations in recurring interactions. Analogy and metaphor, as based on a relationship between a source and target content, provide one basis for sender–receiver communications, essentially involving proposals to send content from one subject matter for incorporation in another. Whether or not the content sent is adopted then depends on the way in which communication in the scientific community arbitrates the proposal. Here the tension between the likeness and unlikeness of a candidate analogy or metaphor is important, since grounds exists for both acceptance and rejection.

McCloskey's explanation of how such cases are resolved emphasizes the idea of scientists as storytellers. Theories may be very technical and formal, but they are often explained in narrative form or as an account of "how things work." This narration gives an explanation of why a theory makes sense – in this sense it is an explanation of the explanation. This wider framework, then, presents an overarching rationale that provides justification for parts of the theory that may not in themselves seem plausible. That is, they make sense in the larger context. From this perspective, we can see why analogies and metaphors which may initially seem problematic come to be accepted. They are appropriate to a larger story, and thus scientists come to re-evaluate the apparent unlikeness they exhibit as really not an unlikeness at all.

Relevant readings

Maxwell, James Clerk (1965) *The Scientific Papers of James Clerk Maxwell*, ed. W.D. Niven, New York: Dover.
>Includes Maxwell's methodological reasoning about the use of metaphor in science.

Samuels, Warren (forthcoming) *Essays on the Invisible Hand*, Cambridge: Cambridge University Press.
>A survey and analysis of the the invisible hand idea based on exhaustive research into the many uses of the concept in economics.

Witt, Ulrich (forthcoming) "Novelty and the Bounds of Unknowledge in Economics," *Journal of Economic Methodology*.
>A discussion of the nature of novelty in an evolutionary framework.

Focus 6.2   Paul Feyerabend

Paul Feyerabend (1924–1994), born in Vienna, Austria, was a professor of philosophy at the University of California, Berkeley for more than three decades. He served in the German army in World War II, and was wounded in the German retreat on the Eastern Front. After the war he studied sociology, history, and physics, before specializing in philosophy. His dissertation supervisor was Viktor Kraft, a former member of the Vienna Circle and the center of a postwar Austrian philosophy club called the "Kraft Circle." Feyerabend wrote his thesis under Kraft on basic observation sentences (or "protocol sentences") which were thought by the logical positivists to provide the foundations of scientific knowledge.

Shortly after completing his degree, Feyerabend met the well-known Cambridge philosopher Ludwig Wittgenstein when the latter gave a lecture to the "Kraft Circle" on his later thinking. Wittgenstein's early thinking had been much admired by the logical positivists, but he was to repudiate much of it after the war. Feyerabend became interested in Wittgenstein's new ideas, and subsequently read the proofs of Wittgenstein's *Philosophical Investigations*. He received a British fellowship to study with Wittgenstein in Cambridge, but Wittgenstein died and Feyerabend decided to study instead at the London School of Economics under Karl Popper, who he had also met after the war in Austria.

Popper was already known as a falsificationist critic of logical positivism from his 1934 *Logik der Forschung*, later translated as *The Logic of Scientific Discovery* (see Chapter 3). In his lectures and seminars at the LSE, Popper argued against the idea that there existed a well-defined scientific method and in favor of a set of simple rules that should be followed by scientists. Feyerabend was influenced by this thinking, and when he returned to Vienna, he translated Popper's two volumes of *The Open Society and Its Enemies* into German, and began writing papers on the quantum theory in physics in an effort to apply Popper's approach. He subsequently developed the view – contrary to that of his philosophy thesis and logical positivist thinking – that observation statements were not objective reports of experience and theory-independent, but were determined by the theories used to explain observations. In this he also reflected Wittgenstein's arguments – in his *Philosophical Investigations* – that meaning depends on the context in which expressions are used.

When Feyerabend first moved to the University of California in 1960, he encountered Thomas Kuhn and read Kuhn's *Structure of Scientific Revolutions* in draft form. Following his views developed in the study of physics and Wittgenstein's philosophy that meaning is determined contextually, Feyerabend concluded that scientific terms had different meanings in different theories, and thus, much as Kuhn had reasoned, were "incommensurable" in meaning across their different uses. He applied this view to the question of how we ought to think about mental phenomena, and, arguing that the language referring to mind and brain are two different, incommensurable ways of speaking, recommended we methodologically give up the concept of the former to speak only in physical terms – a view later known as eliminative materialism.

Generalizing on his work on the subject of "incommensurability," Feyerabend called for a "theoretical pluralism" whereby scientific progress results from many incompatible theories competing with one another. In his "pluralistic test model," theories are tested vigorously against one another, both in their ability to make predictions and as descriptions of reality. Often the weaknesses of theories could only be detected when they were challenged by other theories, and thus Feyerabend reasoned that we ought to multiply the number of theories we are willing to consider. Indeed, his belief in the need for a proliferation of theories was so strong that he argued that theories that were weak in empirical support or even inconsistent with much of the evidence ought to be retained in order to sustain a climate of testability.

By 1970, when he wrote "Against Method: Outline of an Anarchistic Theory of Knowledge," Feyerabend's thinking had moved considerably beyond Popper's falsificationism, and he advanced for the first time his theory of "epistemological anarchism," which he said was inspired by John Stuart Mill's *On Liberty* critique of scientific methodology. Visiting and lecturing at the LSE and University College in London, he also met and befriended Imre Lakatos (see Chapter 4). They made plans to write a dialogue together called "For and Against Method" in which Lakatos would defend a rationalist conception of scientific explanation and Feyerabend would attack it, but Lakatos died in 1974. Instead Feyerabend went on to publish *Against Method: Outline of an Anarchistic Theory of Knowledge* (1975; dedicated to Lakatos), followed three years later by *Science in a Free Society*, which included replies to his critics and also the reviews of *Against Method*.

The key to epistemological anarchism was Feyerabend's conviction that the history of science demonstrates that there are no general methodological rules for successful scientific investigation – apart from the rule that "anything goes." For example, he argued that no methodological rules could explain the Copernican Revolution, and that any attempt to follow such rules might have prevented it. Feyerabend applied his conclusion to logical positivism and all standard methodologies of science, and also to Popper's critical rationalism and Lakatos's methodology of scientific research programs, both of which he regarded still as being "rationalist" in nature. Unsurprisingly, Feyerabend himself was criticized as being "irrationalist" and a relativist. His defense was that he was only drawing out the implications of incommensurability and emphasizing the value of an open, non-dogmatic science. Distancing himself from the term "anarchism," he preferred to label his approach "Dadaist," after the interwar cultural movement begun in Zurich which offered a critique of prevailing standards in art and literature.

Indeed, despite his famous slogan "anything goes," it is apparent that Feyerabend was not really a relativist in the strongest sense of that term. His relativism was more a reflection of his view that we need to be attentive to the clash of positions and even cultures, and derived from his critique of a highly rationalist understanding of science and his view that Reason with a capital "R" was a philosopher's abstraction that was ambiguous and empty. In this regard, his thinking is better characterized as pluralist and postmodernist in its emphasis on openness to exchange and dialogue, whether or not this led to resolution of debate and disagreement, and in its rejection of rationalism as an essential aspect of science.

Relevant readings

Feyerabend, Paul, (1975) *Against Method: Outline of an Anarchistic Theory of Knowledge*, London: Verso.
   Feyerabend's statement of epistemological anarchism.
Feyerabend, Paul (1978) *Science in a Free Society*, London: New Left Books.
   Feyerabend's answer to Popper's *Open Society*.
Feyerabend, Paul (1995) *Killing Time: The Autobiography of Paul Feyerabend*, Chicago: The University of Chicago Press.
   Feyerabend's view of his life.

Focus 6.3   Realism and Causal Explanation in Economics

In Chapter 2 we saw that for Milton Friedman, the value of a model is determined not by how realistic it is but by its ability to make good predictions. Indeed Friedman thought that any attempt to construct a completely realistic model of the economy – like having a perfect photographic reproduction – was nonsensical. All models necessarily leave out a variety of aspects of the economy in an effort to explain what is central to their operation, and accordingly he thought our concern should be with what is involved in building a sufficiently good approximation of the economy.

Does this mean that Friedman is an anti-realist? Taking realism to be the view that the world exists independently of our theories and thinking about it, one could develop unrealistic models and yet still be a realist. This means that realisticness and realism are not identical. Much the same can also be said about social constructivist approaches such as that developed in the sociology of scientific knowledge (SSK) (see Chapter 5). Though the social interests of the scientific community determine a theory's acceptance rather than its compatibility with the way the world is, this need not entail anti-realism (or idealism), since it could still be argued that the world exists independently of our theories but has less influence on their determination than social interests.

What, then, is the place of realism in economic methodology? In fact, there are different forms of realism according to just what it is that is believed to exist independently of our thinking. Commonsense realism takes ordinary objects (buildings, people, animals, etc.) to really exist. In contrast, scientific realism takes the objects of scientific theories (electrons, gravitation, genes, neurons, etc.) to be what really exists. Economic methodologists have debated whether economics should be seen as commonsense realist or scientific realist: on the one hand, economics seems to be about ordinary things such as preferences and prices; on the other hand, these things are defined theoretically, and so may be well removed in meaning from their commonsense understandings.

Another form of realism that is important in economics is causal realism. This is the view that relationships between events in the world cannot be understood simply in terms of regularities or laws, but need also to be understood in terms of cause-and-effect connections. It implies that at some level explanations in economics ought to be formulated in terms of the idea of causal mechanisms. Recall that Carl Hempel's deductive-nomological model of scientific explanation is a regularity- or law-based approach, and that it can fail to provide adequate explanations when we have regularities that are accidental in nature (see Chapter 1). What seems to be missing in these cases is that the explanation fails to capture underlying cause-and-effect relationships.

Economists, it is fair to say, are generally concerned with *causes*. They seek to explain what causes economic growth or what causes changes in prices. It is true that econometrics can only unearth correlations, but the independent/dependent variable equations economists estimate in regression analysis are believed to reflect real cause-and-effect relationships in the world that economists hope to identify through the analysis of data. This is true for even the most instrumentalist of empirical economists. Thus Kevin Hoover argues that Friedman, despite his rejection of realisticness and instrumentalist emphasis on the predictive power of models, was a causal realist, because he was interested in causal mechanisms that govern the business cycle and in the effect of changes that might result from altering the money supply. It follows that good economic models are not just good at making predictions; they are also good for policy prediction when we wish to causally intervene in the economy. This view goes back at least as far as the early development of econometrics, with Jan Tinbergen's interwar call for causal explanations of the business cycle (see Chapter 2).

What, then, is involved in causal explanations? Nancy Cartwright develops a realist account of causal explanations in terms of the idea that in nature we find many "capacities" which, in stable environments, act as if they are "nomological machines" that produce law-like behavior. For explanations in economics, where we usually cannot assume stable environments, we resort to either *ceteris paribus* reasoning or – in some cases – to experiments to isolate these causal relations in the world. Cartwright argues that models, in economics and elsewhere, should be expected to be unrealistic – they are idealizations or approximations of relationships we believe operate in the world, and are usually expressed in mathematical terms. But we nonetheless evaluate models in terms of how well they capture why things happen in the world as they do. Thus

Cartwright is a causal realist in that she believes our explanations aim to capture the nature of a world that is independent of them.

Another realist view that provides an account of causal explanation is the critical realism advanced by Tony Lawson. Lawson argues that economies and societies are open rather than closed systems, and cannot be understood fully in terms of empirical regularities or the constant conjunction of events. Rather we must look beneath these patterns of events and investigate the causal structures, powers, and mechanisms (not unlike Cartwright's "capacities") whose manifestations we find exhibited in different tendencies in economic phenomena and dispositions in economic behavior. Lawson thus rejects empiricist economic methodologies that build explanations out of event regularities, arguing that realism requires we ask what underlying causal factors must be presupposed if we are to account for the phenomena we observe.

Realism, then, plays an important role in economic methodology – if not always an obvious one. In the history of the subject, many economists can be classified as realists. Realism can be contrasted with **conventionalism**, which ignores or puts aside the issue of whether economic theories and models are true or apply to what exists independently of them in the world, and only seeks explanations which are seen as widely accepted and generally agreed upon.

Relevant readings

Cartwright, Nancy (1999) *The Dappled World: A Study of the Boundaries of Science*, Cambridge: Cambridge University Press.
    A statement of Cartwright's views about laws, capacities, and causal explanation.
Hoover, Kevin (2009) "Friedman's Methodological Stance: Causal Realism," in U. Mäki (ed.), *The Methodology of Positive Economics*, Cambridge: Cambridge University Press.
    A critical evaluation of the view that Friedman is an anti-realist.
Lawson, Tony (1997) *Economics and Reality*, London: Routledge.
    The key statement of critical realist thinking.
Mäki, Uskali (1989) "On the Problem of Realism in Economics," *Ricerche Economiche* 43: 176–97.
    Explains the distinction between realisticness and realism.

Chapter 7

Value Judgments in Economics

In this final chapter we move away from our chronological survey of economic methodology to consider a topic that is relevant to all the methodological approaches we have surveyed, and which has often been a significant point of contention for economists: **value judgments** in economics. The approach of this chapter differs from that of earlier chapters in being primarily analytical and paying less attention to historical developments. In addition, the discussion is also more sharply focused on the subject of economics. In this respect, this chapter provides an introduction to the methodology of normative reasoning in economics treated as an important dimension of economic methodology.

Value judgments are evaluative types of statements that range from appraisals ("That is an excellent book") to prescriptions with no ethical content ("You should use this tool in this way") to ethical prescriptions or moral judgments ("It's morally wrong to steal"). Appraisals usually include language that is evaluative or that expresses an opinion. Prescriptions usually include language that recommends or expresses what ought to be done or should be the case. Generally, value judgments of all kinds are said to be normative. Only some of them are concerned specifically with ethics and morality, where the concern is with the fundamental aspects of "good" and the appropriate rules for right conduct. In contrast to all of these, statements that avoid appraisals or prescriptions are generally thought to be positive or value-free.

The standard view of most economists is that economics is a positive, value-free science with no place for value judgments of any kind. Widespread acceptance of this view dates back to the 1930s and Lionel Robbins's (see Focus 2.1) influential claim that economics and ethics are "two fields of inquiry" between which "there is a logical gulf fixed which no ingenuity can disguise and no juxtaposition in space or time can bridge over" (Robbins 1935: 148).

The standard view also captures the received view thinking of the logical positivists of the Vienna Circle, who asserted that only two kinds of propositions can be regarded as scientific knowledge: analytic and synthetic *a posteriori* propositions (see p. 10). Since value judgments are neither, they have no place in science – or indeed in economics. The logical positivists thus characterized value judgments as expressions of feeling or attitude rather than as scientific statements, a view shared by Robbins. Their view is known as emotivism (a form of non-cognitivism in ethics) from the idea that expressions of value are just "emotings" such as "ugh" or "ahh."

Some two decades later Milton Friedman (see Chapter 2) echoed this view, stating that: "Positive economics is in principle independent of any particular ethical or normative judgments" (Friedman 1953: 4). Friedman also associated scientific statements with predictions, and clearly value judgments are not predictions. Today, many economics textbooks begin with a short statement about how the positive and the normative (as a general way of referring to value judgments) are entirely separate subjects of investigation. Economists are regarded as being concerned with the former as proper to the domain of science, leaving policy-makers and the public to deal with the latter in the domain of opinion. The view of economics that is emerging from this approach is one in which economics operates as a value-free science, and society then decides what value judgments to apply to its results.

This view, however, does not stand up to any reasonable examination. Indeed, it can be shown that value judgments enter into economics in a number of distinct ways: in the way in which the economy is investigated, in the often value-laden character of the concepts employed by economics, in the ethical views implied by the fundamental propositions of standard economics, and in how explanations in economics incorporate ethical values and moral norms.

It is true that we can distinguish the language of value judgments and evaluative statements from that of language that states facts. The former includes "ought"-type terms (both explicitly and implicitly), while the latter excludes them, and restricts itself to "is"-type terms. But economics as a subject of investigation does not preserve this distinction, despite its frequent claims of doing so, which means that values and facts are mixed up together in the subject, and value judgments play a larger role than is generally appreciated.

Here we explain this in four different ways:

(i)   in terms of the **methodological value judgments** made by economists;
(ii) in connection with the **value-ladenness** of economic concepts and explanations;
(iii) according to how value judgments in economics support particular ethical views; and
(iv) in connection with how explanations in economics need to accommodate the ethical values and moral norms that people observe.

Methodological value judgments

Methodological value judgments in economics are evaluative judgments which economists make with respect to the methods and approaches they choose to employ in their investigation of the economy. These are not the sort of value judgments which make ethical judgments about moral right and wrong, but are nonetheless normative in that they involve prescriptions or recommendations about how one ought to carry out economics. Indeed, the standard claim expressed by Robbins, Friedman, and many textbooks that economics ought to be a value-free science is itself a methodological value judgment, in that it tells how we ought to practice economics. In essence, methodological value judgments are practical or pragmatic – "how to do it" sorts of judgments – rather than ethical or moral value judgments. This is very much what Kuhn referred to when he spoke of the "disciplinary matrix" that operates in normal science (see Chapter 4).

The most important methodological value judgments in economics involve three kinds of choices made by economists regarding how economics should be carried out: (i) the choice of the subject matter to be investigated; (ii) the method to be used in investigating that subject matter; and (iii) the criteria, standards, and norms used to assess and judge the validity of the investigation's outcomes.

Choice of subject matter

The choice of the subject matter to be investigated produces a point of entry. Since there is no necessity that a given subject matter be approached in any one particular way, the economist must make a methodological value judgment about what kinds of topics are worthy of investigation.

In neoclassical economics, for example, a key point of entry is the activity of choice, and economics is accordingly said to be about the choices made by people. This contrasts with the thinking of the eighteenth-century classical economists, such as Adam Smith and David Ricardo, who were interested in such topics as growth and distribution in the economy as a whole, and for whom these subjects were their point of entry.

Clearly, the methodological value judgments economists make about their points of entry and topics of investigation have a strong influence on what they identify – and indeed define – as the subject matter of economics. These kinds of value judgment are sometimes related to economists' ethical views, but they may also be independent of their ethical views, so that even when economists keep their own ethical opinions to one side, they still have to make value judgments of the methodological kind.

Methods of investigation

Economists also make value judgments about the methods or approaches they believe should be used in an investigation of the economy. For example, neoclassical economists investigate the choices made by people in terms of the theory of rational choice, which explains individuals' choices in terms of a set of conditions that apply to their preferences (completeness, reflexivity, and transitivity in risk-free situations).

However, there are other ways of explaining people's choices that violate these conditions on preferences (for example, that people's preferences may be "framed" by context), and there are also explanations of choice that say very little about preferences (for example, that people act out of habit).

Similarly, the classical economists made significant methodological value judgments when they employed the labor theory of value to investigate the role of growth and distribution in the economy. Whatever method or approach the economist adopts, then, reflects a methodological value judgment about how the investigation ought to proceed. Further, just as nothing necessitates one particular entry point into economics, so nothing necessitates one particular type of approach to it either, so economists must always make some sort of methodological value judgments.

Standards of validity

Economists also make methodological value judgments with respect to the criteria, standards, and norms that are used to assess the validity of the outcomes of their investigations. What counts as a valid result can involve many considerations, some of which have been explored in previous chapters (see also Focus 3.3). One important question concerns whether or not an explanation can be shown to be empirically adequate. But, as we have seen, there have been many views of what counts as empirical adequacy in this sense.

- Popper believed scientific results were not valid unless they had withstood attempts to falsify them, and even then he asserted that they were only provisionally valid. At the same time, empirical adequacy is not always emphasized, as many contributions in the history of economics have been theoretical, mathematical, and based on *a priori* thought experiments.

- Kuhn, by contrast, argued that normal science achieves its validity by providing solutions to puzzles within well-established paradigms. Clearly, economists have a range of views about what ought to be accepted as good explanations in economics, and this variety of views is a further measure of the extensive nature of methodological value judgments in economics.

In conclusion, we may say that these three forms of methodological value judgments concern the conduct of inquiry in economics – or how one carries out economics, rather than the outcome of one's inquiry. Many economists recognize that value judgments arise in economics in this way, but nonetheless argue that, in contrast to the conduct of inquiry, the content of economics that results, that is, the subject apart from how people investigate it, is a value-free, or value-neutral subject matter.

Accordingly, their view is that once economists have made their decisions about how to proceed, economics can be regarded as a fully positive subject. Put differently, the only value judgments that pertain to economics are methodological ones. Against this, however, some argue that the very concepts and explanations of economics themselves are value-laden in the sense that they incorporate values that derive from their investigation. On this view, neither the subject matter (or content) of economics nor the way in which economic inquiries are conducted is value-free. Let us consider, then, whether economics' content can be thought to include values.

The value-ladenness of economic concepts and explanations

The case for saying that the content of economics is value-free rather than value-laden goes back to the distinction we make in language between evaluative assertions and fact-stating assertions. This **fact–value distinction** is famously associated with "Hume's guillotine" – the idea that statements using "is" language are completely different and cut off from those using "ought" language. David Hume had argued that that no inferences from the former can be made to the latter, or in other words that statements using "is" language never imply statements using "ought" language.

G.E. Moore later argued that attempting to infer what people ought to do from claims about the nature of the world committed the "naturalistic fallacy." According to this view, as long as economics is formulated in the value-free language of "is" statements, its content can always be thought to be positive and value-free. This view has been widely accepted by economists. For example, in his 1994 prestigious American Economics Association Ely Lecture Nobel Prize-winning economist Kenneth Arrow asserted:

> I am old-fashioned enough to retain David Hume's view that one can never derive "ought" propositions from "is" propositions. The two issues, method and value, are distinct. (1)

Gunnar Myrdal (1898–1987, 1974 Nobel Prize with Friedrich von Hayek, "for their pioneering work in the theory of money and economic fluctuations and for their penetrating analysis of the interdependence of economic, social and institutional phenomena"), however, held an entirely different view of the matter.

> A disinterested social science has never existed and, for logical reasons, cannot exist. The value connotations of our main concepts represent our interest in a matter, give direction to our thoughts and significance to our inferences ... contrary to widely held opinions, not only the practical conclusions from a scientific analysis, but this analysis itself depends necessarily on value premises. (1–2)

Myrdal's argument against the traditional view can be expressed as follows: economic concepts and explanations cannot be formulated in genuinely value-free language, even when using only "is" statements, since these statements invariably conceal evaluative terms that imply hidden "ought" statements. In other words, "is" statements and "ought" statements can never be fully separated in ordinary speech, because on closer examination the former implicitly contain the latter.

Essentially Myrdal's argument rests on a claim about the "depth" of meaning of the terms we use to identify concepts in economics. He believed that the terms used by economists cannot be defined strictly in relation to other economic concepts in a given explanation, but must also be seen as having a broad range of additional meanings and associations for people that come from outside the context of the explanation in which they are employed.

He gave the following examples of a number of terms that contained additional meanings: productivity, equilibrium, balance and adjustment. These latter meanings and associations typically involve values. Take, for example, the important microeconomic concept of perfect competition. In economics, perfect competition is defined in terms of the perfect information assumption and the assumption that when there are many firms, they are all unable to influence the price level. But the broader idea of "competition" for people outside of economics has many meanings that go well beyond the economist's definition. Moreover, this extended set of meanings is usually accompanied by various value judgments regarding the desirability or undesirability of competition ("competition is good" or "competition is harmful").

Of course, economists can always say that they are only interested in their own technical meaning of a term. But this does not eliminate the term's other meanings, and nor does it guarantee that economists will not also think in terms of these more extended meanings of the concept. It is also difficult to see how a concept in economics could ever be made a purely technical term, since that would require that it should have no ordinary associations whatsoever, thereby making it irrelevant to explaining the economy!

Myrdal's view complicates our understanding of the content of economics, and it makes a reasonable case for saying economics is value-laden rather than value-free. But it does not tell us anything about the extent of the problem. It could be the case that the value-ladenness of economic concepts has little influence on economic explanations, and thus might be regarded as incidental. Myrdal's own view was quite the opposite: he believed that important value connotations could never be removed from economics and social science. Economics, that is, is strongly value-laden. This value-ladeness of economic concepts, moreover, generates an "economic point of view" that makes economics a thoroughly normative system. Interestingly, Myrdal again echoes much of Kuhn's notion of the "disciplinary matrix" (see p. 105):

> The student of economics is taught "to think in economic terms." This means chiefly – or so we are repeatedly told – that he should cultivate the ability to see and understand economic phenomena, rapidly and exactly, in a specific light, i.e. observe them from a particular point of view and classify them according to certain theoretical categories. The actual choice of viewpoint and categories will, of course, depend, in the last resort, on the underlying epistemological approach. Once one has grown accustomed to thinking within the frame of the inherited normative system, which offers the assurance of a "beaten track," it becomes difficult to step aside and inspect the system from outside.
>
> (Myrdal 1953: 22)

At the same time, obviously many concepts and explanations in economics have relatively little extra-economic value-laden content. Indeed, many concepts in economics are substantially technical, and arguably have very little extra-economic meaning. Consider the concept of an input–output table (developed by 1973 Nobel Prize laureate Wassily Leontief, "for the development of the input-output method and for its application to important economic problems") that refers to one way of explaining production interconnections between industries. This concept has limited popular meaning beyond the definition employed by economists. This does not mean, of course, that people do not make value judgments about the desirability or undesirability of thinking of an economy in terms of input–output relationships, but compared to other cases (such as the concept of competition) they are rather weakly attached to economists' understanding of the concept. Why, then, should they even be considered part of the economics concept? Might the economists' concept of an input–output table be essentially value-free?

Myrdal's view was that economic explanations always possess a substantial political significance, and so he would have insisted that even seemingly value-free concepts in economics, such as the input–output table, will always end up being value-laden. But note that this response is rather about the use and conduct of economics, and does not prove that every single economics concept is value-laden in a significant way. Some indeed appear to be, but others appear not to be.

We must conclude, then, that concepts and explanations in economics can be – but need not be – strongly value-laden. It depends on the concept and the uses to which it is put. This, however, still refutes the standard completely value-neutral view of economics content. It also creates a problem for us in that it still leaves us with no way of judging the extent or seriousness of value-ladenness in explanations in economics. On the one side we have Myrdal's view that it is a serious issue; on the other there is the possibility that a more "technical" economics might be consistent with a somewhat "weakened" value-neutrality view in which values underlie economic explanations, but have no special implications for any *particular* ethics or politics.

This suggests that we might be better able to assess the role that value judgments play in economics by examining particular theories and explanations. Further, rather than simply asking whether the concepts in economic explanations are value-laden, let us ask whether when we do find value-laden concepts in economic explanations whether they play any special role in promoting particular ethical theories (that is, theories about what is morally good or right and wrong, as well as the grounds for such judgments) to go along with those theories and explanations in economics. Such theories and explanations would then be strongly value-laden by virtue of implying specific moral judgments.

By comparison, cases where no particular moral judgments were implied would be weakly value-laden. Thus, instead of just looking at the "depth" of the meaning of the concepts used by economists, we will examine the role value-laden concepts play in theories with respect to promoting certain moral judgments. The example we will consider will be standard rational choice explanations.

The ethical commitments of rational choice explanations

Rational choice theory sees individuals' choices as rational when their preferences satisfy a set of formal conditions that allow us to regard those preferences as "well behaved." For example as noted above, individuals' preferences need to be transitive (meaning that if a is preferred to b, and b is preferred to c, then c cannot be preferred to a). Immediately we see a value judgment being made in terms of the meaning of the term "rational."

Though the concept of rationality used by economists is defined in a technical way in terms of the conditions required of preferences for making rational choices, for many people the meaning of "rational" includes the idea that it is good to be rational. This, of course, is a value judgment. Indeed, this value judgment is reinforced by rational choice theory's explanation of rationality in terms of a set of conditions individuals' preferences *ought* to satisfy in order that their choices qualify as being rational. By stating what conditions preferences ought to satisfy, rational choice theory prescribes how individuals ought to choose in order to be rational. Thus, given that people often assume that being rational is good, rational choice theory relies on this value judgment to effectively say how individuals should choose in order to achieve the good state of affairs of being rational.

Rational choice theory, then, is value-laden in the sense of employing an important value judgment. To determine, however, whether it is strongly or weakly value-laden, we should go on to ask whether this value judgment implies any particular moral judgments and ethical views. Let us say a bit more, then, about what is involved in making rational choices.

Specifically, making rational choices means choosing so as to satisfy one's preferences (as the theory understands preferences). Satisfying preferences is, of course, just one interpretation of what making a rational choice might mean, since there are other ways in which we might explain how making a choice could be thought rational. For example, one could say a rational choice involves relying on reasons that others find persuasive. Or one could say that making a rational choice involves drawing on one's most firmly held beliefs. Interpreting rationality in terms of preference satisfaction, then, is only one way of explaining a rational choice, and thus involves what was explained above as making methodological value judgments, specifically, as concern the choice of subject matter and the method of investigation.

In rational choice theory, then, the definition of making a rational choice is in terms of choosing in such a way as to satisfy one's preferences. Further, acting so as to satisfy one's preferences is also explained as making oneself better off, so that being rational and satisfying one's preferences is precisely what it means to make oneself "better off."

This is often described in terms of maximizing individual utility. Sometimes maximizing utility is said to be a matter of acting selfishly, but such a definition is a mistake. One can make rational choices that satisfy one's preferences when those preferences concern making others better off: these preferences are sometimes called altruistic or other-regarding preferences. In this case, one makes oneself better off by making others better off. Maximizing utility, then, simply involves making rational choices that satisfy one's own preferences, whatever they may be and for whomever they benefit.

This understanding, it can then be seen, implies a particular set of moral judgments, because it provides a particular ethical interpretation of what it means to be better off. The idea of being "better off" makes a direct reference to the idea of what is "good" in life – a key concept of ethics. But there are, of course, many ethical views of what constitutes the good in life – and, accordingly, what people regarded as making one "better off:"

- One might be said to be better off when one is able to fulfill one's moral duties and act responsibly, whether or not this satisfies one's preferences.

- One might be said to be better off when fulfilling one's commitments to others, though this could in fact be contrary to one's preferences.
- One might be thought better off if able to develop one's capabilities.
- Or one might be said to be better off when one is able to act according to principles of justice, though this could be entirely irrelevant to what one's preferences might be.

In standard rational choice theory, however, one is only better off when acting in such a way as to satisfy one's preferences. With the good and the idea of being better off defined in this way, an ethics of the right and wrong things to do must always be formulated in these terms, rather than in terms of matters such as duty, commitments, capabilities, or justice. Both moral judgments and one specific set of grounds for them thus flow from how the theory is value-laden and how it employs a particular set of methodo- logical value judgments.

The philosophers Daniel Hausman and Michael McPherson go further, explaining the basis for rational choice theory's identification of being better off with satisfying one's preferences in terms of another important value judgment that underlies rational choice theory – namely, the ethical principle of "minimal benevolence." This principle says that, all things considered or putting aside other considerations (economics' standard *ceteris paribus* clause), people *ought* to be able to make themselves better off by satisfying their preferences. That saying this requires a value judg- ment reflects the fact that there are other ways people might be thought to be made better off. One could pose as an alternative ethical principle, for example, that people *ought* to be able to make themselves better off by acting virtuously or according to their duties, commitments, capabilities, or justice. Rather than relying on the principle of minimal benevolence, one might then rely on some principle that says people ought always do what is believed to be right, *ceteris paribus*. For Hausman and McPherson, however, it is the principle of minimal benevolence that completes the nor- mative picture underlying standard rational choice theory.

Notice that a substantial amount of the normative force which the prin- ciple of moral benevolence has, or of its persuasiveness as a specific "ought" prescription, lies in the implicitly broad scope of its *ceteris paribus* clause. Essentially that clause allows us to disregard other theories of being bet- ter off such as concern duty, commitments, capabilities, and justice. This effectively isolates only that set of moral judgments that the preference sat- isfaction view of being better off entails, making it possible to talk about the specific ethical view to which rational choice theory is committed. Having done this, economists can make clear recommendations about policies that make people better off in terms of preference satisfaction, and should these policies produce, say, what others judge to be unjust outcomes, this can be ignored because it falls in the *ceteris paribus* clause.

There is more to rational choice theory's ethical view, of course, in the form of the famous Pareto optimality principle, which offers a basis for policy recommendation in economics by treating preference satisfaction as the good. The Pareto principle prescribes policy changes that make at least one person better off without harming any other person as measured in terms of individuals' preference satisfaction. This involves an additional value judgment, since one might alternatively recommend policies that made some people better off and some people worse off if the gains to the former exceeded the losses to the latter. This latter principle is used, in fact, in cost–benefit analysis, where the goal is to maximize the net gains in people being better off across individuals.

The usual defense of the Pareto principle vis-à-vis cost–benefit analysis is that changes that make no one worse off are seen as "less controversial" than those that involve net gains, but also some losers. That is certainly true, but this does not make the Pareto principle any less of a value judgment. At the same time, this avoidance of controversy comes at the cost of relevance, since there are essentially no real-life circumstances in which a policy change does not harm someone. Nonetheless, the additional value judgment that comes with the Pareto principle is that absence of controversy is such an important good that even where net gains are extremely high and losses very small, the recommendation of this kind of outcome should be ruled out.

Cost–benefit analysis, in fact, is widely employed in real-world economic policy-making. It is for the purely practical reason that policy changes have winners and losers, and one way to evaluate such changes is to calculate the costs and benefits for each in order to determine the overall outcome. At the same time, there is nothing that prevents policy-makers from also considering other ethical issues side-by-side these cost–benefit judgments. Whether a change in policy infringes on individuals' rights, is perceived to be unjust, or worsens inequality are among the considerations that have been raised. Policy-makers, then, typically proceed in a more eclectic manner, or pluralistically, taking into consideration multiple ethical perspectives. However, whether thinking in terms of the Pareto principle or in terms of some sort of cost–benefit analysis, the economist is still employing a particular theory of ethics with a set of implied moral judgments about what people *ought* to do.

The important point in this respect is that economics is rarely free of ethical implications, and the issue is rather whether our economic theories are adequate to our ethical thinking or bias it toward certain views of right and wrong. Indeed, were economics free of all value judgments, it would provide no basis for policy recommendations of any sort!

To return to the argument regarding weakly and strongly value-laden economics, standard rational choice theory is not just value-laden, in the sense that it employs a set of value judgments (namely, people are better off in acting on their preferences, the principle of minimal benevolence, and the Pareto principle) and a set of important methodological value judgments regarding the nature of choice, but it is also strongly value-laden in virtue of implying a particular set of moral judgments and a particular view of the foundations of ethics.

We may contrast standard rational choice theory, then, with other theories of choice that are also strongly value-laden but promote other views of moral right and wrong. We can also contrast it with economic explanations that are only weakly value-laden. In this latter case, value judgments may be involved, including methodological ones, but not the sort of value judgments that provide a basis for moral judgments and a particular view of ethics. The economic analysis of input–output relationships in production is one such example of this. Methodological value judgments underlie this type of explanation, but the sort of value judgments that support ethical claims about what is morally right and wrong do not.

This is not to imply, however, that economic analysis *should* be at most weakly value-laden. Determining what the goals of economic explanation ought to be is itself a methodological value judgment. Clearly in some circumstances it is an advantage for an explanation to be strongly value-laden if economic policy-makers hope to realize outcomes that have a certain moral quality.

Consider the Easterlin paradox that cross-sectional country data and within-country time-series suggest that there is no clear relation between economic growth of income and happiness. Most people believe that economic growth increases happiness. Suppose, then, that policy-makers wish to promote happiness as an economic outcome, and call upon economists to recommend policies that will help to achieve this goal. To explain how this might occur, economists would need to develop economic models of people that makes happiness rather than preference satisfaction their objective. The value judgment this entails is that happiness is good, and the associated ethical view would be that people ought to be able to achieve this good. This would therefore lead to the development of a strongly value-laden economics in the sense of supporting ethical claims about what is morally right and wrong, because this sort of analysis answers the questions posed by policy-makers.

Accommodating ethical values and norms

There is a fourth way in which economics incorporates value judgments. Irrespective of whether or not an economic explanation is strongly or weakly value-laden, economists often find themselves called upon to explain behavior that is believed to be motivated by or influenced by ethical values people have and by the moral norms they observe. In such circumstances, economists then need to fit their accounts of economic behavior to include motivations that operate in ethical life, making the values and norms people observe part of their economic explanations.

It is true that in offering such explanations some economists will seek to reinterpret moral motivations as the disguised pursuit of self-interest (a reductionist argument), but we saw above – in connection with standard rational choice theory – that maximizing utility need not be understood as acting selfishly or strictly in terms of self-interest, for example, as when we say people act to satisfy altruistic preferences. Indeed, there are no restrictions on the content of people's preferences in rational choice theory, or what sorts of things people prefer. Rational choice theory only employs a set of formal conditions that apply to preferences if their choices are to be regarded as rational – it says nothing about the kinds of things individuals prefer or their motivations for preferrring them.

An altruistic preference, we saw, is one that places a value on someone else being better off, rather than on serving one's own personal interests. One way of representing such a preference is in terms of consumption externalities whereby the satisfaction of another person's preference raises one's own utility. Though such a preference could be linked to any number of the ethical values held by people, such as kindness toward others, fairness, equality, etc., economists need not explain which ethical values lie behind a set of altruistic preferences or how they underlie those preferences. They only need be able to explain how people might exercise such preferences when they are said to act in the interest of others. In this case, then, an economic explanation accommodates an ethical phenomenon. We might say that the economic explanation conforms to the moral landscape.

This type of explanation goes back to the writings of Adam Smith, who used the concept of compensating differentials to explain differences in wages in labor markets reflecting what contemporary theory refers to as differences in preferences for different kinds of employment. Smith was interested in explaining why less desirable jobs, such as those that are dangerous and dirty, are paid higher wages than jobs that are more desirable. Contemporary labor markets also exhibit this variation in wages reflecting the differences in desirability of jobs, and one reason we might emphasize that explains why people consider some jobs desirable is that they involve charitable purposes. If we suppose that the many people who choose to work in charitable organizations do so because they are motivated by their ethical goals, then in this case the explanation of wage differences accommodates the ethical values people possess. As with altruistic preferences, there is no need to explain what those values are or how they underlie people's preferences, but the economic explanation nonetheless must incorporate the fact that people do possess ethical values.

Another type of ethical phenomenon economists have increasingly sought to explain are moral norms. These are the widely held rules or conventions about what is right or wrong – they are relatively free-standing in that they are not tied to any particular set of ethical values, and indeed are often subscribed to equally by people who hold different ethical values. In this respect again, economists need not concern themselves with the question of why certain norms exist – this remains the concern of moral philosophers and social scientists – but only with the impact of these norms on the shape of the economy.

Consider the fact that there are many market interactions in economies that depend on the concept of trust with respect to people's responsibilities for fulfilling the terms of contracts. One basis for the confidence people have that contract terms will generally be fulfilled is the presence of moral norms which guide people's interactions. Moral norms effectively govern people's expectations about what they can count on. Whether or not self-interest is at play in people's observance of moral norms, those norms themselves are nonetheless framed as what people ought to do.

Implicit in the idea of an economic contract, then, is the idea that people *ought* to observe the norm of complying with contracts. But when one speaks of contracts, one must recognize that they presuppose the existence of private property. Thus one reason people believe contracts should be observed is their respect for the institution of private property. Here again, then, economic explanations incorporate value judgments and ethical views of right and wrong. Indeed, the latter are often so much a part of how economists explain the economy that it is difficult to say where economics ends and ethics begins.

One further example can be made to emphasize this point. Though standard rational choice theory makes no claims about the content of people's preferences, society does express values about what people's preferences should be.

- First, most societies reject malevolent preferences, or those that concern doing harm to others.
- Second, individuals may have preferences that are not in their own best interest, so that satisfying them cannot really be said to make them better off.
- Third, if we allow that people's preferences are influenced by the information they have about the world, we can see that in some circumstances a lack of information may lead people to express a preference they would not express were they better informed.

In all three of the cases outlined above, social values play a role in determining what people's "rational" preferences ought to be, where this generally means their being informed and ethically acceptable. This, of course, involves a different meaning of the term "rational" from that used when we consider standard rational choice theory. But for rational choice theory to underlie real world economic policy-making, it needs to accommodate how people might wish rational choices to be "rational." Thus, if they are to be useful, economic explanations of people's choices need to be structured so as to incorporate society's value judgments.

Economics as a useful subject

This last point suggests a fitting conclusion to our discussion of value judgments in economics, and one that offers us a further perspective on economic methodology. When we say explanations in economics need to incorporate people's value judgments to present a more appropriate picture of the world, we assume implicitly that economics needs to be useful for people in economic life. Indeed, it is hard to imagine how economic explanations might be produced that totally disregarded their usefulness. Is it even possible to describe and explain economic life in such a way as to have no significance or meaning whatsoever for people's own understanding of the economy? Quite the contrary, economic explanations always aim to inform us about how their economic life works, and thus they always address people's concerns and interests, which in turn reflect their values.

Thus the ideal of economics as a positive, value-free science seems to have been misconceived from the start. A thoroughly value-free economics would be useless because it would tell us nothing about our concerns, interests, and values. Why, then, has being a value-free science been a long-standing goal of economics?

Here we must go back to the historical character of economic methodology, and in particular to the important influence of the philosophy of science advanced by the logical positivists. In the social turmoil of the first half of the twentieth century, the Vienna Circle hoped that science could be a refuge for objective thinking about the world that seemed impossible in all other arenas at a time of great social conflict.

Accordingly, they established the ideal of a science that could not be abused by politics and ideology, framing this ideal in terms of the goal of value-free science. They were correct to assert that science should not be manipulated in order to promote political and ideological ambitions. But using science constructively is not the same as abusing it, and one of the greatest values of science is its usefulness. Economics, then, can be useful, also value-laden, and not politically manipulative and ideological. The important thing is to be clear about the value judgments that are being employed in any particular theory.

Perhaps Keynes's words from the very end of his 1936 *The General Theory of Employment Interest and Money* offer us both the proper caution and insight into how we should see the discipline of economics:

At the present moment people are unusually expectant of a more fundamental diagnosis; more particularly ready to receive it; eager to try it out, if it should be even plausible. But apart from this contemporary mood, the ideas of economists and political philosophers, both when they are right and when they are wrong, are more powerful than is commonly understood. Indeed the world is ruled by little else. Practical men, who believe themselves to be quite exempt from any intellectual influences, are ususaly the slaves of some defunct economist. Madmen in authority, who hear voices in the air, are distilling their frenzy from some academic scribbler of a few years back. I am sure that the power of vested interests is vastly exaggerated compared with the gradual encroachment of ideas. Not, indeed, immediately, but after a certain interval; for in the field of economic and political philosophy there are not many who are influenced by new theories after they are twenty-five or thirty years of age, so the ideas which civil servants and politicians and even agitators apply to current events are not likely to be the newest. But, soon or late, it is ideas, not vested interests, which are dangerous for good or evil.

Looking backward: looking forward

Toward the end of the nineteenth century the American social reformer Edward Bellamy projected the course of the century to follow by imagining how people might look back upon the twentieth century from the year 2000. In fact, he was really looking backward at his own century, hoping that it held clues to the future, but he thought this exercise in imagination might enable him to see things his contemporaries overlooked. Some one hundred years later, just past the end of the twentieth century, we find ourselves in a similar position. We would like to know how economic methodology might develop in the future, but we have only its past to go on. Like Bellamy, we cannot look back on the present from a time in the future to view how economic methodology will develop. Nonetheless, like Bellamy the past is something we do know about, and it tells us us much about the foundations on which economic methodology has developed to date. Perhaps "foundations" is the wrong word to be used in this context, or perhaps we should recognise that there are multiple foundations and therefore many possible future directions for the development of economic methodology. This book has sought to describe those foundations.

Exercises

1   Give examples of the different kinds of methodological value judgments.
2   What is the basis for the strong distinction between positive and normative economics found in so many textbooks?
3   How did Myrdal argue that economics is value-laden?

4   What value judgments enter into standard rationality theory? What methodological value judgments?

5   How do cost–benefit judgments differ from Pareto recommendations?

6   What are moral norms, and what role do they play in economic analysis?

7   In economics, various types of unemployment are distinguished: frictional, natural, cyclical, structural, and voluntary. Identify the implicit values these concepts may convey.

8   Robbins defines economics as "the science which studies human behaviour as a relationship between ends and scarce means which have alternative uses." Identify the kinds of values that are implied by this definition.

Relevant readings

Arrow, Kenneth (1994) "Methodological Individualism and Social Knowledge," *American Economic Review* 84(2): 1–9.
   Arrow's view of some of the main principles of neoclassical economics.
Bellamy, Edward (1967) *Looking Backward: 2000–1887*, ed. by J. Thomas, Cambridge: Belknap Press of Harvard University Press.
   Bellamy's famous tract and a good example of utopian reasoning as a form of explanation.
Blaug, Mark (1998) "The Positive-Normative Distinction," in John B. Davis, D. Wade Hands, and Uskali Mäki (eds), *The Handbook of Economic Methodology*, Cheltenham: Edward Elgar Publishing, pp. 370–4.
   An influential account of value judgments in economics.
Easterlin, Richard (1974) "Does Economic Growth Improve the Human Lot? Some Empirical Evidence," in Paul David and Melvin Reder (eds), *Nations and Households in Economic Growth: Essays in Honor of Moses Abramowitz*, New York: Academic Press, pp. 89–125.
   Easterlin's original finding regarding happiness and economic growth.
Hausman, Daniel and Michael McPherson (2006) *Economic Analysis, Moral Philosophy and Public Policy*, 2nd edn, Cambridge: Cambridge University Press.
   A comprehensive introduction to the relationships between economics and ethics.
Myrdal, Gunnar (1953) *The Political Element in the Development of Economic Theory*, translated by Paul Streeten, London: Routledge.
   Myrdal's work in which he introduced the idea of implicit values.
Myrdal, Gunnar (1958) *Value in Social Theory*, ed. and intro. Paul Streeten, London: Routledge.
   Myrdal's main statement regarding values in economics.
Sen, Amartya (1987) *On Ethics and Economics*, Oxford: Basil Blackwell.
   An infuential account of the historical connections between ethics and economics.

Focus 7.1   Logical Positivism and Ordinalist Utility Theory

Every new student of economics learns that individual behavior is explained as utility maximizing, and that utility is understood in terms of preferences and indifference curves. They learn that an individual can only say whether one bundle of goods is preferred to another (or the individual is indifferent between them), and that the individual cannot say how much more one bundle of goods is preferred to another – that is, how much more utility the individual would get from one bundle compared to another.

If an individual were able to say by how much he preferred one bundle of goods to another, it would be necessary to measure utility. This is the concept of cardinal utility, employed by Alfred Marshall, A.C. Pigou, and other early neoclassical utility theorists, and which was central to the "old" welfare economics. Using money as the measuring rod of utility, and assuming that money exhibits diminishing marginal utility, they generally argued that economic policy should transfer wealth from the rich to the poor, since this would increase total utility within society.

The current concept of utility, which entered economics in the 1930s under the influence of John R. Hicks (1972 Nobel Prize) and Roy Allen, and which only requires that individuals can compare bundles of goods, is ordinal utility. It provides the basis for the "new" welfare economics formulated in terms of Pareto recommendations, and underlies the First Fundamental Theorem of modern welfare economics that a perfectly competitive economy maximizes social welfare by a Pareto-optimal allocation of resources (see Focus 1.3). Pareto recommendations only require that one person be made better off (according to their own preferences) without making anyone else worse off, and thus avoid making any (cardinal) interpersonal comparisons of utility across individuals, as are involved in the "old" welfare economics.

Indeed, one of the main reasons for economists' adoption of ordinal utility theory was their skepticism regarding interpersonal utility comparisons as expressed forcefully by Lionel Robbins in his *An Essay on the Nature and Significance of Economic Science* (see Focus 2.1). The *Essay* is famous for advancing the standard textbook definition of economics as the allocation of scarce resources across unlimited ends. It is also famous among historians of economics for changing the conception of economics from being concerned with a single domain of life – material welfare in the eyes of Marshall – to being a subject concerned with the whole of life, and thus an entire branch of practical reason. But for economists, the *Essay* was crucial for its critique of interpersonal utility comparisons, which Robbins argued are meaningless. His argument was that we cannot compare the utility of two persons by saying cardinally how satisfied they each are from the goods they consume, because in his view there is no objective basis on which two individuals' degrees of satisfaction can be compared.

> It is a comparison which necessarily falls outside the scope of any positive science. To state that A's preference stands above B's in order of importance is entirely different from stating that A prefers n to m and B prefers n and m in a different order. In involves an element of conventional evaluation. Hence it is essentially normative. It has no place in pure science. (p. 139)

This, in turn, meant that the scope of economic policy should be appropriately narrowed.

> Hence the extension of the Law of Diminishing Marginal Utility... is illegitimate. And the arguments based upon it therefore are lacking in scientific foundations... [and do] not justify the inference that transferences from the rich to the poor will increase total satisfaction. (p. 141)

Robbins, then, provided the key argument for economists for moving from the cardinal to the ordinal concept of utility and for the re-direction of economic policy by arguing that interpersonal comparisons of utility were conventional and normative, and therefore did not belong in science.

He thus portrayed economics as a science essentially in the same way the logical positivists had understood science when they demarcated science from pseudo-science. The influence of the logical positivists was at its height when Robbins wrote the *Essay*, and for them only analytic and synthetic *a posteriori* statements were scientific, where the latter could be demonstrated by observation. As interpersonal utility comparisons concerned satisfaction from consumption, they seemed untestable, and therefore could only be conventional, normative, and meaningless. It was this methodological judgment, then, that justified Robbins' effective call for banishing the cardinal utility concept from economics and reframing of welfare economics.

However, we have seen that the logical positivists' attempt to demarcate science and pseudo-science was not successful, that empirical concepts are often theory-laden, and that economic concepts are often value-laden. In addition, psychologists have shown, contrary to the assertions of Robbins, that it is quite possible to measure the subjective satisfaction individuals receive from consumption, so that interpersonal "utility" comparisons can indeed be made.

This has led in recent years to the development of "happiness" indices that provide methods for measuring individuals' subjective well-being, and the rise of the "happiness" approach to economic policy that recalls the broad scope of the "old" welfare economics. At the same time, there has been a development of non-utility approaches to making interpersonal comparisons across individuals that measure well-being in objective rather than subjective terms, such as the capability approach, in which individuals are compared according to such measures as educational level and health care access.

The legacy of logical positivists in economics, then, is a mixed one. On the one hand, their commitment to empirical science has been sustained – and arguably strengthened signficantly – in postwar econometric and more recent experimental economics practice. On the other hand, their goal of demarcating science from pseudo-science has been largely abandoned as the variety of approaches in economics multiplies with an increased appreciation of the many "foundations" on which economics can be developed. In economics, like in physics, there is no unifying framework. For that reason, the philosopher of science Nancy Cartwright prefers to characterize both disciplines as a patchwork: "we live in a dappled world, a world rich in different things, with different natures, behaving in different ways. The laws that describe this world are a patchwork, not a pyramid" (p. 1).

Relevant readings

Cartwright, Nancy (1999) *The Dappled World: A Study of the Boundaries of Science*, Cambridge: Cambridge University Press.
Anti-reductionist view by one of the leading philosophers of science.
Cooter, Robert and Peter Rappoport (1984) "Were the Ordinalists Wrong About Welfare Economics?," *Journal of Economic Literature* 22: 507–30.
A re-appraisal of the "old" welfare economics vis-à-vis the "new" welfare economics.
Kahneman, Daniel and Alan Kruger (2006) "Developments in the Measure of Subjective Well-Being," *Journal of Economic Perspectives* 20(1): 1–24.
An introduction to the "happiness" approach.
Layard, Richard (2005) *Happiness: Lessons from a New Science*, London: Penguin.
An influential analysis of happiness in economics.
Meikle, Scott (2001) "Quality and Quantity in Economics: The Metaphysical Construction of the Economic Realm," in U. Mäki (ed.), *The Economic World View*, Cambridge: Cambridge University Press, pp. 32–54.
A discussion of the change in economics from being concerned with a single domain of life to a branch of practical reason.
Sen, Amartya (1999) *Development as Freedom*, New York: Knopf.
An introduction to the capability approach.

Focus 7.2   Neutral Science?

The standard view of science makes a sharp distinction between social goals, science, and policy, all of which can be pictured as a triptych:

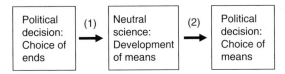

This view that these distinctions can be drawn is mirrored in the economist's distinction between positive economics and normative economics. As such, John Neville Keynes (see Focus 2.1) defined a positive science as "a body of systematized knowledge concerning what is," and a normative science as "a body of systematized knowledge relating to criteria of what ought to be, and concerned therefore with the ideal as distinguished from the actual; an art as a system of rules for the attainment of a given end." It was this distinction that Milton Friedman used in his article "Methodology of Positive Economics" (discussed in Chapter 2). He viewed positive economics as being "in principle independent of any particular ethical position or normative judgments."

This view, expressed by Neville Keynes and Friedman, is shared by many other economists. It is also reflected in many economic policy research institutions across the world. Take, for example, the US National Bureau of Economic Research (NBER), which describes itself on its website in the following terms:

> a private, nonprofit, nonpartisan research organization dedicated to promoting a greater understanding of how the economy works. The NBER is committed to undertaking and disseminating unbiased economic research among public policymakers, business professionals, and the academic community.

An even stronger expression of a particular institute's neutrality is given by the Netherlands Bureau for Economic Policy Analysis (CPB), founded in 1945, with Tinbergen as its first director:

> The result of an analysis will never be a straight recommendation on a particular course of action. Often, CPB will describe an exchange: for instance, an exchange between solidarity and labour participation or between environmental ambitions and economic growth. Everything has its own price. CPB delivers economic arguments; the final choice – in which other considerations appropriately play an important role – will be made by politics.

...The bureau's credibility stands or falls by the objectivity and scientific quality of its analyses.

Thus, the usual assumption is that when economic policy-makers use economic models, there is a one-way flow from the political choice of ends to the development of economic models (arrow 1), and then a one-way flow from the economic models thus framed to the choice of means to achieve the social goals that lie behind economic policy (arrow 2). In practice, however, the requirements and questions of policy-makers play an important role in the development and revision of those very models, the arrows move in both directions, and the models provide a bridge between the positive and normative domains of economics. They provide a clear focus for the people involved – modelers and policy-makers – to interact and share their expertise.

Arrow 1 assumes that society determines the range of ends that scientists thereupon investigate how to attain, but the opposite is also true: through creating new technologies scientists generate new ends. In this respect it shares some similarities with Say's law idea – in the sense that supply creates its own demand. In a more realistic model of the scientific process, arrow 1 would need to point in both directions. A particularly famous example of this is the letter by Einstein to the then US president Franklin Roosevelt, discussing Fermi's research and alerting him about the possibilities of building an atomic bomb (see Focus 7.3).

Another instance of this two-way flow concerns who determines whether economic variables are considered to be endogenous or exogenous. The endogenous variables are those that the model explains, whereas the exogenous variables are those that come from outside the model, and are not explained by it. Which variable is endogenous and which is exogenous is not an intrinsic feature of the variables but is ultimately the choice of the modeler. Endogenizing a variable, moreover, provides a means of dealing with it. Only after a variable, say the interest rate, is endogenized can a specific value of it function as a policy target. Sometimes, then, scientists determine which variables can possibly be modeled as endogenous, for technical and/or theoretical reasons, and as a result arrow 1 points to the right. For example, business cycles are today modeled as stochastic fluctuations, that is, as exogenous phenomena. For a number of years, they have not been a subject about which economists and politicians have had much interest. In the interwar period, however, business cycles were of much greater concern to both economists and politicians, and the latter pressed economists to model business cyles in such a way as to create policy levers that would function as means for evening out these cycles. In this case, arrow 2 needs to point in the reverse direction.

SSK (discussed in Chapter 5) has shown how deeply science is embedded in society, and Chapter 7 has highlighted how problematic in practice it is to maintain a sharp distinction between positive and normative science. These studies tell us that the figure above must be regarded as too simplistic, and should be replaced by a more complex one:

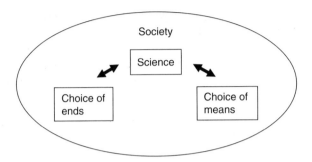

Indeed, scientists do not operate in isolation from society in a hermetically sealed "ivory tower" uninfluenced by society's goals and views of how to address them. As a set of investigative practices science maintains a relative autonomy from the uses to which science can be put, but scientists themselves are every bit as present in the real world as are non-scientists.

Relevant readings

den Butter, Frank A.G. and Mary S. Morgan (eds) (2000) *Empirical Models and Policy-Making: Interaction and Institutions*, London and New York: Routledge.
   A collection of articles written by practitioners and academic economists that explores the interaction between modelers and policy-makers and their institutional arrangements.

Focus 7.3   Naturalistic Legitimation

In our present-day society science occupies a privileged position. This has been attained as the result of its undeniable past successes in the areas of medicine and technology. Thanks to developments – or progress – in these disciplines over the last two centuries death rates have fallen dramatically and the standard of living has increased across much of the modern world. These successes have created the widely shared belief that science is intrinsically good; science improves the quality of our lives and also increases the survival chances of the human race. Science, that is, legitimizes itself by its own natural achievements, a type of justification often referred to as naturalistic legitimation.

   Such legitimation implies that any external interference with scientific processes may impede its progress. But this still begs the question: can we leave scientists to their own business, or should society intervene from time to time to keep scientific development on an "acceptable" track? This, for example, is the question underlying many of the current debates surrounding research into the area of genetic engineering.

The problem of the legitimation of science is echoed in similar problems in the areas of political science and economics. One of the basic questions in political science is the legitimation of power through the idea of a social contract. If one assumes that human nature is inherently social, then no such contract is required. This view is perhaps most explicitly expressed in the political philosophy of anarchism, whose adherents would consider that any such contract would be harmful to society. On the other hand, if one assumes the opposite – "homo homini lupus," that is, "man is a wolf to man" – then one would defend the need for such a contract, as the political philosopher John Locke did most famously at the end of the seventeenth century.

The related question in economics is whether matters should be "left to the market" (*laissez faire*) or whether governments should intervene in markets. The naturalistic legitimation of the market is given by the First Fundamental Theorem of Welfare Economics which asserts that market equilibria are Pareto optimal (see Focus 1.3). According to this theorem, any intervention in the market harms Pareto efficiency. If one doubts the (empirical) application of this theorem to actual society, or if one doubts whether a Pareto welfare distribution is an equitable distribution, one would defend (at least some) restrictions on the market system.

The naturalistic legitimation of a system or process is most severely criticized whenever a system encounters a crisis. Just think of the worldwide economic crisis and the Depression of the 1930s which led many economists to become Keynesians in the decades that followed. Or think of World War II with its unprecedented holocaust, which was the main motivation for a new global social contract formalized in the Universal Declaration of Human Rights, adopted and proclaimed on December 10, 1948 by the General Assembly of the United Nations. In science, however, its own naturalistic legitimation was most severely disputed when the atomic bomb was set off above Hiroshima. This event and the effects of the deadly radiation for many years to come showed an opposite, horrifying face of science: science was capable of damaging the quality of life and even threatening the survival of the human race.

The idea to develop nuclear weapons, it should be emphasized, came not from society *per se*. To imagine the possibility of building such a weapon, one needs to be in possession of specific physical knowledge. It was the scientists themselves who informed society about this possibility in a now famous letter to then US president Franklin Roosevelt, dated August 2, 1939, and most likely written by Leo Szilard, though signed by Albert Einstein.

The splitting of the uranium atom in Germany in December 1938 plus continued German aggression in the war led a number of physicists on the allied side to fear that Germany might be working on the development of an atomic bomb. Among those concerned were the physicists Szilard and Eugene Wigner. But Szilard and Wigner had no influence on those in power. So they explained the problem to Einstein who did. The first part of the letter explains the urgency of the matter:

> Some recent work by E. Fermi and L. Szilard, which has been communicated to me in manuscript, leads me to expect that the element uranium may be turned into a new and important source of energy in the immediate future. Certain aspects of the situation which has arisen seem to call for watchfulness and, if necessary, quick action on the part of the Administration. I believe therefore that it is my duty to bring to your attention the following facts and recommendations:
>
> In the course of the last four months it has been made probable – through the work of Joliot in France as well as Fermi and Szilard in America – that it may become possible to set up a nuclear chain reaction in a large mass of uranium, by which vast amounts of power and large quantities of new radium-like elements would be generated. Now it appears almost certain that this could be achieved in the immediate future.
>
> This new phenomenon would also lead to the construction of bombs, and it is conceivable – though much less certain – that extremely powerful bombs of a new type may thus be constructed. A single bomb of this type, carried by boat and exploded in a port, might very well destroy the whole port together with some of the surrounding territory. However, such bombs might very well prove to be too heavy for transportation by air.

The eventual result of this proposed line of research was the Manhattan Project where "Little Boy," the ironically named Hiroshima bomb, was designed and built.

Another of those involved with the Manhattan Project was John von Neumann, who was a consultant of the Los Alamos Laboratory from 1943 onward. Von Neumann is well known in economics for his *Theory of Games* (written with Oskar Morgenstern), but in science he is perhaps most famous as an early developer of the digital computer.

In his testimony before the Special Senate Committee on Atomic Energy in 1946, von Neumann acknowledged that science "has outgrown the age of independence from society" and should be regulated by society:

> It is for the first time that science has produced results which require an immediate intervention of organized society, of the government. Of course science has produced many results before which were of great importance to society, directly or indirectly. And there have been before scientific processes which required some minor policing measures of

the government. But it is for the first time that a vast area of research, right in the central part of the physical sciences, impinges on a broad front on the vital zone of society, and clearly requires rapid and general regulation. It is now that physical science has become "important" in that painful and dangerous sense which causes the state to intervene.

Considering the vastness of the ultimate objectives of science, it has been clear for a long time to thoughtful persons that this moment must come, sooner or later. We now know that it has come.

In addition to these dramatic developments, the rise of "big science" after World War II, requiring large amounts of funding, made society aware of the necessity of a legitimation of science on alternative grounds, and of the need to think about eventual desired directions along which science should develop. More recent discussions on genetic engineering and stem cell research show that these issues of legitimation continue and remain part of science, including economics. Could the global financial crisis of 2008 been foreseen, and therefore prevented?

Relevant readings

von Neumann, John (1963) "Statement of John von Neumann before the Special Senate Committee on Atomic Energy," in A.H. Taub (ed.), *John von Neumann, Collected Works, Volume VI*, Oxford: Pergamon Press, pp. 1499–1502.
   An impressive statement calling for state intervention by someone who describes his political ideology as anti-communist.

Glossary

Analogy. Transference of an often familiar conceptual content appropriate to one subject to another, often still unfamiliar subject, in order to re-characterize the meaning of the latter.

Analytic propositions. Statements or propositions that are tautological, that is, true by definition.

Anomaly (Kuhn). An anomaly is an observation, experimental result, etc., which violates the **paradigm**-induced expectations that govern **normal science**; a puzzle that resists being solved in a paradigmatic way.

Axiomatization. Syntactic reduction of a **theory** to a set of axioms.

Case study research. An empirical inquiry that investigates a phenomenon within its real-life context, a circumstance in which the boundaries between phenomenon and context are not clearly evident.

Ceteris paribus **clause.** The clause indicating that all other influences and factors do not change; in Latin, literally "with other things the same."

Confirmationism. The view that **laws** do not express certain knowledge but probabilistic knowledge. The degree of confirmation indicates the likelihood that something will happen according to this law.

Context of discovery. The historical, psychological, or accidental context in which a theory is discovered. According to the **received view**, this is of no concern to philosophers of science.

Context of justification. The rational reconstruction of a theory according to specific **demarcation criteria** for the purpose of its justification.

Conventionalism. The standpoint which ignores or puts aside the issue of whether theories and models are true or apply to what exists independently of them in the world, and only seeks explanations which are seen as widely accepted and generally agreed upon.

Correspondence rule. A rule that specifies an experimental or measurement procedure to connect a theory to a phenomenon.

Deduction. Logically correct inference.

Deductive-nomological (DN) model of explanation (Hempel) (also known as the covering-law model of explanation). The view that all scientific **explanations** take the form of deducing a statement of what is to be explained from at least one universal **law** (*nomos*) combined with a set of true statements of initial conditions.

Demarcation criterion. Any principle that distinguish science from pseudo-science or non-science.

Descriptivism (Samuelson). A methodological standpoint that regards theories as a set of axioms, postulates, or hypotheses that do nothing other than accurately describe observable reality.

Disciplinary matrix (Kuhn). A set of elements constituting a discipline. These elements are: symbolic generalizations, metaphysics, values, and a **paradigm**.

Duhem–Quine Thesis. The argument that no theory can ever be conclusively **falsified**, because we necessarily test the theory in conjunction with its auxiliary assumpions and background conditions. A refutation does not clarify what has failed: the theory or one of these background assumptions.

Econometrics. The study of economic phenomena by the application of mathematical and statistical methods. A theoretical structure of the phenomena under investigation is presumed.

Economics of science (ES). The application of the standard tools of welfare economics, externalities, and public goods to determine the optimal level of scientific research.

Economics of scientific knowledge (ESK). The study of science by applying economic theories and concepts to the behavior of scientists.

Edinburgh School Strong Programme. A sociological study of science approach based on the strong assumption that all scientific knowledge is socially constructed.

Empiricism. The view that knowledge arises out of experience.

Epistemological pluralism. The view that there exist multiple kinds and forms of knowledge, none of which can be shown to be superior to or reducible to the other.

Epistemology. The philosophy of knowledge.

Explanation. Answer to a *why* question.

External validity. The validity of results outside the laboratory setting in which they were obtained.

Fact–value distinction. The strict distinction between statements using "is" language and those using "ought" language.

Fallibilism (Popper). The view that all theories are fallible and that a view to the contrary leads to dogmatism.

Falsifiability (Popper). A hypothesis is falsifiable if empirical evidence is conceivable which is incompatible with this hypothesis.

Falsification (Popper). Rejection of a theory by empirical observations contradicting the implications of that theory.

Falsificationism. A methodological standpoint that regards theories as scientific if and only if they are **falsifiable** plus the methodological rules that forbid **immunizing stratagems**; naive falsificationism holds that any theory that is falsifiable is scientific, whereas sophisticated falsificationism holds that a theory is scientific only if it has corroborated excess empirical content over its predecessor.

Formalism (Hilbert). A philosophy of mathematics which considers mathematics to be a rigorous game of manipulating symbols devoid of meaning according to certain formal rules agreed on in advance.

Gender (feminist) perspective. The perspective identifying the role that gender plays in science.

Hard core (Lakatos). The purely metaphysical beliefs that unite the protagonists of an **scientific research program** and which cannot be abandoned without abandoning the entire viewpoint that constitutes the program; the hard core is surrounded by the "protective belt" of testable theories.

Historicism (Popper). The view that history develops inexorably and necessarily according to certain principles or rules, or, in other words, that there are **laws** which determine the course of history.

Immunizing stratagem (Popper). Ad hoc adjustment in a theory to protect it against refutation.

Incommensurability (Kuhn). The methodological standpoint that two competing **paradigms** cannot be compared. This may be because: (1) there are no independent standards of evaluation; (2) within a new paradigm old concepts acquire new relationships resulting in a misunderstanding between the two paradigms; or (3) the two groups of scientists see different things when they look at the world.

Induction. The process of inferring general **laws** from particular events or individual observations.

Instrumentalism. A methodological standpoint that regards all **scientific theories** and hypotheses as being nothing more than instruments for making predictions.

Laboratory studies approach. A microsociological approach to the study of science. This approach is called the laboratory studies approach because the first scientific sites and locations studied were laboratories.

Law. True empirical generalization without exceptions and not restricted to any domain (for example, time period or spatial region).

Logical positivism. A version of empiricism which originated with the Vienna Circle. Its program sought to purify science of all metaphysics and regarded only **analytic** and **synthetic** *a posteriori* **propositions** as scientific knowledge.

Logicism. Originally, the philosophical standpoint that mathematics is an extension of logic; more generally, it also means that all scientific language should be considered an extension of logic.

Metaphor. The result of a successful **analogy**, such that its source is forgotten or becomes relatively unimportant.

Methodological pluralism. The view that there are no meta-criteria by which one methodology can be shown to be superior to all others.

Methodological value judgments. Evaluative judgments with respect to the preferred methods of investigation.

Normal science (Kuhn). Research providing solutions to puzzles, that is, well-defined problems whose solution is assured and which are solved according to specific rules and by meeting specific standards, as suggested by a **paradigm**.

Novel fact (Lakatos). Facts that are improbable, or even forbidden, in the light of the existing theory.

Operationalization. Defining theoretical terms completely in observation terms.

Operationalism (Bridgman). A version of **empiricism** in which the meaning of a theoretical term is nothing more than the way it is measured.

Paradigm (Kuhn). Concrete problem-solutions that provide models or examples from which spring a particular tradition, "school," of scientific research.

Pluralism. The view that multiple competing positions can obtain at the same time.

Positivism. Empiricism in which the senses are the only source of knowledge.

Postmodernism. A critique of modernism which evolved from poststructuralism.

Predicate. A part of a sentence stating something about the subject.

Problem of induction (Hume). Observations can only justify singular statements and never general statements.

Problem of invariance. The problem of finding invariant (stable) relationships outside the laboratory.

Realism. The view that the world exists independently of our theories and thinking about it.

Realisticness. The approach in which only statements that are descriptively correct in all their details are considered to be empirically valid.

Received view, also the standard view. The dominant **logical positivist** program in the philosophy of science.

Reductionism. The assumption that different types of knowledge can be "reduced" to one specific form of knowledge.

Reflexivity (Barnes and Bloor). The principle that science study should be studied according to the same principles as science is studied.

Relativism. The view that truth and knowledge are not objective and a feature of the way the world is, but rather something that varies according to historical and social context.

Rhetoric approach. The approach that considers science as being primarily about persuasion, and studies scientists' tools of persuasion.

Scientific research program (Lakatos). A cluster of interconnected theories deriving from a common **hard core**.

Scientific revolution (Kuhn). A scientific revolution is a **paradigm** shift, that is, a revolution that occurs when an existing paradigm is superseded by a rival.

Scientific theory. The systematic organization of concepts, principles, and **explanations** in a particular domain of investigation.

Semantics. The meaning and interpretation given to the terms and expressions of a statement or theory.

Situational analysis (Popper). Reconstruction of the problem situation the agent faces to explain the agent's choice as a response to that situation.

Sociology of scientific knowledge (SSK). The study of science by applying sociological theories and concepts to the behavior of scientists and organization of science.

Symmetry thesis. The principle that, according to the **received view**, **explanation** and prediction employ the same **DN model**.

Syntactic view of theory. The view that a **theory** is defined as an axiomatization in a formal language.

Syntactics. The logical structure of a statement or theory.

Synthetic proposition. A non-**analytic** statement or proposition about the world that is either true or false.

Synthetic *a posteriori* proposition. A **synthetic proposition** that can be shown to be true by experience.

Synthetic *a priori* proposition. A **synthetic proposition** is known *a priori* if its truth or falsity may be known prior to any appeal to experience, except the experience than is required to understand the proposition.

Theory-laden observation (Hanson). An observation is theory-laden if the truth or falsity of the observation statement is determined by appealing to a theory.

Triangulation. The strategy that more than one method should be used to validate an observation on the grounds that we can have more confidence in a certain result when different methods are found to be congruent and yield comparable data.

Value judgments. Evaluative types of statements that range from appraisals to prescriptions without ethical content to ethical prescriptions or moral judgments.

Value-ladenness. When concepts or statements incorporate implicit value judgments and normative prescriptions.

Verifiability principle. The logical positivist criterion for meaningfulness, which says that a statement is meaningful only if it is empirically verifiable, that is, its evidence derives from sense data.

Name Index

Subject Index